A LITTLE FARTHER

A LITTLE FARTHER

366 Thought Provoking Readings
that Apply the Bible to Everyday Living

A Daily Devotional from
Ulster's Best Known Evangelist

W P NICHOLSON

Compiled by Stanley Barnes

AMBASSADOR INTERNATIONAL
Greenville, South Carolina • Belfast, Northern Ireland

A LITTLE FARTHER
© Copyright 2005 Stanley Barnes

ISBN 1   84030 165   1

Ambassador Publications
a division of
Ambassador Productions Ltd.
Providence House
Ardenlee Street,
Belfast,
BT6 8QJ
Northern Ireland
www.ambassador-productions.com

Emerald House
427 Wade Hampton Blvd.
Greenville
SC 29609, USA
www.emeraldhouse.com

CONTENTS

◆ 6 'HE WENT A LITTLE FARTHER'

◆ 7 BIOGRAPHICAL INTRODUCTION

◆ 9 JANUARY

◆ 41 FEBRUARY

◆ 71 MARCH

◆ 103 APRIL

◆ 135 MAY

◆ 167 JUNE

◆ 199 JULY

◆ 231 AUGUST

◆ 265 SEPTEMBER

◆ 299 OCTOBER

◆ 331 NOVEMBER

◆ 363 DECEMBER

HE WENT A LITTLE FARTHER

He went a little farther, praying in Gethsemane
He went a little farther and in His agony
His sweat, like drops of blood, showed His love for you and me
He went a little farther though it led to Calvary.

He went a little farther, God's well beloved Son
He went a little farther and the victory He won
Redemption's plan accomplished as His life He freely gave
He went a little farther, a guilty world to save.

He went a little farther and those who follow Him
Must go a little farther to bring God's harvest in.
To pray, to go and find them, to give, not count the cost.
To go a little farther, that they might reach the lost.

Marjorie Boreland

BIOGRAPHICAL INTRODUCTION

William Patteson Nicholson was born on the 3rd April 1876, near Bangor in Co. Down, N. Ireland. He was the fourth son of Captain John C. Nicholson and his wife Ellen.

After a wild youth spent at sea as a merchant seaman, he eventually returned home, and on the 22nd May 1899 he was converted to Christ as he was sitting at his mother's fireside awaiting his breakfast.

He subsequently trained at the Bible Training Institute in Glasgow, which was founded by D L Moody. After completing his studies there he was appointed as an evangelist by the Lanarkshire Christian Union. His preaching engagements took him to many countries including the United States, Australia and South Africa, but his greatest work was done in his native Ulster, where he preached in the language of the shipyard men, and like his Master, the common people heard him gladly.

In the midst of Civil War in Northern Ireland his preaching was marked with fearlessness, faithfulness and fruitfulness, and this is best summarised in the booklet 'From Civil War to Revival Victory.'

These daily readings have been carefully selected from his published writings. As each day unfolds the reader will find inspiration to 'journey a little farther' spiritually each day of the year. They also provide an opportunity to become familiar with the thoughts of a great evangelist and soul winner.

May the Holy Spirit come, through these readings, and burn anew in the heart of every reader.

Stanley Barnes
September 2005

JANUARY

1 ◆ A Little Farther

2 ◆ A Little Farther in Believing

3 ◆ A Little Farther in Prayer

4 ◆ A Little Farther in Love

5 ◆ A Little Farther in Holiness

6 ◆ A Little Farther in Giving

7 ◆ Be Alert

8 ◆ Keep Thyself

9 ◆ The Peril of Uncounted Cost

10 ◆ Adaptation

11 ◆ Presumptuous Pride

12 ◆ The Curse of the Church

13 ◆ Take Advantage

14 ◆ Christ Unknown

15 ◆ Tugging at the Wrong Skirt

16 ◆ Untapped Resources

17 ◆ A Child of God

18 ◆ The More Abundant Life

19 ◆ Overgrown Babes

20 ◆ The All Sufficient Saviour

21 ◆ Perfect Peace

22 ◆ Known in Hell

23 ◆ Pre-Pentecostal Believers

24 ◆ Testing

25 ◆ The Sovereignty of the Spirit

26 ◆ Perfection's Sacred Height

27 ◆ The Christian's Power

28 ◆ Care Forbidden

29 ◆ The Christian's Ambition

30 ◆ God's Way of Appropriation

31 ◆ The Singing Side of Salvation

A Little Farther

And he went a little farther…
Matthew 26 vs. 39

How swiftly time flies. We are being hurled on to eternity at a terrific pace, and the older we become the swifter seems the speed. Here we are at the beginning of another year and it seems such a short time since we began the one just ended. Wouldn't life be a very monotonous thing if it were one long drawn-out spell? God in His wisdom has seen to this and therefore our lives, however long or short, are divided into specific periods. That is, they are broken up to relieve the monotony. We have years, months, weeks, days, hours, and minutes. Then we have day and night. We have spring, summer, autumn and winter. I believe the Lord has not only done this to relieve the monotony, but to make us take notice of the flight of time, and if we are wise, take stock of our lives.

This short phrase we are now considering is a condensed biography of our Lord's life 'in the days of His flesh.' No matter how you look at Him and compare Him with others, you always find Him 'a little farther,' but how much it is – He is the Incomparable Christ.

These words give us a glimpse into the life of Christ. Have you ever seen a field all fenced in with boards? You find a knothole and you put your eye to it and you see the whole field. So these words are just like that in the life of Christ. It doesn't matter along what line you look at Him, you always find Him 'a little farther' than any other. May it be true of us at the end of this year, if the Lord tarries or spares us that 'he went a little farther,'

I am willing to go anywhere as long as it is forward.
David Livingstone

A Little Farther in Believing

But without faith it is impossible to please him: for he that cometh to
God must believe that he is, and that he is a rewarder of them
that diligently seek him.
Hebrews 11 vs. 6

It is strange how deficient and weak we are in faith in spite of all the precious promises in His word and His providences in our lives daily. If the Lord rebuked them in the days of His flesh for their littleness and weakness of faith, what must He think and feel about us, seeing all the knowledge we have of His faithfulness and love in the past and present of our lives. The many deliverances we have had; the answers to our prayers; the supply of our money and varied needs; and yet we are so weak and deficient in our faith. If He had ever deceived us or failed us, we might have some excuse for our want of faith in Him; but He never fails or forsakes us. So may we during this New Year go 'a little farther' and dare to believe in Him, even when and where we can neither see nor understand His dealings in our lives. If we are to please Him, then we must have faith in Him, for 'without faith' it is impossible to please Him. We may serve Him and do much work for Him, only by having faith in Him. You say, why is that? Well, you and I would never be pleased with anyone, however much they did for us, if they didn't believe in us. We are only pleased with friends because they have confidence or faith in us. So it is with our Lord. 'Lord increase our faith.' For we live by faith, we walk by faith, we overcome by faith. It is not a once-for-all, but a continuous faith. 'Through faith we'll win the promised crown.'

Keep on believing Jesus is near.
Keep on believing there's nothing to fear.
Keep on believing this is the way.
Faith in the night as well as the day.

Expect great things from God, attempt great things for God.
William Carey

3 JANUARY

A Little Farther in Prayer

Continue in prayer, and watch in the same with thanksgiving;
Colossians 4 vs. 2

This is the Christian's vital breath, and we only live as we breathe. This was the big thing in the earthly life of our Lord. He spent whole nights in prayer. He ever lives to make intercession today. It is strange the way we deal with prayer, although we know how important it is. We give it the least of all places in our lives. We will make and take so little time for prayer. If there is any religious exercise that pleases God and grieves the old devil, it is prayer. Satan will move earth and hell to prevent us, for he trembles when he sees the weakest sinner on his knees. This is why he does away with prayer in our lives and churches. We are powerless when we are prayerless. Let us resolve that this year we will 'go a little farther' in prayer and praying. One thing we may be sure of and that is, when we come to die and stand at the judgment seat of Christ, we'll never have to ask forgiveness for praying too much or spending too much time at it. Praying time is never wasted time. Was there ever a time in the history of the world when we needed to pray as in these days of unrest, revolution, want and distress of nations, when men's hearts are literally failing them. Our Governments and leaders are bankrupt – in God alone is our help. Let us this year cry to God day and night for a mighty worldwide revival that will hasten and usher in the coming of our blessed Lord.

Oh, what peace we often forfeit,
Oh, what needless pain we bear,
All because we do not carry
Everything to God in prayer.

As it is the business of tailors to make clothes and of cobblers to mend shoes, so it is the business of Christians to pray.
Martin Luther

A Little Farther in Love

My little children, let us not love in word, neither in tongue;
but in deed and in truth.
I John 3 vs. 18

This is truly the Laodicean age. 'The love of many waxing cold.' A lukewarm, a tepid condition abounds on every hand, in the Church and amongst Christians. In fact we have got to the place where we decry 'fervent' or boiling love. We are told not to be emotional or enthusiastic (some call it fanaticism) in our love to Christ. No wonder He spues us out of His mouth.

Let me love Thee more and more,
Till this fleeting life is o'er,
Till my soul is lost in love
In a better brighter world above.

However well and warmly we may have loved Him we have never loved Him too well or too warmly. May this New Year show a marked increase in our love to Christ and one another. Was there ever a day when the devil was working overtime at creating differences and divisions amongst God's people? Instead of fighting Satan and sin we are fighting one another. We hate one another for the love of God. What a spectacle to the world. However much another Christian may disagree with us, or even go wrong in creed and doctrine, we must never hate or cease to love him. We must only hate the wrong in life and doctrine. We will never see eye to eye down here, but we can abound in love one to another. So let us hate sin heartily, and love Christ and Christians fervently. This is the 'hallmark' of a true Christian; "By this shall all men know ye are my disciples, if ye have love one to another."

One loving heart sets another on fire.
Augustine.

A Little Farther in Holiness

*Having therefore these promises, dearly beloved, let us cleanse
ourselves from all filthiness of the flesh and spirit,
perfecting holiness in the fear of God.*
II Corinthians 7 vs. 1

There are those who boast they got everything when they were
converted. They don't believe, they say, in religion by instalments.
Their natural life is lived on the instalment plan. They didn't receive
everything when they were born. Neither do we receive everything
when we are born again. It is contrary to the teaching of the Bible and
the experience of Christians of all ages. There can be no holiness until
we are born again, and there can never be any progress in holiness of
life and service until we are fully yielded and baptised and filled with
the Holy Spirit. But when we are yielded and filled, we are to be
continually and increasingly yielded and filled, and thus perfect
holiness in the fear of the Lord. We are to leave, not forsake, the
principles of the doctrine of Christ, and go on to perfection. We are to
grow in grace, for 'without holiness no man shall see the Lord.'
Holiness is an indispensable condition for securing the favour of God,
attaining peace of conscience, and preparing the soul for communion
with God here and hereafter. Holiness is the work of the Holy Spirit.
When I am willing and fully yielded, He works in me to perfect me in
every good work, working in me that which is well pleasing in His
sight, and as we work out our own salvation, God works in us; Christ
is our sanctification or holiness. The Spirit is the worker; His word is
the instrument He uses.

Thy Holy Spirit, Lord alone can turn the heart from sin,
His power alone can sanctify and keep us pure within.

He leads none to heaven but whom He sanctifies on the earth.
John Owen

A Little Farther in Giving

For all these have of their abundance cast in unto the offerings of God: but she of her penury hath cast in all the living that she had.
Luke 21 vs. 4

Everything we have is the Lord's. We are not our own. He has trusted us with money, however much or little. We are not proprietors – we are trustees. He is not dependent on our giving, for the silver and the gold are His, and the cattle on a thousand hills – the earth and the fullness thereof. But He allows us to show in a tangible and practical way our love for Him. Money is an acid test. It precipitates what is in us. How many there are who are thieves and robbers in God's sight. They have, and are, robbing God of tithes and offerings. Let us begin this New Year by at least tithing our income, not after we have paid all our expenses, but by giving God His tithe first. If we do, He will bless us by pouring out an uncontainable blessing. Our lives and faith will be enriched in every way. You ask, what is the tithe? It is the tenth, or two shillings in every pound. I believe once you begin this, you will never give it up, or merely continue giving the tenth – you will increase your giving so that it will be tithes and offerings. Tithing becomes such a rich means of grace to our own lives we will fall in love with God's plan. If this is done, there will be no lack for God's work at home or abroad, especially abroad. There never was a day when missionary money was so scarce, because the devil is impounding the money in every way he can and crippling foreign missionary enterprise thereby. A word of warning – be very careful and prayerful how you spend God's tithe. Don't let one penny support any Church or society that does not ring true to the Book and the Blood. Be careful also to support missions that are evangelising, not merely educational or humanitarian ones. It is our business to preach the Gospel to every creature and by all means save some, and this cannot be done without money, so let us all be tithers.

Treasures in heaven are laid up only as treasures on earth are laid down.
Anon.

Be Alert

Lest Satan should get an advantage of us; for we are
not ignorant of his devices.
II Corinthians 2 vs11

When you got converted, received Jesus Christ, the devil did not die. Sin has not been put into hell, where it will be put one of these days. You are in an alien country here, with an alien nature and an alien body; and you have, as such, inherited what will keep you busy for the rest of your days. Some people think they will never be tempted while they are Christians. You will not be long till you get an eye-opener. There are perils without and perils within, perils around, perils above and perils beneath. The reason why a good many people fail is their ignorance of these things; or, if not ignorant altogether, they fail because they underestimate their peril and under rate the subtlety of the enemy.

The devil does not keep to his own side of the road, but drives in where we least expect him.

C H Spurgeon

Keep Thyself

Take heed unto thyself.
I Timothy 4 vs. 16

You remember how, in the Old Testament, in 2 Chronicles 26, a young fellow became king; and then, when he became lifted up, he sought to take the very position of the High Priest, although the Lord tried to show him the peril and to safeguard him against it. The danger lies with us to-day just as much as with those in olden time. The Lord sought to discover Peter to himself. 'You are going to deny me.' 'Deny you? I will die for you!' 'Satan has desired to have you, that he may sift you.' But is spite of it all, poor Peter rushed on to ruin and sorrow. If the Lord shows us ourselves, it is a terrible thing not to pay heed to it. When you are at a railway junction, and the lines separate one from another, you know that at the beginning of their separation it is as sharp as the blade of a knife, but what a difference at the end! Beginnings may be very little in the matter of sin, but look at what they are at the end. If you are getting away from the main lines of truth, if you are getting it wrong on any moral question, as you value your own soul, I beseech you to heed the Word.

The devil has a great advantage against us, in as much as he has a strong bastion and bulwark against us in our own flesh and blood.
Martin Luther

The Peril of Uncounted Cost

Lest haply after he hath laid the foundation, and is not able to finish it,
all that behold it begin to mock him.
Luke 14 vs. 29

It is one thing to make a start. The first step is not the hardest, but the last. 'Lord, I will follow thee whithersoever Thou goest,' protested one candidate; and you know the reply: 'The foxes have holes and the birds have nests, but the Son of man has not where to lay his head'; and then it was 'Good-bye, Jesus.'

When the storm occurred on the lake there may have been an inclination to say, 'Thank you, I am a fair-weather Christian.' But 'Except a man forsake all that he hath, he cannot be my disciple; except a man deny himself, and take up the cross daily, he cannot be my disciple.... Which of you, going to build, does not count the cost?' The Christian life is a life of battle and building and the Lord would have us to count the cost. Many a pilgrim has made a good start and a bad ending, because he did not count the cost of the persecution - of being ostracised, maligned, misrepresented and hated of all men. It is better never to make the move than to make it and make a mess of it

Salvation without discipleship is 'cheap grace'.
Dietrich Bonhoeffer

Adaptation

No man that warreth entangleth himself with the affairs of this life; that he may please him who hath chosen him to be a soldier.
II Timothy 2 vs. 4

You can never get a man out of a bog hole by going in beside him. A lot of the so-called social work in churches is carried on with the motive, 'We have got to keep the young people,' and so we have all sorts of questionable things going on.

One minister put it, 'After all, it is the same Gospel but it is a re-adaptation.'

I asked, 'How many are you getting with it?'

'Oh, well, not many yet.'

'How many do you get out of that gang for the prayer meeting?'

'We have not got a prayer meeting.'

Oh, let there be a complete and constant abandonment to the Lord. It is not merely an act, but an attitude; not only a crisis, but a process; we should not only be filled with the Holy Ghost, but be in process of being filled. The crisis is when you make the surrender, and by faith receive; and the process is walking in the light as He is in the light and being filled with all the fullness of God day in and day out.

If you are in with God you are out with the world.
Rodney (Gipsy) Smith

Presumptuous Pride

Wherefore let him that thinketh he standeth take heed lest he fall.
I Corinthians 10 vs. 12

It is sometimes unsafe for the Lord to bless a man. You remember that, in the case of Gideon, the Lord said, 'I want to boil down your crowd,' - the crowd that had the fluttering around the heart. After that the Lord said 'you have too many yet,' and Gideon had to reduce the 10,000. And the Midianites were like the sand by the seashore! The Lord said: "If I gave victory by the 10,000, they would vaunt themselves and say 'We have got the victory.'" People sometimes say: 'at the last Convention I got deliverance from my temper. I do not need to bother about it now, I got such a cleansing'; or, 'I will never be bothered with doubts and fears, and never have any scare about whether anybody hears me sing, speak, or pray.' You are in a perilous condition. Yes, one of the perils of your life, and mine, is that of presumptuous pride.

We may easily be too big for God to use us, but never too small.
D L Moody

The Curse of the Church

But they, supposing him to have been in the company ...
Luke 2 vs. 44

The mother and earthly father of Jesus went on their journey home 'supposing him to be in the company'; but they were wrong. There are many who often make the same mistake. I have been twenty-five years on the job, and I am more helpless in God's hands than ever; but this spirit I speak of is the curse of the Church. 'Oh, we know the kind of men that should be elders and deacons.' But all we can see is the outside of the rascals. We are for showing God how to do things, and we make shipwreck of the whole thing. I don't know anything that the devil harps on more than this one thing - 'Look at the success God has given you, look at your experience; you can take advantages and liberties with God.' But in the sight of God we are all bankrupt. All our victory is of God that no flesh should glory in His presence.

Give unlimited credit to our God.
Robert Murray McCheyne

13 JANUARY

Take Advantage

*But grow in grace, and in the knowledge of our Lord
and Saviour Jesus Christ...*
II Peter 3 vs. 18

Take advantage of all the means of grace. If you begin to neglect private devotion, perils will manifest themselves. Read your Bible. If you get into the habit of neglecting the means of grace and the Church, then look out! When a 'twicer' at church becomes a 'oncer' it is like Lot pitching his tent towards Sodom. People compromise by their Sunday reading, and by the use of tobacco for their infirmities. Get busy winning men and women to Christ, and try to get believers filled with the Holy Spirit. Remember, God has only one business, and that is saving men. For that one thing He gave all He had, and is doing all He can. God's work is a saving work. If you are not engaged in a saving work, then do not say you are doing God's work. The only way you can keep a bicycle standing is by keeping it going; and we human beings are like that.

> The growth of grace is the best evidence of the truth of it; things that have no life will not grow.
> Thomas Watson

Christ Unknown

....therefore the world knoweth us not, because it knew him not.
I John 3 vs. 1

What is the good of your trying to get the world to know you? Christ lived a sinless life among nine of a family, and they - at one time even His mother - 'believed not in him.' The world knew Him not. Now, look down the chapter; - Whosover keeps on sinning hath not known Him. Whosoever keeps on abiding does not keep on sinning. Whosoever keeps on sinning hath not seen Him or known Him. He who keeps on sinning is of the devil. Whosoever is born of God doth not commit sin - that is, he won't live in sin. If I were to take a fish out of the water and put lungs in it, it would never live in the water again. Christ has taken me out of the old, and put me in the new, so that I could not live in the old now. Show me a happy backslider, and I will show you a truthful liar, a virtuous harlot, and an honest thief. 'Marvel not if the world hate you.'

> The world is a thistle head; it points its prickles at you no matter in which direction you turn.
> Martin Luther

Tugging at the Wrong Skirt

Marvel not that I said unto thee, Ye must be born again.
John 3 vs. 7

I met a woman in Glasgow once, who told me she had ceased to believe in the Lord and to pray. I asked her, "Why?" She told me her boy - her only son - had been drafted into the army and sent to France; and she had asked to Lord to spare him, and believed He would. But her boy was killed, so she threw up her 'religion', and ceased to believe in God, or pray, or go the church, or read her Bible. "God doesn't answer prayer. It is no use praying or believing," She had thrown everything overboard.

I said to her; "Keep quiet a wee minute until I ask you a question; 'Are you born again?'"

She said, "I'm a Presbyterian."

"Never bother about that," I said. "Are you saved? Are you born again?"

"No," she said.

"Well," said I, "you were tugging at the wrong skirt, knocking at the wrong door, if God isn't your Father. Why didn't you apply to Satan?"

"I never heard the like of that!" she said.

Then I showed her, her need, and how to be born again, and she entered into light; and now she has the privilege of a child of God, to present her petitions before Him.

> Prayer is a living thing; you cannot find a living prayer in a dead heart.
>
> C H Spurgeon

Untapped Resources

Let us therefore come boldly unto the throne of grace that we may obtain
mercy, and find grace to help in time of need.
Hebrew 4 vs. 16

When I was working as an evangelist in one city, I got acquainted with a wealthy man who said to me one day, "Whenever you want me, there is a key to get in by that private door whenever you like." He was a very busy man, making a lot of money; and, he not having the time to spend it, some of us did the spending of it for him. One day, when I was coming out of his room, a man I knew said to me, "What were you doing in there? I would give £10 for every minute you spend in there." At that rate, twenty minutes' time there would be worth £200! That was great.

But do you know anything about your privilege of access to God? King George could not help you very far to access into the presence of God Almighty, with whom nothing is impossible. What a privilege to have!

Suppose you had the privilege of taking whatever you liked in a big warehouse and you came out with only a pocket-handkerchief in your hand. You would be called a fool. And yet that is how many people treat their privilege of access to God. What do you come out with when you get to God? Remember, it is written, "whatsoever you shall ask in my name I will do." Many are living half-starved and poverty stricken lives, in spiritual beggary, and yet all these resources are at their disposal. May the Lord help us to rise to our privileges.

All the storehouses of God are open to the voice of faith in prayer.
D M McIntyre

A Child of God

But as many as received him, to them gave he power to become the sons of
God, even to them that believe on his name.
John 1 vs. 12

There is a lot of rubbish talked as if every one was a child of God. God is not the Father of dogs and cats; He is the Creator of them. He is not the Father of the devil or the damned, but He is the Creator of them. There is not a child of God in hell, or on the road to it, and there never will be.

A dear old maid said to me once, "I suppose you have children?"

"Yes."

"I suppose you love them?"

"Yes."

"If your child was in pain, and you could alleviate it, you would do it?"

"Yes."

"You say God is a Father?"

"Yes."

"And God's children are in hell?"

"I did not say so."

She asked, "Who is in hell?" And I replied, "Children of the devil." The Lord has a home for His crowd, and the devil has one for his crowd. If universal fatherhood is right, then Unitarianism is right, and that is the main plank of Mohammedanism and the other isms.

When you repent of your sins and believe in Christ, when you come to the conscious realisation that you are a guilty soul and see in Christ all that your heart needs, you become a child of God.

Faith lays hold of Christ and grasps Him as a present possession,
just as the ring holds the jewel.
Martin Luther

The More Abundant Life

There is a river the streams whereof shall make glad the city of God...
Psalm 46 vs. 4

The river of God is full, but we are the streams - the channels through which the water of life should flow and bring life and gladness to other lives. In this Gospel according to John we read also the same thing but in another way. The Lord says: "I came that they might have life, and that they might have it more abundantly" more abundant, overflowing life. But the sad thing among Christian people today is that their life, instead of abounding with life, is a kind of a hospital, sickly, anaemic, miserable Christian life. When you go into a hospital you see the people lying on their beds, sickly and pale, weak and worn. Is it life? Oh, yes, there is life there, but it is a very low stage of life. It is not a life that you would covet or envy. And if you will go to a large sanatorium you will see people there in various stages of life, but it is not an enviable kind of life. But you just watch those girls and boys as they tumble and roll and jump out of the schoolhouse! You wonder how their bodies were ever made to stand such exertion, such energy. They cannot be kept in for eight or nine hours with such exuberance of life; they must be allowed out three or four times during the sessions. They have overflowing life.

Let God have your life. He can do more with it than you can.
D L Moody

Overgrown Babes

Therefore leaving the principles of the doctrine of Christ,
let us go on unto perfection...
Hebrews 6 vs. 1

'Let us go on unto perfection'. The word there is the word 'Maturity.' How many men and women are just overgrown babies! Something has arrested their development. They are twenty or thirty years in Christ, but they are nothing but big babies. Instead of the church being an armoury for drilling, it is a nursery and the minister is a wet nurse, and every Sunday he has a bottle with a wee teat. They can sing, "Like a mighty army moves the Church of God," or "Onward Christian soldiers, marching as to war," but they are babies all the same. Instead of taking 16-inch guns, we have a whole lot of go-carts with big babies. Instead of gun carriages and ammunition carriages it is baby carriages.

I am persuaded that nothing is thriving in my soul unless it is growing.
Robert Murray McCheyne

The All Sufficient Saviour

I can do all things through Christ which strengtheneth me.
Philippians 4 vs. 13

Of all the personal letters Paul wrote, that to the Philippians is the only one where there is no word of condemnation. They are all words of commendation. There never was any trouble in that church except with a couple of old maids, who were like a couple of Kilkenny cats with their tails tied together hanging over a clothes line. Now see what he says in ch. 4 vs. 11: "I have learned..." everywhere and in all things I possess the secret both to be full and to be hungry..."I can do some things?" No, "I can do all things," - all things but give up tobacco? All things but govern myself? All things but control my tongue? All things, but, but, but. Wonderful Jesus! Wonderful Saviour! I can do all things.

> Christ's performances outstrip his promises.
> Nehemiah Rogers

Perfect Peace

Peace I leave with you, my peace I give unto you...
John 14 vs. 27

I was once in lodgings where there was only one little boy of six years. One Saturday afternoon he came in saying, "Oh, my head! I have such a sore head." Before the night was over he was unconscious, and he died of tubercular meningitis. He was their only child. The mother never let him out of her arms. Neighbours offered help. But she held on to the child. When the breath had left the wee body they said, "Give it to us, we will dress it." No, she dressed it herself. When the funeral came she watched the procession making its way from the door; then she went back to her bed and slept twenty-four hours of unbroken sleep, after which she got up and went back to her work.

Some who did not know any better said, "Tell me, did you love your boy?"

"Does a mother love her only child? Do fish swim? Do birds fly?"

"Why were you not in hysterics like the others? Why did you not cry with inconsolable grief?"

The peace of God, that passeth all understanding, had guarded her heart and mind. I preached for six weeks in that town, but that sermon of hers did more than all the six weeks preaching.

Peace is not real peace until it has been tested in the storm.
Eric Hayman

Known in Hell

And the evil spirit answered and said, Jesus I know,
and Paul I know; but who are ye?
Acts 19 vs. 15

When I was in charge of a church in Glasgow one of the converts made a request that caused a laugh. He prayed "Lord give me a good reputation in hell with the devil." Afterwards I said to him, "Johnny, I want to see you. Now, listen! I do not want to put a curb on you, but I would not say a thing to make us laugh at the prayer meeting."

He said, "I did not say it to make you laugh. I was praying the desire of my heart; I got it in God's Word." I said, "Where?" He replied, "Do you remember where the devil said 'Jesus we know, and Paul we know, but who are you?' I would not like the devil to have to say to me 'Who are you?' I do pray that God will give me a good reputation with the devil."

For every daredevil there should be a 'daresaint'.
Billy Sunday

Pre-Pentecostal Believers

...he shall baptize you with the Holy Ghost and with fire:
Luke 3 vs. 16

So many converted people are living before Pentecost in their experience instead of after Pentecost. They know Christ as their personal Saviour, but not as the Baptiser with the Holy Ghost and fire. They have been to Calvary for the cleansing blood but they have never gone to Jerusalem for the Pentecost, which would enable them to live lives of holiness, boldness and power. As a consequence they have a feeling of disappointment regarding Christ and His salvation. They expected victory and power when they came to Him for salvation, but instead of that it has just been the reverse. They haven't heard about the Baptism with the Holy Ghost and fire, that it is their birthright blessing. You remember the Ephesian converts were just the same. Paul asked them, "Have ye received the Holy Ghost since you believed?" They said, "We have not so much as heard whether there be any Holy Ghost." So many are just in the same plight today. No wonder their lives are so unsatisfying and unsatisfactory to Christ and to themselves.

The Holy Spirit is a living person and should be treated as a person.
A W Tozer

Testing

Being forty days tempted of the devil. And in those days he did eat nothing; and when they were ended, he afterward hungered.
Luke 4 vs. 2

He may and generally does test our faith, by withholding any manifestation or feeling from us, but only for a time. When Jesus was baptised with the Holy Spirit at the Jordan, He was led by the Spirit into the wilderness to be tempted of the devil for forty days. While there He hungered, and there were wild beasts. But we read: "He came out of the wilderness full of the Holy Spirit," and so will you if you are willing to take Him at His word, and walk by faith and not feeling. You see, dear reader, signs never satisfied any sincere soul. They can be simulated, and they don't last. But the word of the Lord endures for ever. Better a million times one word from the Lord, than all the fanciest feelings and ecstatic experiences one could have; for "heaven and earth shall pass away, but my words shall never pass away." Hallelujah!

I take the promised Holy Ghost,
I take the power of Pentecost,
To fill me now to the uttermost
I take, He undertakes.

Prayer, meditation and temptation make a minister.
Martin Luther

The Sovereignty of the Spirit

Now the Lord is that Spirit: and where the Spirit of the Lord is,
there is liberty.
II Corinthians 3 vs. 17

He never gives you any power apart from His government. It is not my using Him, but His using me. When did you receive pardon? After ye believed. When do you receive power? After the Holy Ghost is come upon you. When does He come? Tarry until. Do not take any credulity, and imagine you have got it when you have not. You know when everything is on the altar, and when there is a willingness to go through with Christ, and take up the Cross; saying, "Jesus, I am going through," glory to God, you know. Then, instead of failure and paralysis, there will be power, joy, victory, peace, and wonderful fruitfulness in God's service.

Thy Holy Spirit, Lord alone can turn our hearts from sin:
His power alone can sanctify, and make us pure within.
O Spirit of faith and love, come in our midst we pray,
And purify each waiting heart! Baptise us with power today.

To be filled with the Spirit is to have the Spirit fulfilling in us all that God intended Him to do when He placed Him there.
Lewis Sperry Shafer

Perfection's Sacred Height

That the man of God may be perfect, throughly furnished unto
all good works.
I Timothy 3 vs. 17

The word 'perfect' is the word 'ready'. What is the perfect Christian? It is the man adjusted to the Head and every member of the body. The adjustment is complete, there are no reservations in the surrender, and the completeness and adjustment is going on to maturity. Might I be guilty of a grammatical mistake? We are completer tomorrow, better adjusted tomorrow, more fully adjusted tomorrow, and all the time we are 'ready for every good work.'

When the Boer War broke out, two or three drunken generals were sent out to make a mess of things; and when they saw things going hard against the British, they sent over to Lord Roberts saying, "Will you take charge of the Expeditionary Force in South Africa?" The reply was, "Yes I will." "When will you be ready to leave?" And he said, "I have been ready for fifteen years." He saw, after the Basuto War that things should have been cleaned up then.

"I want you to teach in Sunday school," and you should be ready to say, "I am your boy."

"I would like you to give your testimony," and the reply should be, "All right, I will do it." "Can you help us in that meeting or hall?" "I am ready."

I ask you, - Are you a perfect Christian, entirely surrendered to your Lord, complete and entire in the surrender, going on more and more surrendering day by day, going on to maturity; and not only that, but ready all the time for every call and demand and command of your Lord? Thank God, this is the word, "he that hath begun a good work in you will perpetuate and perfect that work till the day of Christ." Give Him a chance, and He will perfect you now as to condition, and you will go on to perfection's sacred height.

The nearer men are to being sinless, the less they talk about it.
D L Moody

The Christian's Power

But truly I am full of power by the spirit of the Lord...
Micah 3 vs. 8

We boast about our religion that it is a religion of power. We glory in the Cross of Christ "towering o'er the wrecks of time." It is the marvellous power in Christ and in this Gospel that is our boast. We cannot boast of that too much; but there is a difference between what you read today in the Bible and its manifestation in your life. The world is concerned more about the power in your life than about what you say. They have a right to know and see the expression of that power in your life and mine. The Lord told His disciples "Ye shall receive power." Are you living the powerless or paralysed life? Is your life full of Divine energy or is it a life where the paramount thing is weakness? Here is what the Word of God says, and here is how I live: Do they correspond? Is my life a life of power or of paralysis? Am I being wheeled around like a paralytic invalid? Or am I a mighty man helping in the work of Christ in the strength of God? Is the life full of Divine energy or of human weakness? Is it a life of failure or of victory? Are you triumphing in Christ, or are the devil and the world triumphing over you?

The Christian's birthright is the power of the Holy Ghost.
Lionel Fletcher

Care Forbidden

Casting all your care upon him; for he careth for you.
I Peter 5 vs. 7

How many are so full of worry, care, and anxiety! Take up your Bible and study what God did with worrying people, murmuring people, and you will get a surprise. Whenever you begin to worry or murmur at God, you are charging God's love and will and power. It is a great sin to worry while professing to be in Christ. Thank God, there is a place in Christ where there is "not a shade of worry, not a blast of care," and where all these things are like water on a duck's back. There you have the peace that passeth all understanding, so that you are free to start and serve and help others instead of being merely taken up with your own cares.

> The devil would have us continually crossing streams that do not exist.
> Anon.

The Christian's Ambition

... for I do always those things that please him.
John 8 vs. 29

If you begin to please the Lord you may make mistakes, but the Lord knows you want to please Him. Your judgment, and mine, is not perfect; no man's is. Many a time we do things that we mean to be right, and we try to please God; but because of the infirmity of our judgment we make a mug of it.

You remember the story of the Christian barber who was busy stropping his razor one day when he was about to shave a customer, and he said to the customer, "Are you ready to die?" We smile at that, but all the same the barber was trying to help that man, and no doubt he would learn a bit better after a while. Do you mean to tell me that God will judge that barber the way the customer did? Did that barber try to please his Lord? Certainly, and God will reward him for it while you and I may laugh at his blundering mistake. Outsiders do not see that we are trying to please God, but God knows it. They only see the blundering mistakes you and I make because of the infirmity of our judgment.

> The business of our lives is not to please ourselves but to please God.
> Matthew Henry

God's Way of Appropriation

If ye then, being evil, know how to give good gifts unto your children: how much more shall your heavenly Father give the Holy spirit to them that ask him?
Luke 11 vs.13

There are many people today, some of them well known men, and excellent men, too, who tell us that we ought not to pray for the Holy Spirit, and they reason it out very speciously. They say, "The Holy Spirit was given to the Church as an abiding possession" (and that is true), and then they ask, "Why pray for what you have already got?" To this the late Dr. A. J. Gordon replied conclusively, "Jesus Christ was given to the world as an abiding gift at Calvary. He was given to the world as a whole, but each individual in the world must appropriate this gift for himself. Just so the gift of the Holy Spirit was given to the Church as a whole, but each individual member of the Church must appropriate this gift for himself, and God's way of appropriation is prayer.

We dare not limit God in our asking, nor in His answering.
John Blanchard

The Singing Side of Salvation

Sing unto the Lord, bless his name; shew forth his salvation from day today.
Psalm 96 vs. 2

There are many quiet amiable people who have been brought up in Godly homes, and the Sunday school and Church, and lived religious lives. When they get converted there is not a very great change in their life outwardly. They continue going to their Church and saying their prayers and reading their Bible, and living a decent, respectable sort of Christian life. You would hardly know they have been converted, but when they have been baptised with the Holy Spirit, what a revolutionary change takes place. The disciples before and after Pentecost are an example of this. They are now on fire for the Lord and for the souls of men and women. They not merely love the Lord; they are in love with the Lord. That's a tremendous difference. They live on the singing side of Salvation now, because they are victorious and successful. Christ is not merely a root out of a dry ground to their souls. He is the Rose of Sharon, the Lily of the Valley, and the fairest among ten thousand to their souls. They do not endure salvation - they enjoy it. You see it is the Holy Spirit's work to make Christ real, and make all that He purchased for us with His blood a reality in heart and life daily. So when we receive Him He glorifies Christ in us and to us; and Christ becomes a very satisfying reality to the Pentecostal believer.

Before Pentecost the disciples found it hard to do easy things; after Pentecost they found it easy to do hard things.
A J Gordon

FEBRUARY

1 ◆ Until

2 ◆ The Privilege of His Name

3 ◆ The Downward Tendency

4 ◆ Mortify the Flesh

5 ◆ Conversion

6 ◆ Christ's Gift to the Church

7 ◆ Rehoused

8 ◆ Open Mine Eyes

9 ◆ God's Heaven

10 ◆ The Work of the Lord

11 ◆ Comfort

12 ◆ Influence

13 ◆ Noah's Carpenters

14 ◆ Recognition in Heaven

15 ◆ The Believer and Death

16 ◆ What Must it Be to Be There!

17 ◆ No More Tears

18 ◆ Curiosity about the Future

19 ◆ The Judgement Seat of Christ

20 ◆ The Death of the Righteous

21 ◆ The Great Judgment Day

22 ◆ Heaven a Kingdom

23 ◆ A Fair Wind

24 ◆ A Haven of Rest

25 ◆ Inseparable Twins

26 ◆ On His Terms

27 ◆ Only Soul Winners Shine

28 ◆ Songless Christians

29 ◆ Give up your Name

Until

And behold, I send the promise of my Father upon you: but tarry ye in the city of Jerusalem, until ye be endued with power from on high.
John 24 vs. 49

When Lord Roberts' son was at Spion Kop, he was accompanied by a lot of fine brave young Britishers who seemed careless of danger. They rushed in a battery and it was to certain death. Young Roberts was noticed by one of them to be pale, and was accused of cowardliness; to which the reply was made, "If you were half as scared as I feel, you would take to your heels and run."

There is a courage that can stand firm in spite of all natural timorousness. God can enable us to say, "When I am weak, then am I strong." However paralysed your experience may have been, that may be at an end. "Ye shall receive power." But - "tarry". How long? - "Until." I cannot tell you how long. Tarry until something happens.

The Holy Spirit is God's imperative of life.
A W Tozer

The Privilege of His Name

And whatsoever ye shall ask in my name, that will I do, that the
Father may be glorified in the Son.
John 14 vs. 13

Did you ever give anybody your name? I am always away from home; and every time, before I go away, I have to sign a big document, giving a fellow power to use my name to look after the children and the house, and he signs my name. It is a queer risk! But the Lord has taken that risk, and He says, "Nicholson, here is My name, just go into the bank and get what you want."

Yet many are saying, "Lord, do You think You can afford to give me a penny? Lord, I would like a shilling or two, but I am afraid I would be asking too much." "Whatsoever you shall ask in my name, that will I do" - why - "that the Father may be glorified in the Son." The glory of God is in the name, and the using of it, and He is giving you the use of His name. I say at the Throne of Grace "In the name of Jesus, here is my need." Supposing I go to the banker of our friend Mr. Montgomery and say, "Would you give me £20 for the sake of Mr. Montgomery?" He would be whistling for the police. But supposing Mr. Montgomery gives me a cheque for that amount, I get it at once.

Seven times before Jesus died, in His talk in the upper room in the course of His farewell address He said, "In my name." "I am giving you the use of My name." This is the 'name above every name.'

> To ask in the name of Christ…is to set aside our own will and bow
> to the perfect will of God.
> A W Pink

The Downward Tendency

...So then with the mind I myself serve the law of God;
but with the flesh the law of sin.
Romans 7 vs. 25

There is a lot said about the law of gravity, and the main principle of it is that it attracts everything to the earth. It is only fools and theological professors that talk about things falling up; everything in God's world falls down. But if you hold up your arm, the law of life in it sets if free for the time being from the law of gravity. It does not suppress of destroy the law of gravity, but it counteracts it. A greater law than the law of gravity is the law of life in the arm. It is the same with us in Christ: I am only free from sin as I abide in Christ, and daily and hourly abandon myself to Him. Mr. Moody said one day when he was in Scotland, "After nearly thirty years of serving God, and building up a Christian character, I might go out of this church and in ten minutes' time commit a crime that would wreck those fifty years of Christian character and testimony." We all know the possibility of it. Our only security is in a constant abiding in Christ.

> Though the lions shall one day lie down with the lambs, the flesh
> will never agree with the spirit.
> C H Spurgeon

Mortify the Flesh

For if ye live after the flesh, ye shall die: but if ye through the Spirit do
mortify the deeds of the body, ye shall live.
Romans 8 vs. 13

The curse amongst us is a superficial sense of sin. We are playing with it, we have entered into a great sympathy with it, and we have all kinds of excuses and apologies to make for the accursed thing. God never condones sin; He forgives sinners, but He condemns and destroys sin. He hates sin with a burning white-heat hatred, and when you and I are as near God as we can get, we shall be inflamed not only with love, but with a hatred to sin. Do you make any allowance for it? How do you judge it? Condemn it, in the name of God, and be done with it! It is a terrible peril, whether it comes in the shape of whisky, women, tobacco, worldliness, or anything else. If there is any sin in your life unjudged, drag it out and destroy it in the name of God. You may get a wound like a pinprick, and before you know where you are you have got lockjaw. President Coolidge's son had a blister on his heel, and in a fortnight he was a corpse. Sin is like that in its deadliness; it is a hellish thing: it will blight and curse, but never bless you.

People say - "Oh yes, I lost my temper, but I could not very well help it. Shake hands with me in my weakness." Brother, judge the thing; unveil it in God's presence.

There is a story told of an old Eastern monarch who was supposed to be beautiful - so much so that he kept a veil over his face lest beholders should be dazzled. But one day the veil was blown aside, and he was seen to be what he was in reality, an ugly rascal. Sin is like that.

There is no such cruelty to men's souls as clemency to their sins.
George Swinnock

Conversion

Repent ye therefore, and be converted, that your sins may be blotted out,
when the times of refreshing shall come from the presence of the Lord;
Acts 3 vs. 19

Many people are deceived and think they are exempt from conversion, because they have, as they say, "Always loved the Lord." "They were baptised into covenant grace," and then "They joined the Church." And since then "have lived a fairly respectable, religious life," attending their church regularly and supporting it generously, so they are quite satisfied they are exempt from conversion. They believe others may require it, buy they don't. They do not deny the fact of conversion they just think it is not for them. In fact they are highly insulted and feel indignant if anyone dares to question them about their being converted. The sad thing too, is that very little, if anything, is ever said by their minister, about the necessity and the nature of it. Believe me, dear friend, without conversion you will never enter the kingdom of heaven. The only kind of people there are converted people. Hear the words of the Lord Jesus, "Verily I say unto you, except ye be converted and become as little children, ye shall not enter the kingdom of heaven." So we see the absolute necessity for being converted if we are ever to enter the kingdom of heaven. If you could enter heaven without conversion, you would succeed in making Jesus Christ a LIAR. Remember this one thing - you don't need to be converted if you have made up your mind to go to hell. There are no converted people there.

> To be converted to God means to believe in Christ. To believe that
> He is our mediator and that we have eternal life though Him.
> Martin Luther

Christ's Gift to the Church

But when the Comforter is come, whom I will send unto you from the Father, even the Spirit of truth, which proceeded from the Father, he shall testify of me:
John 15 vs. 26

Stuart Holden made the secret of the victorious Christian life so clear and plain. After one has been born again by the Spirit of God he can live victoriously only by the Holy Spirit. I began to understand that I could not attain this life by self-effort or ceremonies, for it was 'not by might nor by power, but by the Spirit.' It was not an attainment but an obtainment. Christ's gift to His Church. I had been trying to do what the Holy Spirit alone could, and would, do for me. But I must receive Him by faith, on the grounds of grace, and He would sanctify my heart, and apply the Blood, thus cleansing me from all sin and making the victory purchased by Christ on Calvary experiential. As I walked in the light as He was in the light, He would maintain the life of holiness and victory in my life, day by day.

> If Christ justifies you He will sanctify you! He will not save you and leave you in your sins.
> Robert Murray McCheyne

Rehoused

For we know that if our earthly house of this tabernacle were dissolved,
we have a building of God, an house not made with hands,
eternal in the heavens.
II Corinthians 5 vs. 1

One day we will be clothed with immortality and a body like unto His glorious body. What an exchange! Surely we shouldn't be sorry to "put off " this frail, sickly, weak, decaying body when we are promised such a body in exchange? Thank God death need have no terrors for saved men and women. If we can say with the Apostle, "for to me to live is Christ," then we can say "to die is gain." So real and blessed was this to the aged Apostle that he said, "I am in a strait betwixt two, having a desire to depart and to be with Christ; which is far better." May the Lord make this matter of dying a blessed reality to every believer.

> If it be sweet to be the growing corn of the Lord here, how much better to be gathered into his barn!
> Robert Murray McCheyne

8 FEBRUARY

Open Mine Eyes

Where there is no vision the people perish...
Proverbs 29 vs. 18

General Booth, the founder and leader of the Salvation Army, said to some hundreds of his cadets when they were graduating from the training home, "Young men, if I had had my way I would never have had you here for years in this Training Home, but I would have put you in hell for twenty-four hours, so that you might have felt the pains and pangs of the damned, that you might have heard their weeping and wailing, and their gnashing of teeth, and seen something of their torments. I would then have let you out and sent you into the world to warn men and women to flee from the wrath to come. I would be sure of this, you would never take the work easy, or treat it negligently while you were in it."

I feel the old General was about right. Oh! If the old devil can get us to not believe in the fact of hell, then he knows that he has cut the nerve of our energy and effort.

No man can be a Christian who is unconcerned for the salvation of others.
Richard Haldane

God's Heaven

In my Father's house are many mansions: if it were not so,
I would have told you.
John 14 vs. 2

There is no other subject that inflames the heart and fires the imagination more than the subject of Heaven. After being away from home and loved ones for a time, the very thought of going home again fills the heart with joy. Should it not be the same when we think of our Heavenly Home?

When we are thinking of visiting any other country or city, we like to find out all we can about it, so that when we get there we will know what is most interesting and where to look for it, and thus get the most and best out of our visit. Shall we do other about heaven? When the Lord Jesus has taken the trouble to go and prepare a place for us and has given us much information about the place, should we not take time to find out all we can about it, so that when we get there we will not feel as if we were strangers or foreigners? We will feel at home. There are many Christians who know more about the continent of Europe or Great Britain or America than they do about heaven. This should not be.

The light of heaven is the face of Jesus.
The joy of heaven is the presence of Jesus.
The melody of heaven is the name of Jesus.
The harmony of heaven is the praise of Jesus.
The theme of heaven is the work of Jesus.
The employment of heaven is the service of Jesus.
The way of heaven is the blood of Jesus.
The fullness of heaven is Jesus Himself.

Go up beforehand and see your lodging. Look through all your Father's rooms in heaven; in your Father's house are many dwelling places. Men take a sight of lands ere they buy them. I know Christ hath made the bargain already: but be kind to the house you are going to, and see it often.
Samuel Rutherford

The Work of the Lord

Therefore, my beloved brethren, be ye steadfast, unmovable,
always abounding in the work of the Lord, forasmuch as ye know that
your labour is not in vain in the Lord.
1 Corinthians 5 vs. 58

Overflowing in the work of the Lord. How few there are like this in the church today. They are overflowing in the work of making money and in making a successful business. They will spend all their strength and time to succeed. They cannot afford time for recreation or fellowship with their family. Morning, noon and night they are at it. Undoubtedly they are Christian men, but they give you the impression that the things that are real and worth having are the things of this life. They are overflowing with worldly work. They are sadly lacking in the spiritual overflow. The church is neglected. They give a little money or sympathy, but they withhold their services and themselves. They have no time, they say. But they have time for everything else. How contrary this is to the mind of the Lord. We are to overflow in the work of the Lord, not trying to do as little as we can, but trying to do as much as we can. What a blessing we all might be to others if we were overflowing in the work of the Lord. How prosperous and successful the church would be. The most of the work in the church is done by the few who are overflowing. The others are only drags and drawbacks.

Room for pleasure, room for business,
But for Christ the Crucified
Not a place that He can enter
In your heart for which He died.

No man ever yet lost anything by serving God with a whole heart, or gained anything by serving him with half a one.
Thomas V Moore

Comfort

Blessed are they that mourn: for they shall be comforted.
Matthew 5 vs. 4

A missionary out in India had two little children – a boy and a girl. The little girl of three took ill and passed away in a few days; then the little boy took ill also. They saw that it was diphtheria. They were many miles away from the doctor. They heard that one had come to a village some miles away from them. They took up the little fellow and journeyed many miles through the jungle to the village, only to find when they got there that he had gone. All they could do was to watch the little life flicker away. Then they journeyed back again to their station, and laid the two wee darlings in the one grave. The mother said that she never seemed to feel the sorrow until it was all over; then when she came into the home and put away for the last time their toys and garments, it was too much for her. She collapsed. She lay for some days ill; but, speaking about it afterwards, she said the thought that gave her strength and comfort was that she was only separated from them for a short time; she would meet them again and never part. She was able to get up and go about her work again, this glorious truth singing in her heart, Oh, thank God we are only parted for a time. Cheer up, mourning one.

> Ye have lost a child, she is not lost to you who is found in Christ; she is not sent away, but only sent before, like a star which, going out of sight, does not die and vanish, but shines in another hemisphere.
> Samuel Rutherford

Influence

Ye are the salt of the earth.
Matthew 5 vs. 13

This metaphor appeals to the Oriental mind because common salt, being very necessary and precious, has in the Orient an important significance socially as well as commercially. By its use food is made palatable. It also preserves food. Its use in sacrifices gives salt a religious significance. It is the bond of hospitality. When Christ first spoke these words they must have seemed ridiculously presumptuous. How could a Galilean peasant and a handful of fishermen be salt of the earth? Did He think they could keep the world from rotting? It is strange still to reflect that, not withstanding all the miserable inconsistencies of Christians since that time, the whole experience of history has verified these words. There are men today who curl the lip and sneer at it, but they take good care to live where the salt is. Not many choose to live where there is no church.

Your influence is negative or positive, never neutral.
Henrietta Mears

Noah's Carpenters

By faith Noah, being warned of God of things not seen as yet, moved with
fear, prepared an ark to the saving of his house...
Hebrews 11 vs. 7

Noah believed and obeyed God and built an ark. He had many
helpers during the 120 years, but they would not believe, although
Noah preached to them for 120 years. The day came when they were
ordered into the ark, but refused, and that Unseen Hand shut the door.
The rains and floods came, and all were lost. Their last chance had
come, and they refused. You may be a Church officer, a Sunday School
teacher, a singer in the choir, an active Christian worker, helping to
advance Christ's kingdom, and yet be unsaved, and when the
judgment of God comes, be engulfed and damned.

> He sent Noah to preach for one hundred and twenty years and he
> never got a soul beside his own family into the ark.
> D L Moody

Recognition in Heaven

For now we see through a glass, darkly; but then face to face...
I Corinthians 13 vs. 12

So many are perplexed and wonder whether they will know the loved ones who have gone before. The Word of God is very clear about this. We read, "For now we see through a glass, darkly; but then face to face." What sort of a place would it be if we did not recognise each other? Here we know each other very imperfectly. Shall we know each other less there? Nay; we shall know each other better when the mists have rolled away. Peter recognised Moses and Elijah on the Mount of Transfiguration. They were not changed, and that is why he recognised them. How often, when someone is entering death, they have seen someone loved long since but lost awhile! When good Queen Victoria was dying she was heard to say, "Albert, Albert." Her husband, who had died years before, was near her. I knew a lady who told me that when her little child was passing away, she seemed to wake up and her face light up, and she cried, "Papa, Papa." The father had gone some time before. Are we not to believe all this evidence? What makes any place dear to us? Is it not the presence of loved ones there? If we will not know each other we will not know the Lord Jesus. No, no, that could never be. The recognition of the one ensures the recognition of the other.

> We shall certainly not know less there than here. If we know our friends here, we shall know them there. And as we know our friends here we shall know them there.
> Augustus Strong

The Believer and Death

Precious in the sight of the Lord is the death of his saints.
Psalm 116 vs. 15

Let us turn to our Bible and learn something about the believer and death. We are taught it is a sleep. We are never frightened of sleeping. What a blessing at the end of the toilsome day to retire to rest and kindly sleep overtakes us. It is only when sleep seems to evade us for a time that we appreciated the blessedness of sleep. So death will be all that to us, when we reach the end of the road, tired and worn out and weary with life's burdens and trials and joys.

Death is spoken of as an Exodus. What a joyful blessing the exodus was to the children of Israel. No more slavery; no more bondage; no more burdens; no more sorrow and pain. What a glorious deliverance it will be. What release, what freedom and joy. Home at last, Hallelujah!

Death is also represented as a Departure. You have seen the vessel moored to the wharf. The time comes for its departure. The ropes are let go and out she steams into the ocean on her journey to other lands. So it will be with us one day. Sickness and disease and old age will loosen our hold on this life and earth, and when every shoreline is gone we depart to be with Christ, which is very far better.

Take care of your life and the Lord will take care of your death.
George Whitefield

What Must It Be To Be There!

But as it is written, Eye hath not seen, nor ear heard, neither have entered into the heart of man, the things which God hath prepared for them that love him.
I Corinthians 2 vs. 9

I remember reading of a child born blind. He had never seen the beauties or the glories of nature. His loved ones had done their best to make him see by describing them to him; but however well we may describe these things we can never tell them as they really are.

So it was with him. They heard about some clever oculist who had performed some very remarkable operations, and they took the lad to him. He examined him very carefully, and then said that he thought an operation would give the boy his sight, but they were not to be too sure; he would do his best, and if he did not succeed, the boy would be none the worse afterwards, and they would have the satisfaction of knowing that all possible had been done for the lad. The operation was performed. The lad was to keep the bandages on for some days after. At last the day came to take them off, and then it would be known whether the operation had been successful. The excitement was intense. The mother and father and some friends were there. The bandages were removed. The room was darkened. The light was admitted very slowly at first, and then fully. What joy there was when they saw that the lad had his sight. He was taken over to the window of the ward and shown the glories of the early spring. He was silent, and they wondered what was wrong. They looked into his face and saw the tears running down his cheeks. In answer to their questionings he said, "Why did you not tell me what a lovely place I was living in?"

They had done their best, but they had failed to give him any adequate conception of the beauties of nature. So it will be when we get to Heaven. We will say: "The half was never told." Who could adequately describe the glories and the felicities of the Home above, where all is love?

> I wonder many times that ever a child of God should have a sad heart, considering what the Lord is preparing for him.
> Samuel Rutherford

No More Tears

… and God shall wipe away all tears from their eyes.
Revelation 7 vs. 17

"This world is full of sighs, full of sad and weeping eyes." A tear has never dimmed the eye there. I don't know what you women will do when you get there, for tears are your friends in many a time of trouble. I have known many a woman say that she frequently went away and had a good cry to herself. Her tears acted like a sort of safety valve for her. Then what a weapon it is in the hands of women. Just start them flowing, and what man or argument could stand before them? The Lord will see that up there there will be no occasion for them, so they won't be needed. Glory to God! not only unclouded skies, but undimmed eyes for all who gather there.

A Jesus who never wept could never wipe away my tears.
C.H.Spurgeon

Curiosity About the Future

*We have also a more sure word of prophecy; whereunto ye do well that ye
take heed, as unto a light that shineth in a dark place, until the day dawn,
and the day star arise in your hearts:*
II Peter 1 vs. 19

Isn't it strange how men and women will go to this one and the other,
and pay large sums of money, if only they can tell them something
about the future? There is that in every one of us that likes to pry into
the unknown. That is why spiritualism prospers so well these days,
and gypsies and palmists and other emissaries of the devil, with their
delusions. People believe their lies, and yet doubt the Word of God.
You don't need to go to these frauds, for they are just as wise as you
are about the future. You have the Bible in your hand. Go to it, and
there you will find accurately all about what comes after death.

My times are in Thy hand
I'll always trust in Thee;
And, after death, at Thy right hand
I shall forever be.
W F Lloyd

The Judgment Seat of Christ

For we must all appear before the judgment seat of Christ; that everyone
may receive the things done in his body, according to that
he hath done, whether it be good or bad.
II Corinthians 5 vs. 10

Believers "must all appear before the judgment seat of Christ;" to 'receive reward' or 'suffer loss' according to their works on earth. It will not be a question of heaven or hell, since they are all previously in heaven in 'bodies of glory,' but of what reward, if any, they are to get when there. Paul has been with Christ - so has the dying thief - for hundreds of years. How absurd it is then to suppose it has yet to be decided whether they are fit to be there! If we live here, as believers, worldly, pleasure-loving, selfish lives, it will be like hay, wood and stubble, and when the fire hits it, it will go up in a puff of smoke; but if we have lived for the Lord and done our best to win souls, then it will be like gold, silver, and precious stones, that will endure the fire and be to our reward and God's glory through all eternity.

> Only that which is fit for heaven and to live in the perfect presence
> of Jesus Christ will pass.
> Alex Clark

The Death of the Righteous

Let me die the death of the righteous, and let my last end be like his!
Numbers 23 vs. 10

A minister said to an old Scottish saint as she lay dying, "What is it gives you comfort in your dying hour? Is it the love of God?" "Oh, no," she said. He was surprised, and said, "Is it the mercy of God?" "No," she said again; "I have no right to either His love or His mercy." "Then what is it gives you comfort in your dying hour?" "It is the righteousness of God," she said, "for He is just, and the justifier of everyone that believeth."

Jesus Thy blood and righteousness
My beauty are, my glorious dress
Mids't flaming worlds in these arrayed
With joy shall I lift up my head.

Faith wraps itself in the righteousness of Christ.
Thomas Brooks

The Great Judgment Day

And as it is appointed unto men once to die, but after this the judgment:
Hebrews 9 vs. 27

An old Civil War veteran lay dying. His minister came to see him, and as he sat by the bedside of the dying old warrior he wondered what he might say, or wondered what way he might say it; so he said, "John, are you afraid to die?" The old man raised himself up on his elbow and looked with anger and indignation at the minister, and said, "Look here, sir; I have faced death many a time, on many a bloody battlefield, and never was frightened; I have faced it many a time since, and do you think now that I have come to the last of life, I'll be scared? I'm no coward, and I dare you to insult me in my dying hour." He fell back on his pillow exhausted.

The minister was taken all aback for a time, and wondered what he might say now. After lifting his heart to the Lord he said, "John, are you prepared for what comes after death?" "Oh," he said, "that is what makes me scared." How many there are like him! It isn't the thought or the fact of death that scares them. Many a man has faced death with a laugh on bloody battlefields, but when they think about what comes after death, there isn't a man who is not scared.

How calm the judgment hour shall pass
To all who do obey
The Word of God, and trust the blood,
And make that Word their stay!

Christ stands before no man to be judged; but every man stands before Him.
A W Tozer

Heaven a Kingdom

*Hearken, my beloved brethren, Hath not God chosen the poor
of this world rich in faith, and heirs of the kingdom
which he hath promised to them that love him?*
James 2 vs. 5

Heaven is not only a place, but it is a Kingdom. It is as real as any earthly kingdom, but what a difference from the kingdoms of this world. Here we have rulers and kings, but at the best they are only sinners with crowns on their heads. It is necessary for them to be guarded everywhere they go, and they have to maintain large armies and a navy, or they would be dethroned; but in that Kingdom there will be nothing but perfect love between subject and sovereign and among all the people. Neither wars nor rumours of wars are known there. Everyone will have perfect light. None will be crippled or deformed or stunted. Our knowledge will be perfected; the mists will have forever passed away.

There is a land of pure delight
Where saints immortal reign
Infinite day excludes the night
And pleasures banish pain.
Isaac Watts

A Fair Wind

And he said unto them, Where is your faith? And they being afraid
wondered, saying one to another, What manner of man is this! For he
commandeth even the winds and water, and they obey him.
Luke 8 vs. 25

Let us remember that we have the Lord of sea and sky with us, and we can never be lost with Him on board. What a cyclone of passion we have come through; we have almost been sucked into its fatal centre. Sun and stars at times, seemed to have ceased to shine, so dark was the night. We have weathered them all, and will, until we reach the other shore, where the storms of life will be over. Every storm is a fair wind to the child of God, for He is working all things together for our good. They but blow us on our way home.

God promises a safe landing but not a calm passage.
Anon.

A Haven of Rest

And I saw a new heaven and a new earth: for the first heaven and the first earth were passed away; and there was no more sea.
Revelation 21 vs. 1

You never saw the sea perfectly still. It is always in motion. It has a twofold motion; it fluctuates and undulates. It rises and falls and goes to and fro. Isn't that like our lives? What restless creatures we are. We are never satisfied here and never will be until we awake in His likeness. We are always consumed with restless longings, and yearnings. Aims and ambitions have come and gone. Today, we have been up the hill of hope, joy, and faith; tomorrow, we are down in the valley of the shadow of death. Like Noah's dove, we can find no rest on the troubled waters of this life; but we are making for the haven of rest, where we shall forever be at rest and satisfied.

What peace can they have who are not at peace with God.
Matthew Henry

Inseparable Twins

Be careful for nothing; but in every thing by prayer and supplication with thanksgiving let your requests be made known unto God.
Philippians 4 vs. 6

Praising is just as essential as praying. The one has to be acquired and cultivated as much as the other. They go well together if we are to succeed in "saving ourselves from this untoward generation."

The children of Israel were made captive because they served not the Lord their God with joyfulness and with gladness of heart. A growling, grumbling, morbid and morose disposition neither pleases God nor helps us to save ourselves, so let us see to it that we allow nothing to destroy our joy in the Lord and the continued song of praise in our lives. We are to be careful for nothing, prayerful about everything and thankful for anything. This is the sort of life that brings blessing to others in the church and in the world.

In prayer we act like men, in praise we act like angels.
Thomas Watson

On His Terms

If my people, which are called by my name, shall humble themselves, and pray, and seek my face, and turn from their wicked ways; then will I hear from heaven, and will forgive their sin, and will heal their land.
II Chronicles 7 vs. 14

During the centenary year of the great 1859 Revival, a friend who corresponded with W. P. wrote to him shortly before his death to say that there was much preaching in the churches on the '59 revival. The reply was brief and to the point: 'Brother, they could have another, and greater, revival if they would pay the price. God is as keen and able as ever to give revival, but only on His terms.

W. P. Nicholson paid the price and became God's mouthpiece to his generation. Oh, for a prophet for our day, armed with the same truth and empowered by the same Spirit to see 'another, and greater, revival' to the glory of God!

It is easier to speak about revival than to set about it.
Horatius Bonar

Only Soul Winners Shine

*And they that be wise shall shine as the brightness of the firmament; and
they that turn many to righteousness as the stars for ever and ever.*
Daniel 12 vs. 3

At the last the wise will be the soul winner and he alone. Not the man
who built and garnished churches however commendable that may
be; not the man who is successful in business; not the man who pleases
the ear of millions with his song; not the man who thrills the
multitudes with his preaching, but he that 'turneth many to
righteousness shall shine as the stars for ever and ever.'

Those who shine above are soul winners. Many who shine here, as
scholars, as businessmen, as politicians, or in society, will be dark stars
up there. Some of you shine at afternoon teas. There's Mrs. So-and-
so, and her afternoon teas are a dream. Such cake! What tea! What
china! How brilliant she is! How dazzling in her conversation and
social charms and small talk! Do you shine in this - that you win
souls? Some of you shine at church bazaars and jumble sales, chain
teas and sewing meetings, and ballroom buffoonery. You know just
exactly how to do it, never overdoing it and yet never falling below the
line of some giddy soul's applause and flattery. Do you shine in this -
that you win souls.

The devil will allow you to do anything except to get people
converted - allow you to sing and tickle the ribs of a million people to
empty laughter, or make them weep with some earth-born emotion, if
you stop short of getting them converted. He will allow you to preach,
and pack your church by the sheer power of human speech and
impassioned oratory. He doesn't care how big the crowd you draw.
The bigger the better, so long as you stop short of getting them
converted. The devil is concerned about only one thing - getting
people damned. It doesn't matter how it is done or to what
circumstances; he is out for this one thing. And for one thing Christ
came into the world - not to make men happy, not to get them better
wages and better homes, but to get them saved.

Winners of souls must first be weepers of souls.
C.H. Spurgeon

Songless Christians

Behold, God is my salvation; I will trust, and not be afraid: for the Lord JEHOVAH is my strength and my song; he also is become my salvation.
Isaiah 12 vs. 2

I am glad that our religion is a singing religion. The child of God who can't sing is a humbug; I question whether he is a Christian at all. Every Christian is able to sing. I will grant you that his voice may sound like a file on tin, or the croak of an old frog, or the croak of a raven, but it is melody in the heart. It may not be like the song of a canary or that of a nightingale, but the Lord has as much liking for the croak of a frog or the croak of a raven as He has for the song of a canary or of a nightingale. He doesn't expect you and me to sing like canaries or nightingales, but He does expect every one of us to sing. What does he want us to sing? He tells us to sing hymns and psalms. The psalmist, in the fortieth psalm, says: "he put a new song in my mouth" - there is no bigger miracle in the world than a man or a woman saved by God's grace, and singing; and when the world sees it - "Many shall see it, and shall fear, and on the Lord rely."

It is because there are so many song-less Christians, and so many sour Christians, that there are so many unconverted people in the world today.

If Christians praised God more, the world would doubt Him less.
Charles E Jefferson

Give up your Name

To the law and to the testimony: if they speak not according to this word, it is because there is no light in them.
Isaiah 8 vs. 20

Alexander the Great conquered the world when he was 34 years of age, and wept because there were no more worlds to conquer. In his army there was a man who was a coward, and they called him Alexander. Alexander the Great went to him and said, "Man, cease to be a coward, or else give up your name."

I say to you, in the name of Christ; if you call yourself a Christian, and you have doubts about the Bible, for God's sake give up the name "Christian."

A man has no morality who sits in a professorial chair in a college or stands in the pulpit of a church, calling himself a Christian professor or a Christian minister, and casting doubt upon and discrediting the authority and integrity of the Bible. He is not a moral man; he has not got the morality of a highway robber.

> I can't abide cowardice. I refuse to make my God and Saviour a nonentity.
> C T Studd

MARCH

1 ◆ Your Speech

2 ◆ God's Love

3 ◆ We are in Him

4 ◆ A Safe Landing

5 ◆ Stones not Bricks

6 ◆ The Prodigal

7 ◆ Saved and Sure

8 ◆ The Hard Way

9 ◆ The Fellowship of His Sufferings

10 ◆ Face to Face

11 ◆ The Law of Discipleship

12 ◆ Jesus Himself

13 ◆ The Church's Business

14 ◆ The Real Test

15 ◆ Natural Life vs. Eternal Life

16 ◆ Running the Race

17 ◆ The Advent of Faith

18 ◆ A Clean Break

19 ◆ True Repentance

20 ◆ Save Yourselves

21 ◆ Goodbye God

22 ◆ Overflowing Faith

23 ◆ Election

24 ◆ A Glorious Reality

25 ◆ Repentance

26 ◆ A Purifying Hope

27 ◆ Is it a Mark of Love?

28 ◆ Fire! Fire!

29 ◆ The Fullness of the Spirit

30 ◆ Getting your Priorities Right

31 ◆ A Believing Mind

Your Speech

*Seeing then that all these things shall be dissolved, what manner of persons
ought ye to be in all holy conversation and godliness...?*
II Peter 3 vs. 11

When you meet with others - whether in your own home, whether in the street, or in the tram - if anybody were listening to your conversation, would your speech betray you? Would that person know by your conversation that you belonged to Jesus Christ? Would there be that peculiarity about you that men and women would instantly detect and discern that you and I are pilgrims and sojourners, and that we are followers of the bleeding Lamb?

John Bunyan, you remember, was anxious about his soul. A bunch of women gathered every morning at the step of one of their homes, and their conversation was about the Lord and the things of the Lord. John Bunyan stood around the corner, listening. They didn't know, and in that way John Bunyan was brought to a sense of his need, and led to accept the Lord Jesus Christ as his Saviour. When we speak with one another, tell me: is there any mention of the Lord; is there anything about our conversation by which men and women would know that we were really the Lord's?

Whatever moves the heart wags the tongue.
C T Studd

2 MARCH

God's Love

He that loveth not knoweth not God; for God is love.
I John 4 vs. 8

I remember preaching in Moody's church in Chicago - in the old church yonder at the corner. Over the platform or pulpit Mr. Moody used to have the words: "God is Love," brightly lit up by electric light or gaslight. These lights were burning all the time he was preaching. One Sunday night a burglar, who was going to do a job, came along. He peeped in through the church door, and then he opened the door and looked in. He saw these words: "God is Love." He shut the door, and went down the steps, cursing and swearing. The farther he walked along the street the hotter he became, and the madder he became, and the more he cursed and damned. He said, "God is not love. I have been kicked and cursed since ever I was born. I never had a chance. Everything is against me. God is against me. It is not true; it is a lie. God doesn't love me."

But the farther he walked the more he was troubled, and it was not long till he turned back towards the church. When he got to the door of the church Mr. Moody was giving an invitation to his hearers to come to Christ. This burglar walked right down the aisle, fell at the altar, and accepted Jesus Christ as his Saviour.

You may be cast out by everybody, you may be down and out tonight, you may feel heart broken, you may feel as lonely as a man or a woman can be in a big city - and man, I know what that is - as if everybody had turned on you, and you think your life is hardly worth living; or, on the other hand, you may be as respectable as a man or a woman can be, with all your white washed hypocrisy and religiosity and profession: it doesn't matter whether you are up and out or down and out; thank God, He loves you. Shouldn't that be an encouragement to you to come to Christ? He is willing to receive you: "He loved me, and gave Himself for me."

> God so loved that he gave...! And the giving, with Calvary at its heart, was not a trickle but a torrent.
> Paul S. Rees

We are in Him

If a man say, I love God, and hateth his brother, he is a liar:
for he that loveth not his brother whom he hath seen,
how can he love God whom he hath not seen?
I John 4 vs. 20

Dr. Berry, - one of the great Congregational preachers - drew vast audiences to his church over in Birmingham. One night a rap came to his door. He went to the door and found there a poor girl with a shawl round her. She said: "Will you come and get my mother in? Will you come and get my mother in?" He wondered what he could do to get her mother in. The girl said that her mother was lying dying. He went with the girl to her home, and he found her mother lying in bed, dying. He began to tell the mother about the lovely Jesus, the sweet Jesus, and the wise Jesus. The mother said: "It is not that that I want to hear. I want my sins forgiven. They are weighing me down. I want to know that I am saved."

The minister said: "I began to tell her what I had heard from my mother about Jesus, who died for sinners, who shed His blood for sinners; and," he said, "I got her in, and I got myself in." "Many ministers shall say unto me in that day: 'Lord, Lord....' and from the gates of glory they will be hurled to the caverns of the damned.

Out of my bondage, sorrow and night
Jesus I come; Jesus I come;
Into the freedom gladness and light
Jesus I come to Thee.

The most urgent task before the church today is the 'bringing in' of those outside its fellowship.
Guy H. King

A Safe Landing

*Behold, I have refined thee, but not with silver; I have chosen thee
in the furnace of affliction.*
Isaiah 48 vs. 10

We are told not to think it strange concerning the fiery trial. Jesus said, "In this world ye shall have tribulation." Paul tells us to "continue in the faith," and that "we must through much tribulation enter into the kingdom of God." We are to consider Him that endured such contradiction of sinners against Himself, lest ye be wearied and faint in your minds. Ye have not yet resisted unto blood, striving against sin. And ye have forgotten the exhortation which speaketh unto you as unto children, My son despise not thou the chastening of the Lord, nor faint when thou art rebuked of Him; for whom the Lord loveth He chasteneth and scourgeth every son whom he recieveth. If ye endure chastening, God dealeth with you, as with sons; for what son is he whom the father chasteneth not? I believe we often fail because we think no one has ever been tried just as we or for such a long time. We forget that there is no trial but is common to all men. God never promised anyone a smooth passage. He does promise us a safe landing.

*God never would send you the darkness
If he thought you could bear the light,
But you would not cling to the guiding hand
If the way were always bright.
And you would not learn to walk by faith
Could you always walk by sight.*

It is doubtful if God can bless a man greatly without hurting him deeply.
Anon.

Stones not Bricks

Ye also, as lively stones, are built up a spiritual house, an holy priesthood,
to offer up spiritual sacrifices, acceptable to God by Jesus Christ.
1 Peter 2 v 5

The Lord never says in His Word that we are bricks. No. But He does say we are stones. Man makes bricks, but man never made a stone. God makes them. There are too many brick Christians in the Church today, and not enough living stones. You may educate a child in all the ways of Christianity so that it will become proficient, but after all is done and said, you haven't made a Christian out of it. "Ye must be born again." Surely you see dear friends, how imperative it is. "Ye must be born again." I have almost exhausted your patience with my reiteration of this solemn fact. I have done so because you will never see the kingdom of heaven unless you are born again, and I know you want to be in heaven as I do myself, and we all do. Well, don't let the devil deceive you and damn you by some false notion or way.

> All the godly may justly be called Peters; (stones which having been founded on Christ, are fitted for building the temple of God).
> John Calvin

The Prodigal

I will arise and go to my father, and will say unto him, Father, I have sinned against heaven, and before thee.
Luke 15 vs. 18

The prodigal son was led to repent through the failure of his life. He left home and father and started out for the far country and a good time. He had a good time for a while, but it soon ended, and he finished up at the swine trough, feeding pigs, hungry and lonely, forsaken by all his friends.

The Holy Spirit used these very circumstances to produce true repentance, and he came home. What a welcome! His father kissed him before even he washed his face.

This has been the means used by the Spirit in many cases since. It was this that broke my heart and led me home to Christ. As a young man I left home and loved ones. Tired of piety and family prayers I set out to have a good time. I certainly had a good time too, but never truly satisfied, and the good time was transient and intermittent, until at last, disgusted and disappointed with it all, I saw what a failure I was making of my life. My ideas and ambitions were blighted, my heart was dissatisfied and discontented, and my hopes were ruined. This all led home, and soon after to the Saviour. How often the Spirit uses this sense of failure to produce repentance and lead to Christ.

True repentance is personal, permanent, painful and profitable.
John Blanchard

Saved and Sure

Christ in you, the hope of glory:
Colossians 1 v 27

We are saved by believing in Jesus Christ as our personal Saviour, and we are sure we are saved by believing the Word of God. For instance, if you ask me, "Are you married?" I answer, "Yes." You say, "How do you know?" I produce my marriage certificate and show you that. Is that all I have to prove and assure me I am married? If that were all, that would be a queer sort of married life. I have something more than a mere "piece of paper" to assure me I am married. I have my wife! I have something more than a piece of paper to assure me I am saved. I have the Lord Jesus Christ living and abiding within. How many there are in our churches that have gone through the Communicant's Class and would have answered all the questions satisfactorily. They have assented to all the truth they were taught and were told they are now "Believers", therefore ready to become church members. If this is all they have, they are still children of wrath even as others, and on the road to hell, and surer of getting there than ever were before. They are wrapped around with their self-righteous rags and lulled to sleep in a carnal security, and it will be a mighty miracle if they are ever awakened and saved.

Faith rests on the naked Word of God; that Word believed gives full assurance.
H A Ironside

The Hard Way

And the keeper of the prison awaking out of his sleep, and seeing the prison doors open, he drew out his sword, and would have killed himself, supposing that the prisoners had been fled.
Acts 16 vs. 27

It took this unusual earthquake to break the hard-hearted, cruel Roman soldier down and compel him to cry out, "What must I do to be saved?" God has strange ways and uses strange means to bring sinners to their senses and compel them to realise they are lost sinners and need salvation. When sinners become full-grown and become fascinated with the world and its pleasures and sin, they become used to their own notions and ways, no ordinary means will bring them to a sense of their danger, so God uses the unusual. Some sudden calamity occurs, some sudden death of a loved one. Sudden sickness overtakes them; their health vanishes; their money takes wings and flies away. One strange thing after another comes like a bolt out of the blue, until their life is one succession of tragedies; until like the jailor, they feel like ending it all by committing suicide. Just at that point they are led to feel their helpless, lost condition, and cry out, "What must I do to be saved?"

There are many everywhere who thank God for the terrible and trying experience that God used to make them conscious of their lost condition and seek to be saved.

> A sculptor does not use a manicure set to reduce the crude unshapely marble to be a thing of beauty.
> A W Tozer

The Fellowship of His Sufferings

For as the sufferings of Christ abound in us, so our consolation
also aboundeth by Christ.
II Corinthians 1 vs. 5

"For as the sufferings of Christ overflow us". Yes, you will find that the nearer you get to the Lord, the more deeply you come into the realisation of the Christian life, the more you will know of the overflowing fellowship and suffering of Jesus Christ. When you are happy you can share your joy with anyone, but when some great sorrow comes into your life, you are very careful whom you share it with. You cannot share it with everyone. So it is with Christ. He only shares His sorrow with the choice ones. The crowd was outside Gethsemane; the eight were at the gate; but it was only James and John and Peter who were with Him in His agony. Can He bring us into that close fellowship? If He can, we will know what it is to overflow or abound in the sufferings of Christ. William Burns of hallowed memory in Scotland and China, was in Glasgow one day with his mother. She missed him and turning back she found him up an alley sobbing and weeping as if his heart were breaking. She asked him if he was ill. "No mother" he said "It is the thud of these Christless feet on the road to hell that is nearly breaking my heart". Do we abound in the sufferings of Christ? It was the passionate desire of Paul's heart "To know Him and the fellowship of his sufferings". If we suffer with Him we shall also reign with Him. It is as we suffer with Him that we will abound in His consolations.

> When I consider my crosses, tribulations and temptations, I shame myself almost to death thinking of what they are in comparison to the suffering of my blessed Saviour, Jesus Christ.
> Martin Luther

Face to Face

And they shall see his face.
Revelation 22 vs. 4

However much we may long to see the loved ones, we will want far more to see the one who saved us and loved us with a dying and undying love. "Him whom having not seen, we love." When the little boy who was operated on successfully, saw, the first thing he asked for was that he might see the one who had given him his sight. It will be the same with us when we get there. It is not a sleep after death, for to be absent from the body is to be present with the Lord and loved ones. When we die we shall awake in His likeness. We will then know everything perfectly. The problems and the perplexities here will all be solved. The knowledge that we longed for here will be ours there. No more mysteries or uncertainties. We shall know perfectly.

Face to face with Christ, my Saviour,
Face to face – what will it be
When with rapture I behold Him,
Jesus Christ, who died for me?
Carrie E. Breck

The Law of Discipleship

And he said to them all, If any man will come after me, let him deny himself, and take up his cross daily, and follow me.
Luke 9 vs. 23

Cross bearing was the law of discipleship when Christ was here on earth in the days of His flesh and is the law today everywhere and for everybody. Notice the words "any man'. It means everyone who would be His disciple today. It includes every disciple or would-be disciple and excludes none. Christ's condition or law of discipleship isn't changed to suit every candidate for discipleship. He will never change the law to secure a disciple. It is for all ages. There are those who would have us distinguish between being a 'Christian' and a 'Disciple'. Jesus knew no such distinction. Notice His words: "There went great multitudes with him and he turned and said unto them," (Luke 14 vs. 25) not merely disciples, but the multitudes.. Then in vs. 26 He said: "If any man" not merely disciples - ANY MAN. Also Mark 8 vs. 34, "And when he had called the people unto him, with his disciples also." Here we have the people and the disciples separately mentioned, showing the law of discipleship was not merely for the disciples alone but for everyone who would be a disciple of the Lord Jesus. How conspicuous and emphatic and repeated this law of discipleship was in the teachings of Jesus. Isn't it very significant and ominous, the silence in our teaching and preaching today? We seem more concerned about making Christ and salvation popular and appealing than we are about the law of discipleship. Our concern in His service seems to be success and large tabulated results. Someone has said: "If we can preach the Gospel, and please the religious, natural, unregenerate man, we are not preaching Christ's Gospel." How true it is. Cross bearing is never popular or pleasing even amongst true disciples, let alone the natural, unregenerate man. We forget we are the salt of the earth, not the sugar.

> The cross of Christ is the sweetest burden that ever I did bare; it is such a burden as wings are to a bird, or sails are to a ship, to carry me forward to my harbour.
> Samuel Rutherford

Jesus Himself

And if I go and prepare a place for you, I will come again, and receive you unto myself; that where I am, there ye may be also.
John 14 v 3

His coming never means a coming of 'someone' or 'something' else, as many would have us believe today. The descent of the Holy Spirit at Pentecost, and since, is not the Second Coming of Christ, because Jesus said HE (not the Holy Spirit) would come again. The angels said, "This same Jesus would come in like manner as ye saw Him go" - not someone else but "this same Jesus". The apostle said, "Jesus HIMSELF would descend from heaven." Notice how guarded and emphatic the words are. Not "Jesus shall descend," but "Jesus HIMSELF".

You see if we make the Second Coming of Christ anything but personal, we strike a blow at the doctrine of the Trinity, for the Holy Spirit is the third person of the blessed Trinity. Then we are told that when Jesus comes again, the dead in Christ will be the first (that corruption will put on incorruption), then we that are alive and remain will be changed and caught up (this mortal will put on immortality), and together we shall meet the Lord in the air. When the Holy Ghost came at Pentecost and when He comes in power at revivals, the dead are not raised and we are not caught up; so you see how absurd it is to speak of His coming again as anything but a personal return.

I am daily waiting for the coming of the Son of God.
George Whitefield

The Church's Business

I pray for them: I pray not for the world, but for them which thou hast given me " for they are thine.
John 17 v 9

The mission of the Church is not the conversion of the world but the gathering out of the Church - the body, the bride of Christ. Then, you say, the Church and the Gospel is a failure. Oh no. They are accomplishing the work they were called and chosen to do. The Church was never intended to convert the world but to witness to the world. Supposing I started a linen factory and was doing fine - making good linen and selling all I made. You came along and asked me, "How are you doing?" I said, "Fine, business is good." You said, "Are you making and selling any boots?" "No, this isn't a boot factory, this is a linen factory." Just image you saying, "Oh, you are a failure. You are not making and selling boots." How ridiculous for anyone to talk like that. It is no more ridiculous than anyone saying that the Church is a failure because she isn't making a better world or saving it. That is not her business. Her business is to witness to all, and the Lord will call out His own.

Witnessing is the whole work of the whole church for the whole age.
A T Pierson

The Real Test

And whosoever doth not bear his cross, and come after me,
cannot be my disciple.
Luke 14 vs. 27

You remember how indignant Peter was when Jesus told them the cruel way He was to be put to death. "Be it far from thee, Lord: this shall not be unto thee." Jesus turned and rebuked him and then said, not only is the cross for me, but for every disciple. "If any man will come after me let him deny himself and take up his cross and follow me." Isn't it just here so many would-be disciples part company with Jesus? The cross fills them with fear and dread. The young ruler was very anxious to gain eternal life, but when he heard the plain, uncompromising conditions: "Sell all... take up the cross and follow me," he went away very sorrowful. It is the same everywhere today. They want the blessing of salvation without the reproach of the cross of Christ. It can't be done, dear reader. No cross, no crown is as true today as when Jesus said, "Ye cannot be my disciple unless you take up the cross."

> You will not get leave to steal quietly to heaven, in Christ's company, without a conflict and a cross.
> Samuel Rutherford

Natural Life vs. Eternal Life

For whosoever will save his life shall lose it; but whosoever shall lose his life for my sake and the gospel's, the same shall save it.
Mark 8 vs. 35

In this startling paradox the word 'life' is used in a double sense. In the first instance in each clause of the sentence, it signifies natural life, with all the adjuncts that make it pleasant and enjoyable; in the second, it means the spiritual life of renewed soul. The deep, pregnant saying of Jesus may therefore be thus expounded and paraphrased: Whosoever will save (i.e. make it his business to save or preserve) his natural life and worldly well-being, shall lose the higher life, the life indeed; and whosoever is willing to lose his natural life for My sake shall find the true eternal life. According to this maxim we must lose something. It is not possible to live without sacrifice of some kind, the only question being what shall be sacrificed - the lower or the higher life: animal happiness or spiritual blessedness? If we choose the higher, we must be prepared to deny ourselves and take up the cross, though the actual amount of the loss we are called on to bear may be small: for godliness is profitable unto all things, having the promise of the life that now is, as well as that which is to come.

Rid me, good Lord, of every diverting thing.
Amy Carmichael

Running the Race

Wherefore, seeing we also are compassed about with so great cloud of witnesses, let us lay aside every weight, and the sin which doth so easily beset us, and let us run with patience the race that is set before us.
Hebrews 12 vs. 1

Dear friends, salvation is no lazy and easy road to heaven, as many seem to think. It's a race, and we are to run with dogged determination the race set before us, looking unto Jesus. Paul could say, "I therefore so run, not as uncertainly (carelessly, lazily): so fight I, not as one that beateth the air: But I keep under my body, and bring it into subjection: lest that by any means, when I have preached to others, I myself should be a castaway". This word is used only 8 times in the original New Testament. (Once 'castaway' I Corinthians 9 vs.27; once 'rejected' Hebrews 6 vs. 8 and 6 times 'reprobate' II Corinthians 13 vs. 5,6,7; II Timothy 3 vs.8 and Titus 1 vs.16). It would seem as if Paul was urged to "run" and "fight" and keep at it, or he might lose more than the reward. He feels he might lose the race by being disqualified.

The alternative to discipline is disaster.
Vance Havner

The Advent of Faith

So then faith cometh by hearing, and hearing by the word of God.
Romans 10 vs. 17

While Peter preached to the crowds in Jerusalem at Pentecost, 3000 and 5000 were led to repent and believe. The Spirit used the word of condemnation and salvation in a wonderful way that day. That is why we should try and bring sinners to hear the Word of God. While they listen the Holy Spirit produces repentance. The old devil will move earth and hell to hinder Christians from inviting sinners to the service and prevent the sinners from attending. Well he knows the means used by the Spirit to produce true repentance in the sinner.

> How precious is the Book divine
> By inspiration given!
> Bright as a lamp its doctrines shine,
> To guide our souls to heaven.
> John Fawcett

A Clean Break

*Neither yield ye your members as instruments of unrighteousness unto sin:
but yield yourselves unto God, as those that are alive from the dead, and
your members as instruments of righteousness unto God.*
Romans 6 v 13

Full surrender. No withholding - friends, time, earthly store. He doesn't demand a perfect surrender, but He does demand an honest surrender. All you know and don't know, without evasion or reservation. He will take nothing less and nothing else. Love so amazing, so divine, demands my life, my soul, my all. You hear a lot today about - Must I give up this or that? You must give up everything. Let the unrighteous man forsake His ways and the ungodly man his thoughts and let him turn to the Lord and He will abundantly pardon. Jesus doesn't save everybody. Oh no. He saves His people. "His name shall be called Jesus for he shall save His people." If you are not willing to belong to Christ you can never be saved. "Now to be Thine, yea Thine alone, 0 Lamb of God I come," must be the language and attitude of your heart. You must break clean, once and for all, with the world, the flesh and the devil. A clean cut, a wholehearted surrender. You cannot serve God and the devil, but you must serve one or the other, all the time. Neither God nor the devil will take part-time service. They both demand whole time, wholehearted surrender. So many would like to make Jesus a Saviour merely from hell. A sort of a fire escape out of hell-fire into heaven, but they want to live as they like and do as they please - enjoy the world and its pleasures and yet escape the world's doom and damnation. It can't be done, friend. You must make a clean break.

If religion be worth anything it is worth everything.
Matthew Henry

True Repentance

This is a faithful saying, and worthy of all acceptation, that Christ Jesus came into the world to save sinners; of whom I am chief.
1 Timothy 1 vs. 15

Every true and repentant and repenting believer feels with the Apostle Paul that he is "the chief of sinners."

The old Puritan said that he had no quarrel with what Paul said when he said he was the chief of sinners, but he did quarrel with him for taking his place. So every true penitent feels the same, in some measure, about it. Paul said there was no good thing in his flesh, but that he was incorrigible, "was not subject to the law of God, and neither indeed could be," and could never please God. Never mind what our definition of repentance may be, let us be sure of this one thing, that there is no repentance unto life - true repentance - where we deny or do not feel utterly sinful and vile, and never can be anything else, apart from His saving grace.

Upon a life I did not live,
Upon a death I did not die,
Another's life, another's death
I stake my whole eternity.

> One of the most fundamental marks of true repentance is a disposition to see our sins as God sees them.
> Charles Simeon

Save Yourselves

Save yourselves from this untoward generation.
Acts 2 vs. 40

These were the closing words of Peter's Pentecostal sermon: the first sermon preached in the Christian Church. What a sermon it was! And what a preacher!

We hardly recognise him. What a change has been wrought in him since Christ died! Before Pentecost what a blustering, blundering coward he was. He could swear and curse better than he could preach. But now see him stand before these murderers of Christ and hear his bold and scriptural words, so eloquently and heroically spoken. No cowardice here; no cursing and swearing now. Goodbye to all that forever. And what marvellous results! Think of it. In Jerusalem of all places: the seat and citadel of all bigotry and hatred of Christ. And Jews, of all people. The very ones who had cried out only a few days prior to this: "Crucify Him! Crucify Him!" Now they are crying out from pricked hearts, "Men and brethren, what shall we do?" Just image! 3000 of them. What a scene! What an event! (O Lord, send us another Pentecost these last of the last days. Surely our hungry hearts cry out for it?) When Peter heard their cry, he immediately stopped his preaching and told them how to be saved - what to do; and with many other words did he testify and exhort, saying, "Save yourselves from this untoward generation."

> Since no man is excluded from calling upon God, the gate of salvation is set open to all. There is nothing else to hinder us from entering but our own unbelief.
> John Calvin

Goodbye God

Then said his wife unto him, Dost thou still retain thine integrity? curse
God and die. But he said unto her, Thou speakest as one of the foolish
women speaketh. What? shall we receive good at the hand of God, and shall
we not receive evil? In all this did not Job sin with his lips.
Job 2 vs. 9-10

The word "curse" in the original means, "bid farewell" or say "Goodbye to God." This is exactly what Satan said to God that Job would do. "Then Satan answered the Lord, and said, Doth Job fear God for nought? Hast not thou made a hedge about him, and about his house, and about all that he hath on every side? thou hast blessed the work of his hands, and his substance is increased in the land. But put forth thine hand now, and touch all that he hath, and he will curse (say goodbye) thee to Thy face." God have him permission to touch all that he had. God could trust Job in adversity as well as prosperity. I wonder how many of us He could trust? God felt confident Job would not let Him down. Satan went out from God's presence to do his dirty work, but remember, he was under God's permission and supervision. He could only do what God permitted and no more. But what a calamity that was, and all in one day. 7000 sheep, 3000 camels, 8000 oxen, 500 asses, and last of all and sorest of all, seven sons and three daughters. What a day and what a calamity! Surely enough to provoke any man to say, "Goodbye to God." But what did Job do and say?

"Then Job arose, and rent his mantle and shaved his head, and fell down upon the ground, and worshipped." (He didn't curse God, or complain or grumble, as many of us have done under far less trying conditions, and sad to say, as many are doing today) "And said, Naked came I out of my mother's womb, and naked shall I return thither: the Lord gave, and the Lord hath taken away; blessed be the name of the Lord. In all this Job sinned not, nor charged God foolishly."

Hallelujah! How pleased God must have been and how chagrined the old devil must have been.

Saints must be best in worst times.
Samuel Rutherford

Overflowing Faith

Therefore, as ye abound in every thing, in faith, and utterance,
and knowledge, and in all diligence, and in your love to us,
see that ye abound in this grace also.
11 Corinthians 8 vs. 7

We are to overflow first of all in faith. There are some who have not got enough faith to warm their souls, and they have little comfort in this life and not a very lively assurance and hope for the life to come. My! but it is a grand thing to meet a Christian overflowing with faith. What a rebuke it is to our own lack of faith and what an inspiration to us. We are to abound, we are to overflow in faith. And it is not to be a dummy's faith. There must be utterance. Of course the majority of ladies are overflowing in that line, but it is not this kind of utterance. It is not talking about dress, society gossip, but it is talking about the Lord and the things of the Lord. It is marvellous how many dummies there are in God's family and how many dumb people are in God's house. They will talk about politics; they will talk about baseball; and they will talk about baby until they weary you. Just get a company of ladies together and put a baby amongst them. Before many minutes they will be talking all kinds of things, in all kinds of languages and they will talk and talk and talk. Dear me, how little there is of the overflowing utterance of the things of the Lord. Some will say "Oh I am so retiring" or "I am timid and shy". If you would only surrender your heart to the Lord you would be overflowing in utterance. "Out of the abundance of the heart the mouth speaketh" Then again we are to abound in knowledge. Knowledge concerning our Lord and the things of the Lord, and we are to abound in all diligence, not laziness, not lethargy, not in apathy. My! What a crowd of tired folk there are in the church today. On Sunday morning if it is raining or snowing, they cannot go to church, but they will go out in any kind of weather for anything else, and when it comes to doing anything or giving any time for the Lord, how very tired they become. How soon they flag, and how soon they are clear down and out, but if it is anything for society, they are full of energy, life and diligence.

So many Christians badly need a faith lift!
John Blanchard

Election

Wherefore the rather, brethren, give diligence to make your calling and election sure: for if ye do these things, ye shall never fall:
11 Peter 1 vs. 10

"Ye will not come unto Me," said Jesus. I believe the old coloured preacher explained it well when preaching on election. He said if a man wants to be elected to some Government office, he must stand for election and if he gains the majority vote he is elected. So it is with the sinner. If he is to be elected to eternal life he must stand for election, and if he does he is most surely elected. What ridiculous folly on our part to sit still and say, "If I am elected I'll be elected, and if not I'll not." Such a fatalistic attitude as that is dishonouring to God and damning to the soul. Fatalism is eternally fatal for the soul. Believe at once and be saved. You are able to do it, and will be held responsible for not doing it.

> Let a man go to the grammar school of faith and repentance before he goes to the university of election and predestination.
> George Whitefield

A Glorious Reality

Marvel not that I said unto thee, ye must be born again.
John 3 vs.7

Oh! It is a glorious reality. Sitting at my mother's fireside waiting for breakfast one Monday morning between half-past eight and a quarter to nine o'clock, I accepted Jesus Christ as my personal Saviour, and immediately I was born again and knew it. I said to my mother, "Mother, your prayers are answered and your anxiety is ended. I am saved." Her joy was unspeakable and full of glory. Are we supposed to believe our senses when they tell us about natural things, but when they come to give evidence about spiritual things, then they are liars? Such nonsense. And yet there are many who think this is so. How do I know honey is sweet? I have tasted its sweetness. How do I know fire burns? I have felt it burn. How do I know that red is red, or black is black, or green is green? I have seen it. How do I know one note of music from another? I have heard them. How do I know a thing has an evil smell? Because I have smelt it. Are we not to believe our senses? What can we believe if we can't believe them? Are my senses not as dependable about spiritual things as they are about natural things? Certainly they are. I have seen the Lord. I have felt the Lord: I have tasted - the Lord is good. "That which was from the beginning, which we have heard, which we have seen with our eyes, which we have looked upon, and our hands have handled of the Word of Life," was John's way of putting it, and it is ours, too. We would as soon doubt our own existence as doubt the reality of this fact - we are born again.

The new birth is not only a mystery that no man can understand; it is a miracle that no man can undertake.
John Blanchard

Repentance

The Lord is not slack concerning his promise, as some men count slackness;
but is longsuffering to usward, not willing that any should perish, but that
all should come to repentance.
11 Peter 3 vs. 9

We may under-rate, or may even dislike it. Am I right in saying "repentance" is the most unpopular word in the whole vocabulary of religion? Has not every sinner a strong prejudice against repentance? Is it not so, that men would rather hear of anything else than repentance? It is utterly repugnant and repulsive to the carnal, unsanctified Christian. He desires and demands forgiveness without any qualification on his part whatever. If this is so with the unsanctified believer, how much more is it so with the unsaved sinner? Whether popular or unpopular, it is the immutable Word of God. It is mentioned 100 times in the Bible. It is used 58 times in the New Testament; of these 25 are to be ascribed to Luke in his Gospel and the Acts, and twelve of the Apocalypse. St Paul uses if five times. Would God command us to repent, and offer it to us if it were unimportant or non-essential? Salvation then cannot be without repentance, anymore than without faith. If I can reconcile any to "the sweet grace" of repentance, and lead you to say with Bengel, "Repentance is a joyful gift and not a matter of sorrow"; and to think of repentance as did one of the old Puritans, who said, " I should like to die repenting"; this article and labour of love will not have been in vain.

Remember, we don't bring repentance to Christ but get repentance from Christ.

> Evangelical repentance is not at the beck and call of the creature. It
> is the gift of God.
> A W Pink

A Purifying Hope

And every man that has his hope in him
purifieth himself even as he is pure.
1 John 3 vs. 3

What should all this mean to us who love His return and look for it?
We should surely see to it that our hearts are pure and clean. "The pure
in heart shall see God." If we really believed in His return we wouldn't
allow impurity of heart. We should be ashamed before Him at His
coming, if we did. Let us therefore cleanse ourselves from all filthiness
of the flesh and the spirit, perfecting holiness in the fear of the Lord,
for His coming is at hand. We should also live separated lives -"in the
world but not of it". What shame would be ours if He came and found
us in the show or dance or card party. What shame and loss will be
ours if we do not live separated lives. Come out from among them and
touch not the unclean thing is His command to us today as we walk
and live as pilgrims and sojourners, as we see the day approaching.
Then as we see the signs of His return multiplying on every hand,
surely it will make us zealous in His service and doing all we can by
all means to save some out of the wreck. We cannot surely be idle or
indifferent when we feel His return is so near. We'll seek to have
ripened sheaves and not faded leaves when He comes.

> The imminent return of our Lord is the great Bible argument for a
> pure, unselfish, devoted, unworthy active life of service.
> R A Torrey

Is it a Mark of Love?

I am therefore become your enemy, because I tell you the truth.
Galations 4 v 16

I was conducting a campaign in West Australia one time. One day I received a letter from a preacher saying that if I would be more like Jesus I would preach more about heaven and less about hell. This made me go to my Bible to find out whether I was unlike Jesus, preaching about hell so much. This is what I found. Jesus spoke about hell about thirteen times, and in awful and gruesome language, and He only spoke about heaven once, "In My Father's house are many mansions."

You would think by the way some talk that they had more love for their fellowmen than Jesus had or has. Jesus is incarnate love. He so loved that He gave Himself for the salvation of men. Do you find these men who talk about loving their fellowmen ever dying or even suffering to save them? Oh no. They sit calmly be their fireside cooing like a turtledove about love, while all the time they don't know the first thing about love.

The one next to Jesus who told more about hell was John, the Apostle of love. As you read the Book of Revelation about hell, how terribly graphic and gruesome is the description. Do you mean to tell me these turtledoves of today have more love, or know more about love, than Jesus or John did? Surely not. But is it a mark of love for men to hide the truth from them because it is awful?

It has always been a mark of the false prophets and preachers that they preached what people wanted to hear.
Peter De Jong

Fire! Fire!

And again he entered into Capernaum, after some days; and it was noised
that he was in the house.
Mark 2 vs.1

I remember we came to a nice Presbyterian-covenanting town. We had a lovely hall (a memorial to the 1859 revival), which seated several hundred. The first week there I never had more than maybe twenty for an audience, and these were mostly dear old women. The town hardly knew I was there or that I was holding an evangelistic mission. I didn't know what to do. One day I met the town crier ringing his big bell and telling about an auction to be held. I got an inspiration. I gave the crier two shillings and sixpence and asked him to lend me his bell. I didn't tell anyone what I was going to do; they would have been shocked and refused to come with me. I got to the top of the main street, took my coat off and tied the arms around my waist; then I rolled up my sleeves and started down the street ringing the bell and shouting with all my might, "FIRE! FIRE!" What a commotion! Windows were flung open; doors banged. The people crowded out from their houses to see me tearing down the street roaring like a madman and ringing the bell and shouting, "FIRE! FIRE!" They thought the town was on fire. We passed the Wee Free Church. They were holding their weekly prayer meeting with about twelve people; out they came. When I got to the bottom of the street where there was a covenanting memorial, I climbed up on it and cried out with a loud voice, "Hell fire is coming, you covenanting Presbyterians, and I am trying to keep you out of it." I got some rubbish thrown at me, but I got my crowd and packed my hall. The minister said that any man who would do that to get people under the Gospel - he would stand by him, and he did; he came night after night to the meetings. The people said, "if he can go, then we will go too." The minister and I became and remained fast friends until he passed away. He was Rev. Dr. Alexander Smellie who wrote the historical classic *The Men of the Covenant*, a moving story of the Scottish Covenanters.

If Christ is in your house your neighbours will soon know it.
D.L. Moody

The Fullness of the Spirit

And be not drunk with wine, wherein is excess;
but be filled with the Spirit;
Ephesians 5 v 18

W.P Nicholson did not limit his experience with the Holy Spirit to a once-and-for-all experience. Rather he considered it to be a succession of new empowering for each new task that the Lord appoints us to do. Like D L Moody he considered himself to be a "leaky vessel" and had to live right under the fountain in order to be kept full. In a sermon entitled Born – Baptised - Filled he draws the distinction between baptism and the process of being filled. "The baptism with the Holy Spirit is a crisis. The fullness of the Holy Spirit is the process - one baptism, many fillings. There is no end or limit to his fullness. We are being filled increasingly and unceasingly. As our capacity enlarges, our fullness increases. There is no such thing as a once and for all fullness. We are being filled unto all the fullness of God, until out of us shall flow rivers-not a river, but rivers. Hallelujah! Rivers of love, joy, peace and all graces of the Spirit."

> Ephesians 5 vs. 18 is not just an experience to be enjoyed but a command to be obeyed.
> D L Moody

Getting your Priorities Right

...for them that honour me I will honour.
I Samuel 2 vs. 30

"Seek ye first (not second or third) the kingdom of God, and His righteousness; and all these things shall be added unto you." (Matthew 6 vs.33) It always pays to serve and love the Lord Jesus. When we put all our affairs into His hands and leave them there, they are safe from all harm and injury. Many times we fall short of realising this promise because, although we leave everything with Him, we soon undertake our own affairs, and as a result we make an awful mess of things and bring pain, loss and misery to ourselves. "Oh, what peace we often forfeit. Oh, what needless pain we bear, all because we do not carry everything to God in prayer" and leave it there.

If you mind the Lord's business the Lord will mind your business.
Ian R K Paisley

A Believing Mind

Be careful for nothing; but in every thing by prayer and supplication with
thanksgiving let your requests be made know unto God.
Philippians 4 vs. 6

William often expressed his gratitude that he had been given a
"believing mind." His life was one of dependence upon the
faithfulness of God to fulfil His promises. A frequent saying of his was
"If you worry you do not trust, and if you trust you do not worry." One
of his favourite texts was John 14 vs.13-14, "And whatsoever ye shall
ask in my name, that will I do, that the Father may be glorified in the
Son. If ye shall ask any thing in my name, I will do it." When preaching
on the problem of prayer, he said, "These words of our Lord Jesus are
as true for us today as they were for the disciples long ago. The Lord
can as truly fulfil them for us today as He did for them. Don't let us
dodge or evade them or change them; let us face them openly and
honestly and put them to the test, and give Him a chance to show to
the world that "He keepeth His promises for ever. Hallelujah!"

> Two things come between our souls and unshadowed fellowship –
> sin and care. We must be as resolute to cast our care upon the Lord
> as to confess our sins to him.
> F B Meyer

APRIL

1 ♦ A Visit to Madame Tussauds

2 ♦ Just as I Am

3 ♦ Blessed Assurance

4 ♦ A Sure Foundation

5 ♦ Holiness and Happiness

6 ♦ Perseverance of Satan

7 ♦ The Christian Life Overflowing

8 ♦ Signposts

9 ♦ Launch Out

10 ♦ The God of Encouragement

11 ♦ Chastening

12 ♦ Nearer Heaven or …?

13 ♦ The God of Jacob

14 ♦ Abram's Partial Obedience

15 ♦ Have Faith in God

16 ♦ Don't Forget

17 ♦ A Block of Marble

18 ♦ Is He at Home?

19 ♦ The Workman

20 ♦ The Job is not Completed Yet

21 ♦ You Belong to Christ

22 ♦ What is a Saint?

23 ♦ Who are Saints?

24 ♦ No Other Way

25 ♦ The Christ of Denunciation

26 ♦ Kangaroo Believers

27 ♦ Rest in His Love

28 ♦ God Proud of the Overcomer

29 ♦ Two Wings

30 ♦ How to Overcome the Flesh

A Visit to Madame Tussauds

And unto the angel of the church in Sardis write; These things saith he that
hath the seven Spirits of God, and the seven stars; I know thy works, that
thou hast a name that thou livest, and art dead.
Revelation 3 v 1

I remember that on one occasion I was up in London, and I went to
Madame Tussaud's to see the waxworks. When I entered the premises
I went up to a woman to put my couple of bob down. It was a wax
figure of a woman! I looked around to see if anybody was watching
the greenhorn, and I said to myself. "I won't be taken in this time," so
I marched past the next woman who was sitting in the place to take
money. I thought it was a figure, too! But there was a big policeman on
the other side, and I though he was a wax figure. Said I, "You can't take
me in this time," and I marched through. The big policeman "nabbed"
me. He said, "Where's your couple of bob?" I gave in; I didn't try to be
wise any more! The wax figure had a name: dead. Presbyterian,
Methodist, Baptist, Plymouth Brother, Christian: A name to live: dead.
Do you know anybody like that - a Christless Christian, a name to live,
and dead? Paul speaks of them as lovers of pleasure more than lovers
of God. They are quite at home in a picture show, but in prayer
meeting they are like old hens in a duck pond! Man alive, they enjoy
themselves in the world and in the pleasures of it, but in the things of
God and the means of grace-they are stones of bread to them,
scorpions instead of fish.

A zealous Saviour ought to have zealous disciples.
J C Ryle

Just as I Am

If we confess our sins, he is faithful and just to forgive us our sins, and to cleanse us from all unrighteousness.
1 John 1 v 9

Charlotte Elliott had been brought into the fellowship of the Church at Easter time. Her godly minister thought she was truly converted and that her soul rested on Christ. One day he he was going past where she lived, and she was coming out of her house dressed for a ball and stepped into a carriage. The old man nearly dropped on seeing that, and he went quickly before the carriage door was closed, and said, "Charlotte, are you saved?" She banged the door closed and got away from the old man, but she did not get away from his question. Instead of dancing till daylight, she was home before midnight, and for a long week her pride was dying. At last she could stand it no more, and she started to seek the minister. As she was making her way to where he lived, she met him on the street, and she said, "I'm delighted to see you. I was making my way to your home, and I have come for two things. First, I apologise to you for my rudeness." "That's all right, Charlotte; I understand it." "Sir, how am I to answer that question you asked me?" "Charlotte," he said, "'just as you are, come to Christ." Just as she was she came to Christ, and some time afterwards she wrote these beautiful words, which have been the means of leading thousands to Him:

Just as I am without one plea,
But that Thy blood was shed for me,
And that Thou bids't me come to Thee,
O Lamb of God, I come.

Just as I am and waiting not
To rid my soul of one dark blot,
To Thee, Whose blood can cleanse each spot,
O Lamb of God, I come.

Come and ten thousand welcomes to Jesus.
John Bunyan

Blessed Assurance

He that believeth on the Son of God hath the witness in himself: He that believeth not God hath made him a liar; because he believeth not the record that God gave of His Son. And this is the record, that God hath given to us eternal life, and this life is in His Son. He that hath the Son hath life; and he that hath not the Son of God hath not life.
1 John 5:10-12.

It is very interesting to know that the reason John wrote his gospel was "That ye might believe that Jesus is the Christ, the Son of God; and that believing ye might have life through His Name." (John 20 vs.31.) When John wrote his epistle, sixty years afterwards, he wrote, "These things have I written unto you that believe on the Name of the Son of God; that ye may know that ye have eternal life." (1 John 5 vs.13.) So that we may have the same "Blessed Assurance" that Fanny Crosby, (the blind hymn writer) wrote and sang about and which enabled and encouraged others down through the years, to sing and shout also. And yet there are many today everywhere who would seek to deprive and deny us this "Blessed Assurance." Men of the world, religious and respectable, many of them would deny us this assurance by saying it is impossible for anyone to be sure they are saved. They say it is the wildest credulity. They look on those who say they are sure of these things as if they were devoid of reason or were utterly presumptuous and blasphemous.

Blessed Assurance, Jesus is mine.

Hallelujah!

Faith saves us but assurance satisfies us.
C H Spurgeon

4 APRIL

A Sure Foundation

He that hath the Son hath life; and he that hath not the
Son of God hath not life.
John 5 vs. 12.

This is God's Word and if I do not believe this record God gives of His Son I make Him a lair. How do I know my sins are forgiven? My Saviour tells me so. Away with fear, for this by faith I know, God's Word shall stand forever sure. What better foundation could you have for your faith? If you had to trust your good works, your prayers, your tears, your sacraments and ceremonies when could you ever feel sure? When would you know you had enough of good works? If we had only the word of man or men however great and good they might be, how could we ever be sure? They might break their word or might change their minds. Glory to God! We have God's sure Word of promise. Heaven and earth will pass away, but My Word shall never pass away. It is unchangeable and unbreakable. Faithful is He that calleth you, who also will do it. You couldn't come to Christ and be cast out. You couldn't believe on Him and not be saved. None perish that trust Him. You can never trust Him too much or yourself too little. God says it. Jesus did it. I believe it and that settles it. Take Him at His Word. Don't call Him a liar or make Him a liar by doubting His Word.

The inward seal of adoption is testified by the outward seal of sanctification. If the Spirit of Christ is in our hearts, the fruit of the Spirit will be exhibited in our lives.

> An inheritance is not only kept for us, but we are kept for it.
> Richard Sibbes

5 APRIL

Holiness and Happiness

But as he which hath called you is holy, so be ye holy in
all manner of conversation;
I Peter 1 vs. 15

Who would ever have thought of linking happiness with holiness especially these days? When we think of or even mention "holiness," we immediately think - long races - sour and dour looks - melancholy and morbid dispositions - in fact, real "kill joys." We certainly never associate happiness with holy living or holy people. The old devil has surely succeeded in maligning God's character and misrepresenting this attribute of His character. Just mention holiness to the young - especially today - and see how soon they cool to your presence and make some excuse for either changing the subject or leaving you. And yet Jesus saw nothing contradictory or incongruous in joining the two together. The late General Wm. Booth, founder of the Salvation Army, said, "blessed" means "hilariously happy." This is altogether contrary to the popular idea today, even among converted people. And because of this misunderstanding they shy clear of the blessing like a "bullock unaccustomed to the yoke." The dictionary says the word "holy" is derived from an Anglo-Saxon word, "halig" which means "healthy." So a holy person is a healthy person, and because of that he is hilariously happy.

The word means, according to Webster, "pure." The word pure means "separate from all extraneous matter, free from mixture, clear, real, blameless, unsullied, untarnished." We speak of pure water, pure air, pure silver, pure gold. The idea is that that which is pure consists of one thing. It is uncompounded, without mixture or adulteration. It has all that belongs to it and nothing else, viz., gold that is free from alloy, unmixed with any baser metal, we call pure gold. Milk that contains all that belongs to milk and nothing else is pure milk. Honey without wax is pure honey. In like manner a heart that is pure contains nothing adverse to God and therefore is "hilariously happy" and couldn't be anything else. Hallelujah! God is called "blessed God" ie. "happy God." You couldn't imagine God being miserable and a "joy-killer," could you? The God who paints the sunrise and the sunset, and a new one every night and morning. The God who puts the song in the breast of the lark and the canary. The God who has given us the lovely flowers and the panoramic scenes of nature, which thrill us. All these beautiful and happiness producing things are unessential. We could live without them but how much happiness we would be deprived of if God hadn't given them to us.

Those that look to be happy must first look to be holy.
Richard Sibbes

Perseverance of Satan

Be sober, be vigilant; because your adversary the devil, as a roaring lion,
walketh about, seeking whom he may devour:
I Peter 5 vs. 8

Talk about the "perseverance of the saints," their perseverance is as nothing compared to the perseverance of Satan. Well he knows that such a life does his cause more harm than ten thousand sermons or books on "Christian evidences" and speaks loudly and powerfully for the glory of God and the advance of His cause on earth. Have you ever noticed how God boasts in such a man? I was going to say, have you ever noticed how proud God is of such a man? Listen, "Hast thou considered my servant Job that there is none like him in the earth, a perfect and an upright man, one that feareth God and escheweth evil"? That is what God boasted about Job to Satan. I wonder could God boast about us to Satan? He can and He will, if we receive and live daily pure, clean-in-heart lives.

Man's chief end is to glorify God and to enjoy him for ever.
Shorter Catechism

The Christian Life - Overflowing

If any man thirst, let him come unto me, and drink. He that believeth on me, as the scripture hath said, out of his belly shall flow rivers of living water. John 7 vs. 37-38

In the fourth chapter of John verse 14 we have His indwelling and sanctifying work; "...the water that I shall give him shall be in him a well of water springing up into everlasting life." The Spirit of God dwelling in you. Eternal life as a well of water, bubbling up in your heart and life. We should know the indwelling of the Spirit in the heart and life day by day. This should be the normal Christian life. There is nothing abnormal about it, and it should be the normal life of every child of God. But when we come into the seventh chapter of John we have the ideal that is in the mind and heart of the Lord Jesus for every one of His regenerate ones; that out of you and me should flow rivers of living water. Not merely born of God, not merely the indwelling of the Spirit of God, but a life overflowing, a life so full that it overflows. Believe me, dear friends, if you can contain your religion it will not be satisfying or satisfactory to yourself or be a blessing to others; only when it is overflowing will it be a blessing to those with whom you come in contact. There is the great river Nile in Egypt. Some English engineers have constructed great dams across that river, and today Egypt is a great wheat growing country. By means of these dams the river is made to overflow its banks and the alluvial soil that is washed down from the mountains is deposited over vast tracts of previously barren lands, bringing life and fertility to the desert, and great crops are raised. While the river was allowed to flow evenly on it - it was not much good to the country, but when it was made to overflow then it became a blessing. So many Christian lives are of little or no service simply because they are not overflowing. The Lord's idea is that we should overflow like the river Nile, our lives reaching out on every side, touching other lives and bringing blessing and benediction to them.

A cup can't hold much, but it can overflow a lot.
Robert Cook

Signposts

And he went a little farther, and fell on his face, and prayed, saying,
O my Father, if it be possible, let this cup pass from me: nevertheless
not as I will, but as thou wilt.
Matthew 26 vs. 39

The first crossroad and signpost is found in the above verse. You will find, as we consider these sign posts, that every one will be marked clearly by one word, viz. "Nevertheless." Christ is at the crossroads in His journey through life. Have you ever considered what would happen if Jesus hadn't surrendered His will to God in the garden that night? We would have no Saviour and no Salvation. But He surrendered His will to the Father and went all the way to Calvary for you and me. As well as being our Saviour, He is also your example and mine. There comes a time in every converted born again life when we refuse our own will and chose God's. The choice may mean a real Gethsemane, a Judgment Hall, a real Calvary, but if we refuse and take our own way we not only ruin our own life and usefulness, but many others may be ruined too. So many seem to think the will of God is hard, harsh, and unreasonable at times. They shrink from it and even shirk it and, as a result, spoil their usefulness here and make others suffer as well. It is natural for us to want our own way and do our own will. We are naturally so stubborn and rebellious, so self willed. When we determine to have our own way and do it, we are being switched on to the wrong road that will mean many a heartache, sorrow and regret. God's will and way may seem rough and harsh, but friend, God's will is good, perfect and acceptable. No matter how it appears at present it can never be anything else. It may mean a very real garden of Gethsemane experience and a very real Judgment Hall where we'll be misjudged and maligned and misrepresented and fearfully mistrusted; a very real Calvary where we hang, a spectacle of scorn, ridicule of shame. In spite of all this dear friends, refuse to have your own way or do your own will. Say it and do it, " Jesus I am going through at any cross or cost."

Once the will of God to me was a sigh; now it is a song.
Francis Ridley Havergal

Launch Out

...he said unto Simon, Launch out into the deep, and let down your nets for a draught.
Luke 5 vs. 4

Let us consider another sign at the crossroads. It too is marked by the word "nevertheless." Luke 5 vs. 4,5. Jesus said unto Simon, "Launch out into the deep and let down your nets for a draught." And Simon answering said unto Him, 'Master, we have toiled all the night, and have taken nothing; nevertheless at thy word I will let down the net.'" "At Thy word." Peter had toiled hard and long and had caught nothing. When Jesus gave the word he did as he was told - "at Thy word" - and enclosed a great multitude of fishes. He took Jesus at His word though it seemed so unreasonable to do it. If anybody knew how and when to fish surely it was Peter. He might have followed his own reasoning and disobeyed Christ. You couldn't have blamed him could you? But although grudgingly, he did obey and the miracle happened and a great multitude of fish was caught. All he had was the bare word of Christ. It is always safe to take Christ at His word and do what He tells us. Have you come to a crossroad in your life regarding some service for Him? You have toiled long and hard, and had little or no success in the past? The Lord has spoken to you in some unmistakable way. You have heard it. You have no question about that, but you hesitate, and are fearful to walk out on the naked word of Christ. It seems so ridiculous and absurd. You wonder what others would say or think. Friend, do not hesitate or linger, launch out. You have His word clear and unmistakable, so launch out. You couldn't have anything surer for your faith and feet as you venture out, than His word. No one can do it for you. You must make the choice and act alone. Don't fail Christ and let Him down. Don't miss the miracle that will happen as you venture out on the naked word of Christ. It is always safe to do His bidding, "Nevertheless, at thy word." Let this be the language of your heart. Let friends and feelings go. Launch Out. "'Tis so sweet to trust in Jesus just to take Him at His word." Hallelujah!

Obedience is the best commentary on the Bible.
Theodore Monod

The God of Encouragement

Nevertheless God, that comforteth those that are cast down,
comforted us by the coming of Titus.
II Corinthians 7 vs. 6

There are many things along life's highway that make us feel very uncomfortable and cast us down. There are those we meet, and have dealings with, who are the means of making us uncomfortable and casting us down. God has not promised us skies ever blue or a flower-strewn pathway. We get rain and clouds as well as sunshine. We get pain and suffering as well as peace and joy. There is a thorn with every rose. The Lord does not hide this from us. He hasn't promised us a smooth and easy passage, but He has promised us a safe landing, "strength from about, unfailing sympathy and undying love." He is the God of all comfort. He knows how to comfort the comfortless and He has many ways of doing this. In Paul's case here the Lord comforted him by the coming of Titus. Thank God the Titus's are not all dead! There are "comforting" believers yet. We meet them on our journey. This word "comfort" is "encouraged" as you see in the margin. Paul was discouraged. He was "down in the dumps." The Lord sent Titus along to encourage him, to relieve him of his dumps or mental malaria.

The church should be the community of encouragement.
Sir Fred Catherwood

Chastening

Now no chastening for the present seemeth to be joyous, but grievous:
nevertheless afterward it yieldeth the peaceable fruit of righteousness unto
them which are exercised thereby.
Hebrews 12 vs. 11.

As we journey along life's highway God is training us. Through each successive task and experience God is educating us. This is not always joyous we are told, but it is always necessary. We are told not to despise it, not to faint. These scourgings are the experience of every genuine, Spirit-born, Blood-washed child of God. It is a mark of your relationship to God and His love for us. If we are without chastisement, whereof all are partakers, then we are bastards and not sons. If we are "exercised thereby," and do not murmur or complain, rebel or fret, it yields the peaceable fruit of righteousness. When sharpening an axe or chisel on the grindstone, it all depends on the angle you hold it on the grindstone, whether you blunt or sharpen it. So in this matter of chastisement. How we are exercised thereby will determine the result in out lives. Friend, don't shirk the chastisements of God and turn aside from them along some other road. If you do you will only bring sorrow and calamity upon you and your loved ones. You may be at this crossroads in your experience; read the instructions on the signpost and journey along God's way for you.

There is nothing more to be dreaded than that the Lord should allow
us loose reins.
John Calvin

Nearer Heaven or ...?

...Behold now is the accepted time; behold, now is the day of salvation.
II Corinthians 6 vs. 2

I remember when I was a student in Glasgow I was holding an open-air meeting late one Sunday night at Gorbals Cross, Glasgow. I was closing the meeting by singing that old hymn of the Church "A day's march nearer home." When we came to the last verse and the last line of the verse, I put my hands to my mouth, and with all the force and voice I had I shouted out, "A day's march nearer.... hell." A man was making his way home after a weekend's debauch. He didn't know there was a meeting and he couldn't see the speaker, but like a thunderclap of doom he heard the awful word, "A days march nearer hell," not home. He was so shaken and awakened he couldn't sleep that night. He got out of his bed and decided for Christ and became a keen out and out Christian and soul-winner. Friend, awake out of your sleep and danger and forsake your sin and accept Jesus Christ now as your own personal Saviour and thou shalt not perish but have eternal life and peace and joy.

All the roads that lead to hell are one-way streets.
John Blanchard

The God of Jacob

...I will sing praises to the God of Jacob.
Psalm 75 vs. 9

There was an old rascal called Jacob. He was so crooked that he could hide behind a corkscrew! He could steal the eye out of your head, and spit in the hole, and you wouldn't know anything about it! You couldn't watch him. He was so crooked that he would even bargain with God. Man, he was a boy! But I will tell you something. You never read in the Bible that God says. "I am the God of Uzza", or "I am the God of Lot," but nearly a hundred times He says "I am the God of Jacob". God says, "I am proud of Jacob. I am his God". One day God, long after Jacob had been converted, brought Jacob from his wife and family and property; got him alone, and God wrestled all night long with that rascal. At last He had a layman for life. Then Jacob began to cling to Him, and God said, "Your name is no more 'Jacob', 'supplanter'. Your name from this day is Israel" a prince with God, a man who has power with God and power with man. "I am the God of Jacob".

There is no telling how much power God can put into a man.
C H Spurgeon

Abram's Partial Obedience

And the scripture was fulfilled which saith, Abraham believed God,
and it was imputed unto him for righteousness: and he was
called the Friend of God.
James 2 vs. 23

Abram was the most illustrious person in ancient history. Venerated by Jews, Christians and Mohammedans. The Father of all them that believe. The progenitor of the nation of Israel. The Friend of God. The one by whom, according to the flesh, our Lord came. The most eminent of all the patriarchs. He was all this and yet we have recorded concerning him, that his obedience to God was only "partial" and not complete. If our Bible were not the Word of God, but merely the word of men, we would never have this record of his partial obedience to God recorded. When God writes a man's biography, He never omits his faults and failings, so as we read their lives, we find them men of like passions as ourselves, however great or pious they may have been.

He was to leave his own country; he was to separate himself from his kindred; he was to go forth unto a land, which God had promised to show him.

The first command Abram obeyed freely, but with reference to the last two he failed. He left Ur, but instead of separating himself from his kindred, Terah his father and Lot his nephew accompanied him. "And Terah took Abram his son, and Lot the son of Haran his son's son, and Sarai his daughter-in-law, his son Abram's wife, and they went forth with them from Ur of the Chaldees, to go into the Land of Canaan and they came unto Haran and dwelt there." (Genesis 11 vs.31.) They stayed here for five years. Five wasted years. The meaning of the word "Haran" is "parched." Partial obedience to any and every call of God will lead us into a parched, dried up Christian life. It was not only true in Abram's experience and day, but it is just as true in our experience and day.

> Faith and obedience are bound up in the same bundle. He that
> obeys God trusts God; and he that trusts God obeys God.
> C H Spurgeon

Have Faith in God

And Jesus answering saith unto them, Have faith in God.
Mark 11 vs. 22

This command is as plain and personal as any commandment Jesus ever gave. There is no misunderstanding it and it is as surely binding on us today as it was on the disciples in their day. It doesn't belong to any particular period or people. It is for all people everywhere and at any period. It is as truly binding on us today as it was any day. We need to remind ourselves of this, for there are those who love to pass on certain Scriptures to others, and for some other time; especially when such Scripture is apt to become difficult in obeying or will mean the cross and cost to them.

It is so easy to repeat this command of Jesus - "Have faith in God." There are only four words in it, but it is altogether another thing obeying it, especially these dark and darkening days we are passing through. It is days like these that sift our faith in God and test our obedience to this command. When the sun is shining and the birds are singing and the flowers blooming and everything is peaceful and lovely, it is easy to keep this commandment, but when the clouds gather and the storm rages and all hope seems gone, it isn't so easy to obey it. Oh! It is so easy to doubt and we are far better at doubting than believing. How we envy the Psalmist as he declares his Confession of Faith - "God is (not "was" or "will" be) our refuge and strength, a very present (not "absent") help in trouble, therefore we will not fear." Hallelujah! If wee David could feel that way in the time of trouble and have such confidence in God, so can we.

> Be careful for nothing, prayerful for everything, and thankful for anything.
> D L Moody

Don't Forget

I know thy works, and thy labour, and thy patience, and how thou canst not bear them which are evil; and thou hast tried them which say they are apostles, and are not, and hast found them liars.
Revelation 2 vs. 2

If you want the world then go for it, but if you want the Church, you must let go the world. Don't forget the blood of Jesus Christ bought the Church. The Church at Ephesus had kept the church roll clean for thirty-five years. They had kept out the 'jack-rabbits' and the 'billy-goats.' 'I've been looking over the church register,' remarked the Lord, 'and you have kept it clean.' Some had been excommunicated; they had been kicked out. Perhaps they had been to the Fair and had got drunk. They had refused the sacrament to them. Would it not clear the air and make people stare if we started this thing today? But no, we have been letting down the wire netting and letting the rabbits come in.

> I looked for the Church and I found it in the world; I looked for the world and I found it in the Church.
> Horatius Bonar

A Block of Marble

For we are his workmanship, created in Christ Jesus ...
Ephesians 2 vs.10

Michael Angelo discovered a large block of marble, covered in dirt and cast aside, where a great building was being erected. He had it brought to his studio, and there carved the most beautiful and perfect figure of a man and called it David. If that block of marble could have spoken it would surely have questioned the treatment the sculptor was giving it. The hammer and chisel were used to do the work of the sculptor, but the design was in the mind of the sculptor. He knew what he was doing. The figure he carved stood over six feet high, admired by thousands, and will stand and be admired as long as time lasts. Because we are saints God is at work in our lives and will perform a work that will be the marvel and wonder of angels for ages to come. Surely, because of this, we will be fully yielded and obedient. Let Him have His way, all the way. We can never trust the Lord too much or ourselves too little. God never does nor suffers to be done, but what we would ourselves, could we but see the end of all events as well as He.

The anvil, the fire and the hammer are the making of us.
C H Spurgeon

Is He at Home?

That Christ may dwell in your hearts by faith;
Ephesians 3 vs. 17

We won't indulge in any habit that would make Him not feel at home in our heart. I feel sure He wouldn't feel at home in the heart of a tobacco slave. Can he feel at home in our social life? Do we belong to the clubs and lodges where He is neither welcome nor wanted? If we frequent picture shows and theatres is it a becoming way of treating Christ? Is He at home in our family life? There is a motto, which is as follows, "Christ is the Head of this House." That is fine and proper, but the next words spoil it, "the unseen Guest." What a shabby, unbecoming way to treat Christ. Paul prayed for these Ephesian saints, " that Christ may finally settle down and feel completely at home in their hearts." May this prayer be answered for us.

Are you truly converted? Are you washed in His precious Blood and born again by the Holy Spirit? If you are you are one of God's saints? Not we may become one, but we ARE one NOW. Don't fear or fail to accept what is ours in Christ. Because we are saints, are we living as becometh saints? If we have failed in the past to so live, friend, will you not now lay down the arms of rebellion and cease all strife. Cry out in the following words:

Have Thine own way, Lord,
Have Thine own way,
Hold o'er my being absolute sway,
Fill with Thy Spirit till all shall see,
Christ only always living in me.
Adelaide Pollard

The Workman

Being confident of this very thing, that he which hath begun a good work in
you will perform it until the day of Jesus Christ:
Philippians 1 vs. 6

If we would only consider for a minute who is the workman at work in our lives, we wouldn't dare even to dictate or rebel because of the way He is doing His work. The hands that are manipulating our lives are the hands of the One who has created the universe. " Lift up your eyes on high and behold who created these that bringeth out their host by number: "he calleth them all by their names by the greatness of His might, for that He is strong in power, not one faileth." When we look around this world we are living in, what miracles are all around us. Do you think God will make any mistakes in His work in our lives? Do you think He is not able to perfect and finish the work He has begun?

"Hast thou not known? hast thou not heard, that the everlasting God, the Lord, the Creator of the ends of the earth, fainteth not, neither is weary? there is no searching of his understanding."

Don't rebel at His way or feel annoyed at Him. Your interference will only mar the work. Our interference only hinders Him and delays His work. He does not expect us to understand what He is doing or how He is doing it, but He does expect we will freely yield ourselves to Him and trust Him implicitly. He never makes any mistakes. There are no errors in the eternal plan. God is working all things together for the perfecting of the saints. We cannot understand, we do not see fully and clearly all He is doing. His ways are past finding out. As high as the heavens are above the earth, so high are His ways above ours. Glory to God! Although we may not see clearly or fully understand, we are assured of this: His ways are perfect. We are more precious to Him than any creation or creature. He created them but He has not only created us, He has redeemed us with His precious Blood.

Let God be God.
Martin Luther

The Job is not Completed Yet

For we are his workmanship, created in Christ Jesus unto good works,
which God hath before ordained that we should walk in them.
Ephesians 2 vs. 10

"Created in Christ Jesus unto good works, which God hath before ordained that we should walk with them." What is a saint? A saint is God's property, also God's workmanship. God is at work developing His inheritance. The riches and glory are to be revealed; the good works are to be manifested. Only God alone can do this work. What a mess we would make of it if the Lord had left the work to us. The treasure is too precious to trust its development to other hands. No other one ever could create a saint out of a sinner. God alone is the workman. It takes all the skill, patience, knowledge and power to perform such a miracle, and God has never done a shoddy job or turned out a jerry building. What a comfort to know we are His workmanship. He has not given the work over to other hands. Through each successive task God seeks to educate us.

One of the largest and purest diamonds ever found in South Africa was given to the British Government, and today it is in the Royal crown. It was given into the hands of the most expert lapidaries in Holland. They studied the diamond for months before they cut and polished it; no apprentice was allowed to touch this work. It was too precious. We are precious to God. What a price He paid for "less than the least of all saints" and for every saint. He and He alone is perfecting us and developing us until one day He will present us faultless (not blameless) before angels and ages.

I can imagine some sneering, sceptical sinner, scoffing and laughing at us being called saints. We have a proverb that says, "Children and fools should not be allowed to see unfinished work." Take your time, scoffing sinner. The job isn't completed yet. It isn't finished. Wait until the work is done, and you will have a chance of seeing if there is any flaw or fault in the finished work.

Christ is preparing saints for heaven and heaven for saints.
Anon.

You Belong to Christ

In whom ye also are builded together for an habitation
of God through the Spirit.
Ephesians 2, vs. 22

A saint is the "Home of God." God does not live in temples built with hands, but dwells in the humble and contrite heart of every saint. We can hardly grasp this truth; let it grasp us. "O what a salvation this; Christ liveth in me." Our bodies are the temple of God. What a privilege! What an honour to be a saint! Never let us hang our heads in shame or blush to own his name. We are God's property - purchased possession. We are His workmanship - wonder of wonders. We are His home - His dwelling place. This solemn fact makes us tremble and wonder how we can live and walk as becometh saints. Let us note this fact, we are now (not will be, but NOW) God's peculiar treasure. His purchased property. We are His workmanship. We are His Home.

I remember the C.C.C.U. men at Cambridge University gave me a beautiful leather coat. I had just finished a 10-day mission there. It was a beauty. Some time after I was in San Francisco, ready to sail for New Zealand. I put my lovely coat down on the dock as I watched our luggage being put on board the steamer. When all was on board, I turned to pick up my coat, but it was gone - someone had stolen it. I have never seen it since. Years have passed away since then. I still own that coat but I don't possess it. It is mine, it belongs to me, but it is no use to me because I don't possess it. Friend, you belong to Christ. He has the right to you - by creation - by redemption! It is your reasonable service to give yourself up to Him. It is the most becoming thing you can do. Do it now. I get tired of these consecration meetings, where many look so sweet and pious as they consecrate themselves anew to Christ. You would think they were doing God a favour. All they are doing is restoring stolen property.

> Consecration is not our giving anything to God. It is our taking our hands off what already belongs to Christ.
> Walter B Knight

What is a Saint?

… and what are the riches of the glory of his inheritance on the saints,
Ephesians 1 vs. 18

"The Inheritance of God". Paul prays for these poor, persecuted believers in Ephesus, "that the God of our Lord Jesus Christ, the father of Glory, may give unto you the spirit of wisdom and revelation in the knowledge of Him, the eyes of your understanding being enlightened, that ye may know what is the hope of His calling, what is the riches of the Glory of His inheritance in the saints." So many say OUR inheritance. No! it is HIS inheritance in the saints. His calling; not our calling. Notice "riches of the glory" in the saints. These poor Ephesian slaves were apt to think and feel they were only poor slaves, bought and sold for about 10 shillings a head. So Paul says, "I am praying for you that your eyes may be enlightened, that you may know you are God's property - God's rich inheritance. Many of us in a very real sense have cried, "Oh to be nothing, nothing." Tell me did Jesus die for nothings and nobodies? Did He leave the bosom of the Father and the worship and adoration of the archangels and angels, come down to this world, despised and rejected and live and die in ignominy and shame on the cruel Cross for nothing and nobody? Did He shed His precious Blood to purchase a bunch of nobodies? May the eyes of our understanding be enlightened that we may know we are "God's property", God's peculiar possession, purchased by the precious Blood of His dear Son. It was the only price adequate. The blood of angels, archangels or saints could never redeem us. Left to ourselves we could never understand this, God alone can enlighten our understanding so that we may know it. Oh may Paul's prayer be answered on behalf of all the saints.

> God does not love us because we are valuable, but we are valuable
> because God loves us.
> Martin Luther

Who are Saints?

...called to be saints:
Romans 1 vs. 8

The word "saint" is used some 119 times in the Bible. It is God's pet name for His people. He never calls them Christians. The word Christian is only used three times in the Bible but never used by God. The First time it is used by the Antiochians. They were a witty people and were fond of giving people nicknames, so they nicknamed the believers of that day "Christians" or "Christ's ones" (Acts 11 vs. 26.) It was certainly a compliment. The followers of Christ were so like Christ they nicknamed them accordingly. Wouldn't it be fine if the world where we live were compelled to nickname us this way? Remember, the Lord never called His disciples "Christians." He had many names for them, viz, friends, disciples, believers, followers, light, salt, witnesses, but His pet name was saints.

The Second time it was used was by Agrippa. He said with a sneer: "Paul almost thou persuadest me to become a Christian. The idea of you trying to make me become such a contemptible thing as a Christian." The word was used by this ungodly ruler; not by God.

The Third and the last time it is used is 1 Peter 4 vs. 16. "Christian" is a word used widely. We talk about Christian countries, Christian people, etc; they are no more Christian than the man in the moon. If you ask anyone, "Are you a Christian?" They feel insulted by you asking them. Ask many who are really saved, "Are you a saint?" They! "O! I'm no saint," yet it is God's pet name for them. A New Testament saint is a blood washed, born again man or woman. If you are saved you are as much a saint as James, John, Peter or Paul or Mary or Martha. I have as much right to be called "Saint William" as ever Peter had to be called Saint Peter, or Paul to be called Saint Paul. The Apostles were fishermen. No moon around their heads. Away with this superstitious balderdash. A saint is a sinner saved by Grace and possessing eternal life.

> The saint is a saint because he received the Holy Spirit, who took up his abode with him and inwardly married himself to the soul.
> Abraham Kuyper

No Other Way

Neither is there salvation in any other: for there is none other name under heaven given among men, whereby we must be saved.
Acts 4 vs. 12

There is no other foundation. There is no other refuge. There is no other remedy for our sin and our guilt. There is no other hope but Jesus only. Only one Saviour and only one way of salvation - by faith in Jesus only. I am the way, THE ONLY WAY. There was an old Roman Catholic woman blind and ignorant. She had been led to Christ late in life, and had never been able to read or write. When she came to die, a priest came to see her and told her that unless she had the last rites of the church she could never enter heaven, etc. As he stood by her bed she said, "Father, give me your hand." He gave it to her and she felt it all over. Then dropping it, she said, "You are no use to me and cannot give me absolution for there is no mark of a nail in your hand." We as Protestants need to learn the same lesson. That if ever we are to be saved, it is faith in Jesus only.

"My hope is built on nothing less
Than Jesus' blood and righteousness;
I dare not trust the sweetest frame,
But wholly lean on Jesus' name.
On Christ the solid rock I stand -
All other ground is sinking sand."

Christ is not only the Saviour but the salvation itself.
Matthew Henry

The Christ of Denunciation

Ye serpents, ye generation of vipers, how can ye escape
the damnation of hell?
Matthew 23 vs. 33

We have come to a place where the Christ of denunciation needs to be preached. Amid the hypocrisies and insincerities which permeate our modern life, we too seldom hear in the pulpit the burning indignation, the splendid scorn, and the fiery arraignment which distinguished the old prophets of God when they looked upon the social sin and corruption in high and low places. The old indignation seems dead. Or are we too cowardly to speak of our convictions? Emerson said, "The pulpit is the coward's fort." We may resent the charge, but we admit it if we keep silent when great moral interests are at stake. It is to be hoped that this wave of foolish and unguarded criticism will soon pass away, and that faithful evangelists will be appreciated. We must evangelise or we will fossilize. We must preach the evangel or we will perish. Oh for a mighty wave of evangelistic zeal and fervour all over the land and in all our churches.

We fear men so much because we fear God so little.
William Gurnall

Kangaroo Believers

Commit thy way unto the Lord; trust also in him;
and he shall bring it to pass.
Psalm 37 vs. 5

There are those who are "Kangaroo" believers. It is a hop and a jump with them - "Sometimes trusting, sometimes doubting." But genuine faith is constant and continuous.

Simply trusting every day, trusting through a stormy way,
Even when my faith is small, trusting Jesus that is all.
Trusting Him while life shall last, trusting till the earth be past.
Till within the jasper wall, trusting Jesus that is all.
Trusting as the moments fly, trusting as the days go by.
Trusting Him whate'er befall, trusting Jesus, that is all.

Whether it is sunshine or rain, summer or winter, day or night, calm or storm, - whether it is easy or hard - trusting Jesus that is all. Our loved ones may die, but like old Job we will say "Though He slay me yet will I trust Him." We may be maligned, persecuted, lied about, still we will continue steadfast, unmovable and unstaggering in our faith in Jesus.

Faith sees the invisible and believes the unbelievable and receives the impossible.
Corrie Ten Boom

Rest in His Love

...but the just shall live by his faith.
Habakkuk 2 vs. 4

Let us, through faith and patience, inherit the promise. It is the patience or impatience that bothers most of us. The Lord told Abraham He would give him a son and He kept him waiting over twenty years before He gave him a son. He kept him waiting until every human possibility of getting one had perished but Abraham staggered not through unbelief and "being not weak in faith he considered not his own body now dead, when he was about a hundred years old, neither yet the deadness of Sarah's womb... but was strong in faith giving glory to God; who against hope believed in hope that he might become the father of many nations, according to that which was spoken." What glory Abraham's faith brought to God and has brought all these centuries. He is the father of the faithful today. Do you remember when Lazarus was sick, Mary and Martha sent word to Jesus; and He abode two days still in the place where He was and said, "I am glad for your sakes that I was not there, to the intent that you might believe." The Lord has far more trouble teaching and training us that even He has given us all we ask. You see we ask for things, and we, and the Lord know we need them, but only the Lord knows whether it is for the best that we receive them just when we ask for them. So let us not be petulant or impatient or even impertinent, but quietly rest in His love and faithfulness. It may seem long between the asking and receiving. Shall not God avenge His own elect, which cry day and night unto Him, though He bear long with them? I tell you He will avenge them speedily. Then we must leave the how with God. How He will answer our prayers is not our business. "God moves in a mysterious way His wonders to perform." His ways are not our ways, but His ways are perfect and past finding out. Let us leave the time He will answer and the way He will answer with Him, but know that He will answer in His own time and way.

> Faith will not always get for us what we want, but it will get what God wants for us.
> Vance Havner

God Proud of the Overcomer

To him that overcometh will I grant to sit with me in my throne, even as I
also overcame, and am set down with my Father in his throne.
Revelation 3 vs. 21

Have you noticed how many promises are made in the Bible to those who live the overcoming life? The first book of the Bible speaks to us about a man being overcome and the last book tells us about a man being able to overcome if he will only trust the Lord. Will you turn to Revelations 2 vs.7. "He that hath an ear, let him hear what the Spirit saith unto the churches: To him that overcometh will I give to eat of the tree of life, which is in the midst of the paradise of God." Then in the eleventh verse we read: "He that overcometh shall not be hurt of the second death."

Abraham was an overcomer and you read of God saying; " I am the God of Abraham." Isaac was an overcomer and you read often of God saying, " I am the God of Isaac." Jacob was an overcomer and how often you read of God saying, "I am the God of Jacob." God was proud to say, "I am the God of Jacob." But you never read of God saying, " I am the God of Esau." And you never read of God saying, "I am the God of Lot." Poor old self-indulgent, sensual Esau. God was ashamed of him. Poor old worldly, compromising Lot, who with his compromising sent his family to hell and turned his daughters into harlots. Do you mean to say God is proud of a man like that? No. Indeed God sees if we are overcomers. What is the result? "I will confess your name." Just imagine, God up there to confess your name and mine before the angels and before the ransomed in glory! And then in chapter 3 vs. 21: "To him that overcometh will I grant to sit with me in my throne, even as I also overcame, and am set down with my Father in His throne." We shall be set in heavenly places with Jesus Christ; we will be set where we will be able to say,

"I am monarch over all I survey,
My right there is none to dispute."

My future is as bright as the promises of God.
Adoniram Judson

Two Wings

*He giveth power to the faint; and to them that have no might he
increaseth strength. Even the youths shall faint and be weary,
and the young men shall utterly fall:*
Isaiah 40: 29-31

That is, man at his best will fail and fall. "But they that wait upon the
Lord shall renew their strength; they shall mount up with wings as
eagles; they shall run and not be weary; they shall walk, and not faint."
God has given us two wings, faith and prayer, but the sad thing is, so
many have allowed Satan to clip them. Instead of soaring above their
foes and failures, they are not able to rise above them and are
constantly overcome by them. "Surely in vain the net is spread in the
eyes of anything that hath a wing." Proverbs 1 vs. 17 (margin). Let us
take God's way and have done with our own.

*So long thy power hath led me, sure it will still lead me on,
O'er moor and fen, o'er crag and torrent till the night is gone.
And with the morn, those angels' faces smile,
Which I have loved long since and lost awhile.*

Every child of God is born with eagle's wings. God means you to
live an heavenly life.
Andrew Murray

How to Overcome the Flesh

...Walk in the Spirit, and ye shall not fulfil the lust of the flesh.
Galatians 5 vs. 16

There are many of whom it can be said that the world and worldliness trouble them very little, but they are victims of the flesh. Their desires, passions and appetites are strong and they are continually being overcome. The Lord here shows us that if we walk in the Spirit – the atmosphere of our lives – we shall not be overcome. We are only able to crucify the flesh by the Spirit. So as we walk in and with Him we do not fulfil the fleshly lusts. As we yield our bodies up to His rule and sway, He cools, cleanses and controls. If we ourselves try to do it we will only fail. Our efforts only aggravate the evil, but if we commit all to Him, He will guide our walk and govern our bodies and lead us in continual triumph. Let us yield every part of our being to His indwelling, give up trying, but never ceasing to trust.

I more fear what is within me than what comes from without.
Martin Luther

MAY

1 ◆ A Holy Man

2 ◆ Cross Bearing

3 ◆ Submit to God

4 ◆ An Empty Christian Life

5 ◆ Selfishness

6 ◆ Compromise

7 ◆ Empty Religion

8 ◆ Empty Worship

9 ◆ Empty Service

10 ◆ Neglected Communion

11 ◆ The Bema

12 ◆ God's Honour Roll

13 ◆ The Lord's Jewels

14 ◆ A Book of Remembrance

15 ◆ A Divine Compulsion

16 ◆ A Holy Affection in the Soul

17 ◆ Fox Hunting

18 ◆ The Little Foxes

19 ◆ Private Devotions

20 ◆ Tithing

21 ◆ Diligent Parents

22 ◆ Church Membership

23 ◆ Family Life

24 ◆ A Mental Reservation

25 ◆ Restitution

26 ◆ The Proof

27 ◆ Our Lord's Teaching

28 ◆ Many Perplexed

29 ◆ The Meaning of Holiness

30 ◆ Chosen to be Holy

31 ◆ Called to be Holy

A Holy Man

...be ye clean, that bear the vessels of the Lord.
Isaiah 52 vs. 11

The Bible teaching of holiness is sublimely simple, viz; a holy man is a clean man, separated unto God. An electric wire if it is to conduct electricity must first be insulated, that is, covered and kept clean. Second, it must be isolated, that is, it must be separated and kept separated. That is why it is held by porcelain fixtures. So a holy man is a clean man, kept clean by the blood of Jesus, and living a separated life. In the world, but not of the world. It is not sinlessness or sinless perfection, but a clean, separated life. We keep our bodies clean. We dress in clean clothes. We live in clean homes. We eat off clean vessels, and we breathe clean air. Our hearts and minds ought to be clean. Why should we love cleanliness around us and not inward cleanliness? We are to be vessels unto honour, sanctified (holy) and meet for the Master's use. God is a clean God, and He wants clean children. He can't use unclean vessels or have communion with them.

A baptism of holiness, a demonstration of godly living, is the crying need of our day.
Duncan Campbell

2 MAY

Cross-Bearing

And whosoever doth not bear his cross, and come after me,
cannot be my disciple.
Luke 14 vs. 27

Many people speak of sickness, circumstances, persecution or marriage as their cross. That is a lot of sentimental poetic nonsense. To Christ, the cross represented all the malicious hatred of the world. The world expressed its hatred when He was nailed to the cross, and it has not changed its attitude since then. It still hates Christ. And it hates us for being His disciples. The cross is as real to the disciple today as it was to Christ nineteen hundred years ago. We can never become popular with the world and be disciples of Jesus. Taking up the cross means a clean cut from the world. If we are unwilling to do this we cannot be His disciples. Becoming good church members and active workers in the church or being decent, good and popular does not qualify us to be His disciples. Being His disciple never makes a person popular.

> Our Lord made discipleship hard and lost many prospective followers because He called them to a pilgrimage not to a parade – to a fight, not to a frolic.
> Vance Havner

3 MAY

Submit to God

Finally, my brethren, be strong in the Lord, and in the power of his might.
Ephesians 6 vs. 10

I tell you friends, if you meet the devil in your own strength, you will find you are no match for him. Submit to God, and in the power of that submission, resist, and you will find that the gates of hell shall not prevail against you. If only we confess our weakness and inability, and submit ourselves, and our foe to God, He will give us such power to resist that the devil will flee from us. Our little boy was ill and was lying in his bed very weak. I had been away over the week-end, and when I came back and leaned over his wee cot, he couldn't say much, but he put his wee arms around my neck, as much as to say, "Could you help me, father?" I felt as if I could give every ounce of my strength and every drop of my blood to help him. It was his helpless weakness that touched me. It is the same with God our Saviour. He is touched with the feeling of our infirmity. When we helplessly turn to Him, all His power is exerted on our behalf. Satan is too much even for the best and strongest of us. We are no match for him. How hard it is to get us to believe that! The only man that ever met and mastered him was the God-man. Let us live this life of submission to God and we will not be overcome, but be overcomers. "They overcame him by the blood of the Lamb, and by the word of their testimony; and they loved not their lives unto death.

Stand up, stand up for Jesus
Stand in His strength alone.
The arm of flesh will fail you
Ye dare not trust your own.

The first step on the way to victory is to recognise the enemy.
Corrie Ten Boom

An Empty Christian Life

Israel is an empty vine, he bringeth forth fruit unto himself: according to the multitude of his fruit he hath increased the altars; according to the goodness of his land they have made goodly images.
Hosea 10 vs. 1

What a grief and disappointment Israel was to God! What wonders He had done for them! He had delivered them from Egyptian bondage and slavery, by power and blood. He had led them through the wilderness, providing for every need of theirs so miraculously and constantly. They never lacked. He brought them into the land of promise – a land flowing with milk and honey. After all this, He has to say about them, "Israel is an empty vine, he bringeth forth fruit unto himself." Before we say a word against these people, let us ask ourselves, "What does He say about our lives, after all He has done for us?" Are we living like them, an empty life?

> Many Christians are still in the wilderness longing for garlic instead
> of grace; melons instead of manna!
> Vance Havner

5 MAY

Selfishness

... He bringeth forth fruit unto himself ...
Hosea 10 vs. 1

"He bringeth forth fruit unto HIMSELF." Everything he says or does is for himself. If the Lord does not give him happy feelings and keep him in good health and please him in everything, he either growls at God or forsakes Him and His service. If he undertakes work for God in the church, it must either pander to his pride or position or prosperity in his business. He joins a church where he thinks he will get the most business out of it. He takes office in the church because it gives him better standing in the community. Everything he does for the Lord is always with a view to his own interests first and the Lord after. The Lord and His work is just a stepladder for him to raise himself on. This is a sure sign of an empty Christian life.

> Far too frequently in this life, we are interested in only three persons; me, myself and I.
> Anon.

6 MAY

Compromise

Their heart is divided...
Hosea 10 vs.2

"Their heart is divided." He doesn't believe in the sort of preaching that demands separation from the world in every way, shape and form. He is broad in his views. He doesn't see any harm in having church dances, concerts, or card parties, or having these things in the homes of the members of the Church. He frequents the picture house more than the prayer meeting. He supports his club or lodge in a way he never thinks of supporting his Church. If the minister dares to mention any or all of these things in his preaching, then he gets angry with him. He wants intellectual preaching, he says, not such vulgarity. He forgets that there is nothing so vulgar as his hypocrisy. A compromising life is an empty life in the sight of God.

> Have I long in sin been sleeping.
> Long been slighting, grieving Thee?
> Has the world my heart been keeping?
> O forgive and rescue me – Even me.
> Elizabeth Codner

Empty Religion

If any man among you seem to be religious, and bridleth not his tongue, but deceiveth his own heart, this man's religion is vain. Pure religion and undefiled before God and the Father is this, to visit the fatherless and widows in their affliction, and to keep himself unspotted from the world.
James 1 vs. 26-27

This empty life manifests itself in our religion, in our worship, in our service, and in our thoughts. Turning to God's Word we there learn what is said about these four things: Empty Religion - isn't this common of our religion today? How little bridling of the tongue there is, and how the Church is hurt by the slander and the gossip of many whose lives are empty. They have a form of godliness, but they have no power. Their religion is only some sort of decent cloak that they wear on the Sunday. It is not their life, and has little to do with their life. Their faith is only a fact and not a fascination.

The jawbone of an ass was a killer in Samson's time. It still is.
Morris Gilber

Empty Worship

Ye hypocrites, well did Esaias prophecy of you, saying, This people draweth nigh unto me with their mouth, and honoureth me with their lips; but their heart is far from me. But in vain they do worship me, teaching for doctrines the commandments of men.
Matthew 15 vs. 7-9

Their worship is empty. They are more concerned about the transitions of men than they are about the commandments of God. They are very particular about the ritual of the worship and would not have any change made that might mean blessing to others. They substitute formality for spirituality. The form is more to them than the spirit. This is the true sign of an empty life. They bow in prayer to the Lord, but it is only with the lips; the heart is not in it. While they are being led in prayer, their thoughts are everywhere and on everything but God. They take the most solemn vows in the church, but they do not make any change in their lives. Their lives are the same through the week as ever. When they sing they sing lies. If their lives tallied with all they sang, what a change there would be in their lives! How obnoxious all this must be to the Lord Jesus! He says: "Who hath required this at your hands? I am weary to bear them."

> Carnal men are content with the 'act' of worship. They have no desire for communion with God.
> John W Everett

Empty Service

A son honoureth his father, and a servant his master: if then I be a father,
where is mine honour? and if I be master, where is my fear? saith the Lord
of hosts unto you, O priests, that despise my name. And ye say, Wherein
have we despised thy name? Ye offer polluted bread upon mine altar; and ye
say, Wherein have we polluted thee? In that ye say, The table of the Lord is
contemptible. And if ye offer the blind for sacrifice, is it not evil? and if ye
offer the lame and sick, is it not evil? offer it now unto thy governor; will
he be pleased with thee, or accept thy person? saith the Lord of hosts.
Malachi 1 vs. 6-8

I do not know more solemn words than these. Is this not true of much
of the service of the Lord today? As long as it does not cost anything,
it is given. If they tried to serve their earthly master as they serve the
Lord they would soon be removed. It is such weariness to them -
anything they do for the Lord. There is no blood in their service. It
does not cost them anything, and therefore does not count. It is only
by the shedding of blood that there can be any remunerative toil. The
least little thing keeps them away from the Church. The poorest
excuse will take them away from their Sunday School class. They are
eager enough when it comes to the pleasures or business of life. No
sacrifice is too great then. They rather delight in it if it does not cost
them a great deal. How sickening this must be to the Lord. Wherever
you find an empty life, you get this empty, costless, bloodless service.

If religion be worth anything it is worth everything.
Matthew Henry

Neglected Communion

*Not forsaking the assembling of ourselves together, as the manner
of some is; but exhorting one another: and so much the more,
as ye see the day approaching.*
Hebrews 10 vs. 25

We have time for the newspaper or novel. We find time to sleep, to eat, to play but no time to read our Bible every day and pray. How can any life be anything but empty, if we neglect the channel that brings in the fullness? You might as well expect to live without eating or breathing as to expect to be filled and yet neglect communion with God. Whatever the cost, let us have done with this neglect and be diligent and we shall know this blessed experience - a life of overflowing fullness. Others are careless about public communion. Once to the Church on Sunday is all they care to go at all. While they are in Church their minds are not occupied with God, but with business and pleasure, or maybe they are not occupied at all, as they sleep most of the time. If we cared for our bodies in the same slovenly way, or our business, we would soon find how empty they would become. Why can we not be as sensible about our spiritual lives as we are about our physical?

No man ever said, at the end of his days, 'I have read my Bible too
much, I have thought of God too much, I have prayed too much, I
have been too careful with my soul.
J C Ryle

The Bema

For we must all appear before the judgment seat of Christ; that every one may receive the things done in his body, according to that he hath done, whether it be good or bad.
II Corinthians 5 vs. 10

What sort of a life are we living? Is it empty? Are we content to continue living such a life? What sorrow and shame will be the portion of such a one at the judgment seat of Christ? The fire, will that day, test our lives, and whatever has been of hay, wood or stubble will be burned and the soul saved as through fire, but it shall suffer loss. Let us in the light of that day, cast everything out of our lives that should not be there, however precious to us or prized by us, and then, when we stand before His Throne, we will not have shame and confusion, but hear Him say: "Well done. Enter thou into the joy of thy Lord." God grant it.

Shall I empty-handed be, when beside the crystal sea
I shall stand before the everlasting throne
Must I have a heart of shame, as I answer to my name,
With no works that my Redeemer there can own?

What regret must then be mine, when I meet my Lord divine.
If I've wasted all the talents he doth lend;
If no soul to me can say, I am glad you passed my way
For 'twas you who told me of the sinner's Friend'

If my gratitude I'd show unto Him who loves me so
Let me labour till the evening shadows fall;
That some little gift of love I may bear to realms above,
And not empty-handed be when comes the call.

He will not say 'Well done' if we have not done well.
Anon.

God's Honour Roll

...and that thought upon his name.
Malachi 3 vs. 16

In spite of the fact that the nation had sunk into a state of political degradation and national decay, there were a few who "spake often to one another" and "that thought upon His name." The church was corrupt; the priests were unfaithful to their sacred trust. They were given to secularising tendencies. There were few devout worshippers. The sacrifices, which were offered at the altar, were despicable and worthless. They seemed to imagine that any animal was good enough for God – the lame, the blind that had become useless for work, the maimed or the torn, the beast that was dying of disease and could not be offered for sale in the market, they would have been afraid to sell. They grudged the best of their possessions to Him who had given them all. Formalism and hypocrisy abounded in all their religious services. Except for this solitary voice of Malachi, prophecy had hushed her harp. In the midst of such degrading and demoralising conditions, religiously and nationally, we have those whose names are on God's honour roll, giving themselves over to meet together for worship and fellowship, and to think upon His Name. Are there those today, as in Malachi's day, who think upon His Name and speak often to one another? Thank God there are. These are the ones whose names are written on God's honour roll. They may be few, unnoticed and unknown, but they are known to God, and He hears and hearkens to their work and meditations. Friend! You may have to live in a worldly, ungodly home, or work in the midst of a wicked, licentious crowd of men. You may belong to a worldly formal church. Thank God! In spite of all this, you may be one of God's "honour roll". If there were those whose names were written there in Malachi's day then we may make sure our names are on God's honour roll today.

> How sweet the name of Jesus sounds
> In a believers ear!
> It soothes his sorrows, heals his wounds
> And drives away his fears.
> John Newton

13 MAY

The Lord's Jewels

*And they shall be mine, saith the Lord of hosts, in that day when
I make up my jewels; and I will spare them, as a man spareth
his own son that serveth him.*
Malachi 3 vs. 17

The past is behind us, and can never be recalled or changed. It will meet us at the Judgment Seat of Christ, but the present and future is ours; let us then resolve by God's grace and enabling spirit that the present and future will record the fact that we are determined to be one of God's honoured ones. Never mind the cost, cross or consequences. Never mind the persecution and sacrifices we may be called on to suffer or bear, as long as we are counted worthy to have our names written on God's honour roll. When we answer to our name on that great review and reward day, all we have ever suffered or sacrificed will seem as nothing compared to the honour of being counted one of God's honour roll men. God says, "They shall be mine." "My jewels" in that day. They are dear and valuable to Him. They represent surpassing beauty. Jewels are nature's loveliest gifts. God's jewels are here incomplete. When the cutting and the burnishing are finished they are to shine as the stars forever and ever. They have been dug from the black caverns of sin; they have been brought from the stormy depths of hell, these blood-bought, grace-preserved, grief-polished "Jewels of God." Hallelujah! - that they should be to the praise of His glory throughout all ages. May we be one of that number.

The manufacture of a saint takes a lifetime.
Alan Redpath

A Book of Remembrance

...and a book of remembrance was written before him for them
that feared the Lord...
Malachi 3 vs. 16

To fear God is to take up His cross, deny self daily, and follow Him at any cost, or cross, never allowing the consequences of such a life to make us terrified by our enemies or compromise one iota, like Joshua and Caleb, who wholly followed the Lord. Their song is:

Jesus, I am going through,
I'll pay the price whatever others do,
I'll take the side of the Lord's anointed few,
Jesus I am going through.

When we measure the lives of so many Christians these Laodecian days, by this yard stick, we can be sure their names are not in God's honour roll. They may be in the Lambs Book of Life. They are neither cold nor hot. They are lukewarm - a disgrace to the church and a disgust to Christ, and a hindrance to the work of God in the world. In the light of these facts can you say 'my name is in God's honour roll'? If not, let me plead with you, dear friend, yield unconditionally and receive the Holy Ghost to purify your heart, and fill you unto all the fullness of God. He will make you a vessel unto honour, meet for the Master's use and prepared unto every good work. Then your name will be written in God's book of remembrance - His honour roll.

> I will place no value on anything I have or may possess, except in relation to Christ's Kingdom.
> David Livingstone

A Divine Compulsion

...spake often one to another...
Malachi 3 vs. 16

Their conversation daily was such that it betrayed them. They were recognised as those whose names were in God's honour roll. If we express no concern for the interests of God and God's work and ways in our lives, in our words, we shall be justly suspected of having little in our thoughts. We should learn to indulge ourselves by our common talk, as well as in our actions. How we shrink from talking about the soul and eternity, about the pilgrim way and celestial city, about God and Christ. How we shrink about giving our testimony, about the love that sought us; the blood that bought us; and the grace that brought us to the fold. Wondrous grace that brought us to the fold and keeps us there day by day. In fact, many don't believe in such conversation. They can talk about politics, society, amusements, even domestic affairs, but they are silent when it comes to speaking one to another about their spiritual experiences. You could walk and live with them for years, and you would never suspect from their conversation that they were even saved. Such are certainly not on God's honour roll. Those on God's honour roll cannot help but speak of the things they have felt, seen and heard. There is a Divine compulsion in them that constrains and enables them to speak often one to another.

The Bible knows nothing of solitary religion.
John Wesley

A Holy Affection in the Soul

Then they that feared the Lord ...
Malachi 3 vs. 16

The fear of the Lord is not the "slavish fear" which dreads the punishment rather than the sin which is the cause of the punishment, but a "filial fear," a holy affection in the soul whereby it is inclined to reverence God and to approve of His words, and ways; to hate the devil and love God, to hate sin and love holiness; to abhor that which is evil and cleave to that which is good. It is to live a life of uncompromising antagonism to the world, flesh and the devil, and a life of whole-hearted devotion and loyalty to God and His word. It is to live daily a life separated from the world and separated unto God.

> No one can know the true grace of God who has not first known the fear of God.
> A W Tozer

Fox Hunting

Take us the foxes, the little foxes, that spoil the vines;
for our vines have tender grapes.
Song of Solomon 2 vs. 15

Fox hunting was a very real and constant work in Palestine. It was never a once and for all job - done and done with. Oh no, the foxes, the little foxes were very numerous and foxy in Palestine, and they were very fond of tender grapes. They were prolific in breeding, and you had always to be on the lookout for them if your grapes were to be spared. They didn't kill or destroy the vines. They merely devoured the grapes when they were tender, and robbed you of your harvest. Isn't this a picture of many a Christian's life today. I wonder is it a picture of your life and mine? Our danger from these little foxes is not that we would be lost, but that our lives become spoiled and unfruitful. We were chosen by Christ to be faithful Christians. If our lives are to be fruitful we will need to give good heed to the words of our text: "Take us the foxes, the little foxes, that spoil the vines; for our vines have tender grapes." If the vines were to be destroyed by some wild and ferocious beast we would always be on guard and never let down our watchfulness, but when they may be spoiled, not destroyed, by the little foxes, we are apt to become careless. If our fruitfulness of life was to be spoiled only by some vulgar, vicious sin, there would be little or no danger of our vine being spoiled. If it was some sudden, violent, open assault of the devil tempting us to some dreadful and disgusting sin, we would be on our guard and resist vigorously and successfully; but when our danger lies in some subtle and insidious "little fox," here is were we often fail. The foxes are so numerous; seemingly so innocent and persistent, that we have become unfruitful gradually, and almost unconsciously, at least for a time. How many Christians gave the promise for a successful and fruitful life and then something came in and was allowed, some little innocent looking fox, and the life gradually became unfruitful.

The permanent presence of the old nature guarantees that in the Christian life there is no victory without vigilance.
John Blanchard

The Little Foxes

Take us the foxes, the little foxes, that spoil the vines;
for our vines have tender grapes.
Song of Solomon 2 vs. 15

Our danger does not always lie in the necessities of life, but in its luxuries. The danger is not in the porridge, but in the partridge. Our danger is not on the battlefield, but in the camp. In other words, our danger does not always lie in some seemingly innocent and necessary and constant appeal to our senses, some "little fox" of recreation and pleasure, and before we are aware of it our life has become unfruitful. The tender grapes have been spoiled. We may still be as active and busy as ever in God's work and in some degree successful. We may be regular in our attendance at the church and meeting, but little foxes are all the time spoiling the tender grapes and making us unfruitful. It is well to know we may be successful in our service for God and souls, and yet be unfruitful. You see, success may be determined by circumstances, opportunity, and natural gifts, but fruitfulness is determined by a life that is yielded fully to Christ and filled with the Holy Spirit. It may be fruitful and not always successful, and it is fruit the Lord desires and expects, not success.

For every one hundred men who can stand adversity there is only one who can withstand prosperity.
Thomas Carlyle

19 MAY

Private Devotions

Take us the foxes, the little foxes, that spoil the vines;
for our vines have tender grapes.
Song of Solomon 2 vs. 15

What about our private devotions? What time do we give to them? Is it our best time and plenty of it? The best time is first thing every day. God first. Or do we leave it till some time later, when we are tired and sleepy? How much time do we allow for our Bible reading and prayer every day? I believe from personal experience and observation, it is here where the little foxes do their deadly work. We become lazy and lie too long in our bed in the morning. Then we haven't time enough for our Bible reading and prayer. We have our home and family duties, or school or business to attend to, certainly we have, and we ought to be diligent about them too; but not neglect our devotions. How readily we excuse ourselves for our neglect and carelessness in this matter. Do you remember how and when you vowed you would take and make time every day for your Bible reading and prayer? It was to be first thing every day. You did well for a time, but what hindered you continuing? The little foxs have been at work. Face the facts friend and get after the little foxes and destroy them, as you will wish you had done when you stand before the Judgment Seat of Christ. There is nor substitute for private, daily bible reading and prayer. You may attend meetings, and you may be busy in God's work, one way or another, all this is no substitute. There is nothing we grow so readily weary in as this, and therefore it is a fertile source of unfruitfulness.

Backsliders begin with dusty Bibles and end with filthy garments.
C H Spurgeon

Tithing

Bring ye all the tithes into the storehouse, that there may be meat in mine house, and prove me now herewith, saith the Lord of hosts, if I will not open you the windows of heaven, and pour you out a blessing, that there shall not be room enough to receive it.
Malachi 3 vs. 10

You remember you vowed you would lay aside a tenth of your income. This was to be peculiarly "God's money." This continued a little time until you prospered and it began to look a large amount to give. Your business prospered or your salary was increased, and when you deducted the tenth, it seemed a lot and you yielded to the temptation and robbed God, and have continued to rob God ever since. No one knows anything about this but God. Your gifts are still generous and regular, but the tithe is not fully given. The little foxes have begun to spoil the tender vines. The little foxes did their deadly work by getting you to pay your accounts or debts first and then tithe what was left, thus robbing God. It is your gross income or earnings you are to tithe. We owe God first and then all other obligations. I wish I had the space to let you know the blessings God has promised to tithers. Look them up yourself and you will see how foolish you are to rob God in tithes, not merely in eternity, but in time; not merely spiritual blessings, but temporal and material blessings. Friend! Let me entreat you, lay that little fox by the heels and destroy it, and begin to be honest with God. Begin and calculate all the little money you have robbed God of, and pay it back as well as begin to give the tenth faithfully and regularly again.

> Give according to your income lest God make your income according to your giving.
> Anon.

Diligent Parents

Train up a child in the way he should go; and when he is old,
he will not depart from it.
Proverbs 22 vs. 6

We are told about Eli, "His sons made themselves vile and he restrained them not." It cost him and his family their lives and the priesthood. Lack of authority in the home has been, and is today, a fruitful source of family sorrow and tragedy. The children never can respect their parents; in that they have never been taught respect and obedience. The family of many a Christian reveals the fact that foxes are at work in the lives of the parents, making them unfruitful. Godly, God-fearing children are not an accident. They are the fruit of their Godly parents' sacrificial, scriptural training. There is much more one might state, but time and space do not permit. Let me plead with you, dear friend, if this article has revealed foxes, little foxes, in your life, spoiling the vines, don't be annoyed and get angry, rather take it to the Lord and heed His command: "Take us the foxes," that is, take hold of them resolutely and definitely and have done with them once and for all, and your life will become fruitful in love, joy, peace, and all the graces of the Spirit. This will never mean that you can become careless, oh no, you will need to watch and pray everyday until life's journey ends, and we will not cease to pray for you, and to desire that you may be filled with the knowledge of His will that ye might walk worthy of God unto all pleasing, being fruitful in every good work and increasing in the knowledge of God, in Jesus' name, Amen.

The best way to beat the devil is to hit him with a cradle.
Billy Sunday

Church Membership

And they continued stedfastly in the apostles' doctrine and fellowship, and in breaking of bread, and in prayers.
Acts 2 vs. 42

Are you a member of a church? This is a public testimony. Be careful about the church you join. If the minister is untrue to the Blood and the Book don't join that church or you will become a partaker of his evil deeds. He may be very genial, scholarly and benevolent man, but if he doubts and questions the absolute integrity and authority of the Bible and the Deity of Jesus Christ, he is a modernist and must be shunned. Don't let denominational sentiment or loyalty to the minister make you a Judas Iscariot—a betrayer of Christ. Ring true to Christ and His Word at any cost or cross. Join some church where you can worship without offence and where your soul will be fed and nourished and fit you for a fruitful life and service. Many are sitting under a ministry that is poisoning their spiritual life, and then wonder and complain they are not enjoying their Saviour and Salvation. You cannot live and thrive on poison. Don't send the children to the church. Take them there and sit together as a family. The children may object. Never mind. While they are in your home and supported by you, they are under your authority. You remember how God said "Shall I hide from Abraham that thing which I do;... for I know him, that he will command his children after him."

An avoidable absence from church is an infallible evidence of spiritual decay.
Frances Ridley Havergal

23 MAY

Family Life

But as for me and my house, we will serve the Lord.
Joshua 24 vs. 15

The Lord was the first "Home maker." What a beautiful home He prepared for the first married couple. The Garden of Eden had everything necessary and beautiful. Satan was the first "Home breaker." What a wreck he made of that first sinless home, and what a sorrow and shame followed. Their first-born was a murderer, and they lost their beautiful home. God is more concerned about the family than the nation. It's the families that make a nation. If the family is wrong, the nation will be wrong. When we are saved we are told to begin work for God in the home. "Go home and tell what great things the Lord has done for you." Especially when we receive the Holy Ghost for holy living and fruitful service, we are to begin at Jerusalem - the home. Many would like to become ministers, evangelists or missionaries in the homeland or abroad, but they don't begin at home. Look around and see the number of children of Christian parents on the road to hell, largely because there was no home religion. The minister on Sunday, or the Sunday school teacher can never substitute for the parents. Parents cannot pass the responsibility on to the Church.

> Holy families must be the chief preservers of the interest of religion in the world.
> Richard Baxter

A Mental Reservation

But Peter said, Ananias, why hath Satan filled thine heart to lie to the Holy Ghost, and to keep back part of the price of the land?
Acts 5 vs. 3

The largest society there is in the Church today is the society of Ananias and Sapphira to those who keep back part of the price. They sing some of the most solemn vows or take them before others. They will sit at the Table of the Lord, pledging their faith and faithfulness to Him, while all the time in their heart, they are keeping back part of the Lord's possession. Their surrender is made with a mental reservation. We may succeed in deceiving our friends and the Church, but cannot deceive God. Friends, we must be honest with God if we are to be blessed. Let us not try and atone for our deficiency in surrender by working ourselves into a state of hysteria and groaning and crying and praying, as if God was unwilling to bless. The moment we unreservedly surrender fully, that moment and only at that moment, will we receive the desire of our hearts.

The greatness of a man's power is the measure of his surrender.
William Booth

Restitution

And if it be stolen from him, he shall make restitution
unto the owner thereof.
Exodus 22 vs. 12

Read carefully the whole chapter and see how detailed and definite the Lord is, regarding this matter. I suppose it is one of the most objectionable subjects one could undertake to preach on, if not the most objectionable, and yet there never was a day when it was more necessary. I believe many who are called backsliders never really decided for Christ, although they professed to do so, because the Holy Spirit brought before their mind some one whom they had wronged, or some one they had robbed in the past, indicating that they would need to make restitution before they could be saved, and they turned away from Christ sorrowfully. It may have been months or years after their professed decision. There can never be real repentance where there has not been an honest effort to make right past wrongs. We can never be forgiven unless we forgive. We cannot and do not love God if we don't love our brother. If we love him we will show the sincerity and reality of our love by confessing our wrong doing and putting it right.

> When we have done harm to our neighbour, we should make restitution, though not compelled by law.
> Matthew Henry

The Proof

Therefore if any man be in Christ, he is a new creature: old things
are passed away; behold, all things are become new.
II Corinthians 5 vs. 17

The proof of the genuineness of Zaccheus' conversion was this. "If I have taken anything from any man by false accusation, I restore fourfold." Jesus replied, "This day is salvation come to this house." Everyone who lived in Jericho and knew Zaccheus would believe in the reality of his conversion when they received £20 for £5 he had stolen from them by overcharging them in their taxes. Wouldn't there be a stir in that old town! Whatever the world may say about Christianity and Christians in general, they surely believe in an experience that makes a man restore, and restore fourfold, what he had stolen in the past. When you see the Philippian jailor washing the bruised backs of Paul and Silas, you can more easily believe that he has a change of heart, and it was a genuine one. However loudly we may profess, if we have robbed or wronged anyone, we cannot make that wronged one believe it is sincere until there be confession and restitution, we make it right as far as we can.

I knew a man who had been a heavy drinker before his conversion. He professed conversion and came right out for the Lord in the wee town where he lived and began preaching in the open-air. Every time he started to preach the publican would come out at the door of the pub and shout, "John, what about the £67 you owe?" John would shout back, "When God forgave my sins He paid my debts." His name and profession was a stench in the nostrils of the villagers. His influence and testimony did more to hinder God's work than all the drunkards combined. Apart from religion altogether, it is only common honesty, to say the least, to make right whatever wrong we may have done, and restore whatever we have taken from another.

It will make us very careful of ourselves, if we consider that we are accountable not only for the hurt we do, but for the hurt we occasion through inadvertency.
John Wesley

Our Lord's Teaching

Therefore if thou bring thy gift to the altar and there remember that thy
brother hath ought against thee: leave there thy gift before the altar and go
thy way, first be reconciled to thy brother: and then come and offer thy gift.
Agree with thine adversary quickly.
Matthew 5 vs. 23

There had been riots in a city we visited for a mission. Shop windows had been smashed and a good deal of property damaged and stolen. Amongst the converts of the mission was an Irishman. He got "well saved," and began making restitution as his conscience directed him. He had smashed a large window during the riots. When this disturbed his conscience, he was frightened of the consequences and the impossibility of paying. However, he found out the name of the Insurance Company who had paid for the window. He went and saw the manager and told him his story; how he had been converted and now wished to make his restitution. The manager was deeply interested in all that the young man had told him, and made an appointment to meet him the next day. When they met he asked the man how he proposed to pay the bill, it was £34. The man was on the dole, but he told him he would pay him by regular instalments. The manager asked him how much would quieten his conscience. He said, "I leave that, sir, with you." "Well," said the manager, "if £10 would satisfy you, it will me." The Irishman wondered how much he could spare out of his dole. He had an old motorcycle that he used for taking him to his "relief work." He began to pray the Lord to send him a buyer for it. He would walk the three miles instead. A few days after, a man offered him £10 for his cycle and he paid the Insurance Company. I wish you could have seen the joy and heard it in results, and what peace filled his soul. Today he is training in the Bible School for full-time work for the Lord. Friends, "there is no other way to be happy in Jesus, but to trust and obey." The witness of the Spirit is given to those who believe and also to those who obey.

> Reformation and restitution do not save. But where one is truly repentant and has come to God in sincere confession, he will want to the best of his ability to put things right with others.
> Harry Ironside

Many Perplexed

Therefore if thou bring thy gift to the altar, and there rememberest that thy brother hath ought against thee; Leave there thy gift before the altar, and go thy way; first be reconciled to thy brother, and then come and offer thy gift.
Matthew 5 vs. 23-24

Many are perplexed about whether the devil is tormenting them or the Holy Spirit convicting them. Our Lord gives us light on this. Listen, "When thou comest to the altar and there rememberest." Where do we remember? At the altar. That is, when you are seeking the Lord about your salvation you may be sure it is the Lord speaking to you. What are we to remember? "That thy brother have ought against thee." So many imagine it is "If you have ought against thy brother." The word of the Lord is: "Thy brother hath ought against thee." That's quite a difference, isn't it? Has your Lord anything against you? You pledged you would give Him a tenth of your income. Trouble came: work ceased: income decreased. So you ceased paying your tithe and hence robbed God. We must first be reconciled to God. "Get right with God." Has our landlord anything against us? Have we paid our rent? Has the grocer, butcher, baker, milkman, doctor, tailor, or milliner anything against us? First be reconciled, and then come. If we are unable to pay let us be honest enough to confess to the one we owe anything to that we will pay as soon as we can. "First be reconciled." You won't have long to wait for the blessing of God and the assurance of your salvation. It is God's way and He will never change His ways to suit us or win us.

> My dear friends get these stumbling stones out of the way. God does not want a man to shout 'Hallelujah' who doesn't pay his debts. Many of our prayer meetings are killed, by men trying to pray who cannot pray, because their lives are not right.
> D L Moody

The Meaning of Holiness

Follow peace with all men, and holiness,
without which no man shall see the Lord.
Hebrews 12 vs. 14

The word "holy" is derived from a root "halig" or healthy. If you were talking about your body you would say it was healthy. If you were talking about your soul, you would say, or ought to be able to say, it was holy. You would be just as correct if you said your body was holy and your soul healthy. Holiness is spiritual health. Sin is soul sickness, and where allowed and entertained there can be no health or holiness. But when we are cleansed by the blood of Christ and filled with the Holy Spirit, we are made holy or healthy. Surely we all want to be healthy in soul and body. That is just exactly what God desires to make us and keep us.

I want to bring you to God's Word, and with as little comment as possible, so you may get away from your own notions or the notions of others and understand your Bibles on this matter. There is a sublime simplicity and clearness about the Bible teaching on holiness. There is much confusion amongst even holiness people. But you find the confusion arises when they begin to define holiness. We all surely believe the Bible teaches it. Let us not so much bother about the definitions, but get into the experience and live it before men daily. This will do more to silence controversy and attract believers to it. The Bible speaks of the beauty of holiness. It is a beautiful thing, and makes our lives beautiful and attractive.

A holy life is the life of God.
William Gurnell

Chosen to be Holy

According as He hath chosen us in Him before the foundation of the world,
that we should be holy and without blame before Him in love.
Ephesians 1 vs. 4

We hear a lot to-day in some circles about 'election,' 'foreordination,' 'predestination,' and the impression they give you is, that it is about salvation and glorification, but never a word about being elected; chosen; to be holy; and yet we are chosen in Him to be holy. We have been predestinated to be conformed to the image of His Son – not a word about salvation. Of course we cannot be made holy without being saved first. But the object of our salvation is for us to be made holy. We also hear some say when this doctrine of holiness is preached or talked about, that it is some new-fangled notion and therefore to be shunned. But notice the words, "Before the foundation of the world." Before ever there was a sun, moon or star, or ever the Sons of God sang at creation's dawn, this was God's choice for you and me.

> The destined end of a man is not happiness nor health, but holiness.
> God's one aim is the production of saints.
> Oswald Chambers

Called to be Holy

For God hath not called us unto uncleanness, but unto holiness...
1 Thessalonians 4 vs. 7

The vilest sinner (let alone every truly converted man) believes when we are saved we should live a clean life. In fact, they even brand anyone professing to be saved and not living a clean life, as a hypocrite of the deepest dye, and rightly so. Well, that is the negative side of our call. The positive side is – We are called to holiness. There are many who turn from uncleanness, but they turn away from the blessing of holiness for some reason or another. But if we are to apprehend that for which we are apprehended in Christ Jesus, we must press toward the mark for the prize of the high calling of God in Christ Jesus and be holy.

I often pray; Lord make me as holy as a pardoned sinner can be.
Robert Murray McCheyne

JUNE

1 ◆ Commanded to be Holy

2 ◆ Christ Died to Make us Holy

3 ◆ Established in Holiness

4 ◆ The Dividends of Discipline

5 ◆ Spiritual Cleansing

6 ◆ Slushy Sentimentalism

7 ◆ A Certified Gospel

8 ◆ Let Him be Accursed

9 ◆ Men Pleasers

10 ◆ A Double Portion

11 ◆ Heed the Plea

12 ◆ Never Popular

13 ◆ Inward Stamina

14 ◆ Goodbye World

15 ◆ So They Went Down to Bethel

16 ◆ Thy Holy Spirit Alone

17 ◆ The Steps and Stops

18 ◆ The Christian Life filled with Peace

19 ◆ Joy

20 ◆ Just Like Grandpa

21 ◆ Comfortable Christians

22 ◆ How Refreshing

23 ◆ Filled with Knowledge

24 ◆ Ways and Acts

25 ◆ Goodness and Beauty

26 ◆ Filled with God's Will

27 ◆ Fruit of Righteousness

28 ◆ The Enthronement of Christ

29 ◆ The Light of the World

30 ◆ Hiding Your Light

1 JUNE

Commanded to be Holy

But as He which hath called you is holy, so be ye holy in all manner of conversation, because it is written, Be ye holy for I am holy.
1 Peter 1 vs. 15-16

Every one of us believes that we are not to kill, steal, or get drunk. Why? Because we are commanded by God not to. Well, here is just as clear and imperative a command – "Be ye holy" – and if we are not holy we are disobedient and rebellious. Never mind what it means. He will teach us about that. We are commanded to be holy. Let us be obedient to His command to be holy. There is a strange mistake abroad that holiness is something quite optional. It is regarded as desirable for certain people and in special circumstances, but its claims are by no means universal. Holiness is regarded as an emotional luxury if not as a spiritual fad. It is as truly an imperative command as any command in the Bible and we can neither evade nor escape the consequences of disobedience to it here or hereafter. We must either obey or disobey the command, but we cannot be neutral about it.

'Be ye holy' is the greatest fundamental of our religion.
Matthew Henry

2 JUNE

Christ Died to make us Holy

Husbands, love your wives, even as Christ also loved the Church and gave Himself for it; that He might sanctify and cleanse it with the washing of water by the word, that He might present it to Himself a glorious church, not having spot or wrinkle or any such thing, but that it should be holy and without blemish.
Ephesians 5 vs. 25-27

Christ died not only to take away our guilt and penalty, but to make us holy and without blemish. We are His church, His bride, and His body. It would be awful if His body was spotted and wrinkled, instead of pure and holy. How terrible to contemplate His bride as a wrinkled and spotted thing. He has made it possible, by His death and dying, to have His Church a glorious Church devoid of all such defects. We are frustrating the purpose of His death by unholy lives and deeds. Anything else than holiness will never let Him see of the travail of His soul and be satisfied.

So in love is Christ with holiness that He will buy it with His blood for us.
John Flavel

3 JUNE

Established in Holiness

And the Lord make you to increase and abound in love one toward another and toward all men, even as we do toward you: to the end He may stablish your hearts unblameable in holiness before God.
1 Thessalonians 3 vs. 12-13

We are to increase and abound in our love one toward another, to the end that the blessing of holiness already received, we may be established in it. You see, this is no transient experience – with us today and gone tomorrow. No. We are to be "established" in it, and the way this is to be done is "grow" and "glow" in love one toward another. Then notice it is blameless, not faultless. We can never be faultless until we see Him face to face. But we can and we may be blameless. We must never confound purity and maturity. Not a few good people mix up things that differ. They confuse holiness with maturity, motive with achievement, love with blamelessness, and the perfection of grace with the perfection of resurrection glory. There are many people dead scared of coming to the place where there will be no more room for improvement. They need not distress themselves about that. All this is to be 'before God'. Isn't that fine and comforting. Not before our family, neighbours, or the world; but before God, even our Father. You see He can see our motives and desires and knows our hearts, and therefore understands us. The world and our best friends often misunderstand us because they don't know our hearts and motives. We may be sneered at and misjudged by all, but we need not be concerned as long as we have His smile and the approval of our own conscience. A lot of people are trying to make everyone see they are holy by certain ecstatic and transcendental experiences and visions or tongues, and they only succeed in making themselves miserable and ridiculous and their friends disgusted. When we have this blessed experience of holiness of heart, we won't need to advertise it. It will be manifested in daily walk and conduct.

An unholy Christian is a contradiction of everything the Bible teaches.
John Blanchard

4 JUNE

The Dividends of Discipline

For they (our parents) verily for a few days chastened us after their own pleasure: but He for our profit, that we might be partakers of His holiness.
Hebrews 12 vs. 10

Isn't this the explanation of many strange experiences in our lives? We have wondered why we were chastened of the Lord. Here we have the answer: "That we might be partakers of His holiness." Many a Christian blesses God for a bed of serious sickness. It was there they were led to yield fully to Him to be made holy. Sometimes money or possessions were taken from us, or maybe health or friends or loved ones, until our hearts and faith almost failed us, but when we came to the end of ourselves and saw the only life worth living was the life utterly yielded and obedient to God, His chastening made us partakers of His holiness. We are so ugly and awkward and rebellious. God has often to chasten us to bring us to the place where we let Him have His way with us.

God chastens us not that he may love us but because He loves us.
A W Tozer

5 JUNE

Spiritual Cleansing

Having therefore these promises, dearly beloved, let us cleanse ourselves
from all filthiness of the flesh and spirit, perfecting holiness in the fear of
God.
2 Corinthians 7 vs. 1

The cleansing here is an act done, and an act done with the perfecting is a process. There will never be a time when we won't require the cleansing blood. For as we walk in the light as He is in the light, we have fellowship one with another and the blood cleanseth – keeps on cleansing – us from all sin. We may have a conscience clear and void of offence today, and tomorrow as we walk in clearer light we see filthiness of flesh and spirit, and we, by a deliberate act, cleanse ourselves. That is, we repent and confess and appropriate by faith the cleansing and thus perfect holiness. If my hands are dirty I cleanse them by water, soap, rubbing, etc., but I cleanse them. Just in the same way we cleanse ourselves by using the means provided for our cleansing. Then this perfecting holiness is in the fear of God. No room for bombast here. No "I am holier than thou" attitude here. It is in the fear of God. Work out your own salvation with fear and trembling, for it is God that worketh in you. Holiness is to be stamped on every ounce and every yard, every minute and every hour, every word and every deed. It will never be a finished job until our latest breath. Notice, "Having therefore these promises, let us." Because we have such promises, God is as good as His promise and will make them good in us. We are not intended to be spiritually sick, or religious invalids. Having these promises, let us perfect holiness, or go on to perfection.

Sanctification is always a progressive work.
J C Ryle

6 JUNE

Slushy Sentimentalism

God judgeth the righteous, and God is angry with the wicked every day.
Psalm 7 vs. 6

These are days when men everywhere have an idea that God is some sort of an old, simple, sentimental mother, too good-natured to punish the sinner here or hereafter. He is such a loving God – so loving that His love conflicts with His justice. In fact He has ceased to be great or holy, just 'love', so called. The sinner can do, as he likes. Live, as he likes. Sin, as he likes. It will all come right in the end they say. God is good. He won't punish, or, if He does, it will be very light and easy, and in the end all will be well in Heaven.

It is a remarkable fact that these very folks don't believe in this slushy sentimentalism when it comes to their own children or criminals in the land. They believe in punishment, and give it too, but "poor" God is all love and pity and so good that you can defy Him, trample under foot the precious blood, and do despite to His Spirit, and He won't punish you here or hereafter. They forget that God's love is mentioned about twenty-eight times in the Bible and God's wrath over sixty times. God is angry every day with the wicked, and knows how to punish the ungodly as well as to bless.

> The holiness of God, the wrath of God and the health of the creation are inseparably united. Not only is it right for God to display anger against sin, but also I find it impossible to understand how He could do otherwise.
> A W Tozer

A Certified Gospel

I marvel that ye are so soon removed from him that called you into the grace of Christ unto another gospel.
Galatians 1 vs. 6

What is "another" gospel? The Word of God is clear and emphatic, so we need not be led astray by the speculations and philosophies of men, be they ministers or professors. Paul says, "I certify you, brethren, that the gospel we preached was not after man," i.e., it was not such as man approves (Weymouth). Our gospel is certified. We love to have certified things. "Certified milk," "certified water," "certified bread," etc. Thank God we have a "certified" gospel.

It is "another" gospel that preaches the Universal Fatherhood of God and Common Brotherhood of Man. The Bible clearly reveals there are two fathers and two families in the world. By nature we are children of the devil, and by regeneration we become children of God. By nature the devil is our father and his works we do. How absurd it is to talk about God being the Father of all! Is He the Father of the devil and his angels or of the damned? You might as well say He was the Father of cows, horses, cats, and dogs, or carrots, turnips, and potatoes as say He is the Father of all. He is the creator of all. There isn't a child of God in hell or on the road to hell. They are the children of the devil. The children of God are either in heaven or on the road there, and sure of getting there. Hallelujah! So the man or angel that preaches the universal fatherhood of God and common brotherhood of man is preaching another gospel, and the curse of God is on him.

Hell is an impossibility if this gospel were true, for God would be a brutal monster if any of His children were in hell. This doctrine does away with hell and the punishment of the wicked, and makes it easy for men to continue in sin, so no wonder such ministers are God cursed.

The gospel cannot stand in part and fall in part.
Cyprian

8 JUNE

Let Him be Accursed

As we said before, so say I now again, If any man preach any other gospel unto you than that ye have received, let him be accursed.
Galatians 1 vs. 9

Another gospel denies the fact and guilt of sin. Any man or minister that preaches sin as a "fall up," or denies man to be a fallen and falling guilty sinner, under the curse and condemnation of God, "is accursed." These days when evolution is making ministers into "monkey" preachers; where man is being deified and God humanised; where they spell man with a capital "M" and God with a small "g;" where man neither desires nor requires a Saviour for he isn't a sinner but the highest result of evolution and is still going higher, divine as Jesus was divine. He may blunder and make mistakes, but he is falling up, and therefore isn't guilty. Such preaching is another gospel, and brings the curse of God on the preacher.

If man isn't a guilty, lost, helpless, condemned-already sinner, then Christ's death was either a mistake or a mere example of love and loyalty. It wasn't a vicarious death. He didn't die the just for the unjust to bring us to God. He wasn't the Lamb of God bearing away the sin of the world. Man is his own saviour and doesn't need a substitute. All he requires to do is to develop the divine spark in him and follow the light of his conscience. Such preaching is preaching another gospel, and is bringing down God's curse upon the preacher.

The theory of evolution is as weak as a rope of sand.
Billy Sunday

9 JUNE

Men Pleasers

For do I now persuade men, or God? or do I seek to please men? for if I yet
pleased men, I should not be the servant of Christ.
Galatians 1 vs. 10

Another gospel seeks to please men. Paul says: Is it man's favour or God's that I aspire to? Or am I seeking to please men? If I were still a man pleaser I should not be Christ's bondservant. How many ministers and church workers are doing this very thing. It doesn't matter whether the man we are trying to please is ourself or someone else. It is another gospel we are preaching.

My friend, the proof that we are under God's blessing and not under God's curse is that we have offended, and are offending you when we preach. If we succeeded in pleasing you, we would only succeed in grieving God and bringing God's curse on our ministry and life. The cross of Christ is always, and always will be, an offence. The preaching of it will always offend, and if we do away with it, we are preaching another gospel, and we are under God's curse.

What a dreadful thing to live under the curse of God instead of God's blessing! How careful we should be as ministers or church workers so to preach the gospel in its purity and sublime simplicity that we will bring the blessing of God upon our own lives and upon our hearers. So our ministry will be unto life and not unto death, unto salvation and not unto damnation. But I fear lest by any means, as the serpent beguiled Eve through his subtlety, so your minds should be corrupted from the simplicity that is in Christ, for if he that cometh preacheth another Jesus whom we have not preached, or if ye receive another Spirit which ye have not received, or another gospel, as I said before, so say I now again, let him be accursed.

No man ought to be in a Christian pulpit who fears man more than God.
William Still

A Double Portion

And it came to pass, when they were gone over, that Elijah said unto Elisha, Ask what I shall do for thee, before I be taken away from thee. And Elisha said, I pray thee, let a double portion of thy spirit be upon me.
2 Kings 2 vs. 9

What a remarkable man Elijah was. We know so little about him. We don't know who his parents were, or what kind of people they were. All we know about him we find in 1 Kings 17, "And Elijah the Tishbite, who was of the inhabitants of Gilead." That's all we know about him prior to his message and ministry. Usually when a prophet enters, we have some account of his parentage. We are told whose son he was and of what tribe, but Elijah drops out of the clouds, as if, like Melchisedek, "he was without father, without mother and without descent," which made some of the Jews fancy he was an angel sent from heaven, but the apostle has assured us that "he was a man of like passions as we are" (James 5) which perhaps intimates not only that he was liable to the common infirmities of human nature, but that, by his natural temper, he was a man of strong passions, more hot and eager that most men, and therefore the more fit to deal with the daring sinners of the age he lived in.

So wonderfully does God suit men to the work he designs them for. Rough spirits are called to rough services. "For ye see your calling, brethren, how that not many wise men after the flesh, not many mighty, not many noble are called. But God hath chosen the foolish things of the world to confound the wise." Why? "That no flesh should glory in His presence." (1 Corinthians 1 vs. 26-29)

Our efficiency without God's sufficiency is only a deficiency.
Vance Havner

Heed the Plea

Until the day in which he was taken up, after that he through the Holy Ghost had given commandments unto the apostles whom he had chosen.
Acts 1 vs. 8

The disciples lived with Jesus for three years, saw His miracles, heard His words, saw the life He lived. Peter cried out to Jesus one day "Why can I not follow Thee now?" Jesus said, "Thou shalt follow me afterwards," i.e., after Pentecost. Friends! His disciples needed it; do we not also need it today? Have we a substitute for it? Can we do without it? Oh, no, it is as necessary and essential today as much as ever. We can never know the abundant life until we have received the "double portion" of the Spirit. We are powerless until Pentecost becomes an experimental reality. "Ye shall receive power, said Jesus, after the Holy Ghost is come upon you." So many today are halted between Calvary and Pentecost. Some may have the Spirit, but are still devoid of the "double portion." As a consequence their lives are like a switch back, up and down, round and round, but coming right back again to where they started, any amount of motion but no progress. They sit in a rocking chair, and get nowhere. Young Christians! heed the plea of an old man, converted over 60 years, and Spirit-baptized seven months after conversion, let nothing hinder you from getting the double portion of the Spirit. You will never know the life that pleases God, walking worthy of the Lord and fruitful in every good work and increasing in the knowledge of God, until you know it.

The church has halted somewhere between Calvary and Pentecost.
J I Price

Never Popular

Let us go forth therefore unto him without the camp, bearing his reproach.
Hebrews 13 vs. 13

It is never popular today to become a Spirit-baptized, Spirit-filled follower of Jesus Christ; it means to go outside the camp bearing His reproach. It means being misunderstood, misrepresented, and maliciously maligned. Certainly never to become popular. If we please men we surely displease God, and grieve His Holy Spirit. It became an absolute necessity as he saw the failure of Elijah, when he fled for his life from the face of Jezebel. Elijah was displaced. Elisha was to be his successor. Elisha felt if Elijah failed where would he come in? So he made that heart felt cry for a "Double Portion" of the Spirit. Isn't it the same today in our lives and surroundings? How many wonderful men who received the blessing and ran well for a while, then slowly, but surely, the fire died out, the fear of man, or the fleshly ambition to become famous and become popular, possessed them. They profess still they are being filled, but the edge has been blunted in their testimony and preaching. The song has died out of the life. The holy hilarity has ceased. They are very decent and respectable. They are very careful not to offend. Poor souls. Truly castaways. Oh! my dear Brethren! Surely we must be assured that "It is not by might or by power, but by my Spirit, saith the Lord." There is no "once for all" fullness of the Spirit, but we need to be constantly and increasingly filled with the Spirit. It is only as we walk in the light as He is in the light that we are being filled unto all the fullness of God.

Be extravagant for God or the devil, but for God's sake don't be tepid.
C T Studd

Inward Stamina

Thus hast asked a hard thing: nevertheless, if thou see me when I am taken from thee, it shall be so unto thee; but if not, it shall not be so.
II Kings 2 vs. 10

This blessing is no easy way of life. The blessing is full but not cheap. It will take all our inward stamina plus the grace of God if we are to obtain this blessing. Elijah said, "Nevertheless, if thou see me when I am taken up from thee, it shall be so unto thee; but if not, it shall not be so." Elijah laid down four clear-cut places he should pass through if he was to receive the "Double Portion." The names of these places are very significant and are as applicable for us today as they were to Elisha in his day. They are four steps, or stages, on the way to blessing. Many today desire the blessing, and begin seeking it with all their heart. They make a good beginning, and some progress, and then become "stuck." You can easily tell them, they begin to despise the blessing by sneering and jeering at it. They say there is no such blessing, or if there is, it is not for them in their desperation. Then they say there is no need for it, they received everything at their conversion. They become discouraged or unwilling to go all the way, they would not make restitution or go through in full surrender. They kept back part of the price. It is no easy way; it means all or nothing.

Let us consider the condition laid down before us in the experience of Elisha. Make it our determination. "Jesus I am going through, I will pay the price whatever others do, I will take the way with the Lord's anointed few, but Jesus I am going through." Be sure and depend only upon the Holy Spirit to carry you through. The arm of flesh will fail you. He can and will work in you, making you willing to go through at any cost or cross.

Ministry that costs nothing accomplishes nothing.
John Henry Jowett

Goodbye World

And it came to pass, when the Lord would take up Elijah into heaven by a
whirlwind, that Elijah went with Elisha to Gilgal.
II Kings 2 vs. 1

Gilgal. Elisha was ploughing one day and Elijah passed by and cast his mantle on him. He immediately left all and ran after Elijah. He left all the oxen, friends and family. He burned the bridges behind him. It was a clear-cut and full surrender, once and for all. The children of Israel were delivered from Egypt by power and blood, and went on their way with God. They did not circumcise the male children born in the wilderness. At Gilgal they were circumcised. The reproach of Egypt was removed. The seal and sign of their relation to the Covenant were observed. It meant goodbye to Egypt with all its leeks and garlic and onions and slavery, to find all their good and manner of life in God. It was manna. The Bread of God. And all their life lived hand to mouth, God's hand to their mouth. It meant all that and more to Elisha. It means all that, dear friend, to you, ere you begin along the pathway to the blessing of the "Double Portion." It is goodbye forever to the world, and worldly sinful pleasures. Goodbye to your gay companions and worldly life and living. There must be no evasion or reservation, but an honest, clean-cut surrender.

God does not ask a perfect surrender, but He does demand an honest surrender. Many get stuck at Gilgal. They are unwilling to give up all. They excuse giving up some particular worldly pleasure or gain. Well, friend, you never get any further until you meet all that is involved by Gilgal.

It is the man who tries to make the best of both worlds who makes nothing of either. And he who seeks to serve two masters misses the benediction of both.
Henry Drummond

So They Went Down to Bethel

And Elijah said unto Elisha, Tarry here, I pray thee;
for the Lord hath sent me to Bethel.
II Kings 2 vs. 2

Bethel. Bethel means communion or consecration. You have turned your back on Gilgal; all your worldly pleasures and companions; now you give yourself and all you possess, unreservedly to Christ. All your time, your talents, every ounce of energy, every drop of blood, every family tie, and familiar friend. Everything, everybody, is given up and Christ becomes your all and all. Jesus said, "If any man come to me, and hate not his father, and mother, and wife, and children and brethren and sisters, yea, and his own life also, he cannot be my disciple." He won't take any less. He demands my soul, my all. "He will be Lord of all or not Lord at all." Let me assure you of this. You won't love your father or mother less, or your brother or sister or wife or children less. Oh, no, but He must be pre-eminent. He will not share His throne with another.

They do not love Chirst who love anything more than Christ.
Thomas Brooks

Thy Holy Spirit Alone

And Elijah said unto him, Elisha, tarry here, I pray thee; for the Lord hath sent me to Jericho. And he said, As the Lord liveth, and as thy soul liveth, I will not leave thee. So they came to Jericho.
II Kings 2 vs. 4

Jericho. The outstanding lesson that Jericho teaches is this. "No confidence in the flesh." A whole week the children were marched around the city, twice on Sunday. God rubbed it in that God alone, and in God's way alone, would victory be won. We are apt to depend, maybe not wholly, but depend a little on the flesh, or ceremonies. This life is a life of faith. A life of utter dependence on the Holy Spirit, every day and all day long. Let me urge, dear friend, don't sell your birthright for a mess of pottage, but go through and receive the blessing, the "Double Portion," and enter into all we have in Him and keep on going day by day. Amen. Many fail here. They have passed through Gilgal and Bethel, but here, at Jericho they think they are capable of doing something of the flesh to help them on to victory. It only leads to disaster. We must learn at Jericho. It is not by might or by power, but by My Spirit alone.

If Christ waited to be anointed before He went to preach, then no young man ought to preach until he too, has been anointed by the Holy Ghost.
F B Meyer

The Steps and Stops

And fifty men of the sons of the prophets went, and stood to view afar off:
and they two stood by Jordan.
II Kings 2 vs. 7

Jordan. The place of death. Dead to the world, and worldly ways and opinion. Dead to our aims and ambitions. Dead to self in every way, shape and form. It is no longer "I" but "Christ." I crucified. Christ enthroned and glorified in the heart and life. I live yet not I but Christ. These are the steps and stops into blessing. There is no other way. It is a rugged way. It is the way of the Cross. We cannot avoid or evade it if we are to possess the "Double Portion". The Lord is no respecter of persons. It is the only way and sure way. When we pass through these four places we can be assured of the blessing. Remember, we do not deserve or buy the blessing by going through these places of testing. We only qualify for the blessing. The blessing is received by faith on the ground of grace. It is not of works lest any man may boast. Christ is God's unspeakable gift to a dying world. The Holy Spirit is Christ's gift to His church, i.e., His born again people. We do not attain this life of blessing. We obtain it. Does the condition laid down here in His Word frighten you? Are you scared to venture? It is a life of unclouded communion, unceasing peace, unspeakable joy. The absence of all worries, fear or care. It is a life of abundant and abounding life. A life of constant victory and soul-saving service. What will be the outcome of such a blessing? It is a life hid with Christ in God.

His forever only His; who the Lord and me shall part.
Ah, with what a rest of bliss Christ can fill the loving heart!
Heaven and earth may fade and flee, first born light in gloom decline;
But while God and I shall be, I am His, and He is mine. Hallelujah!

The vision must be followed by the venture. It is not enough to stare up the steps. We must step up the stairs.
Vance Havner.

The Christian Life filled with Peace

Now the God of hope fill you with all joy and peace in believing, that ye may abound in hope, through the power of the Holy Ghost.
Romans 15 vs. 13

We are not only to be filled with hope, but peace; instead of unrest and dispeace; and instead of being contrary and having a controversy with God, we are to be filled with the peace of God, which passeth all understanding and misunderstanding.

There are two kinds of peace mentioned in the Bible. There is peace with God, through our Lord Jesus. (Romans 5 vs. 1). Every true believer has this. We have peace with God. Not will have, but a present possession.

Then there is the peace of God, which passeth all understanding. That is something deeper which all do not enjoy. They say they can't understand it. Have peace when in sorrow, or persecution or poverty or pain? Certainly they can't understand it, for it passeth all understanding, but it is real and true all the same.

The first peace is determined by my union with Christ. The second is determined by my communion with Christ. The first we receive by Faith, the second we receive by obedience. We are to be filled with the twofold peace.

Stayed upon Jehovah
Hearts are fully blest
Finding as He promised
Perfect peace and rest.
Francis Ridley Havergal

Joy

Now the God of hope fill you with all joy and peace in believing, that ye
may abound in hope, through the power of the Holy Ghost.
Romans 15 vs. 13

And we are to be filled with joy. My friends, the Christian life is not a groaning, gloomy life. The Lord doesn't want us to be emptied, only to be filled with moans. Nothing the world affords can be compared with the things the Lord would fill us with. What peace or joy, that the world affords, can be compared with this fullness of joy that the Lord wants you and me to be filled with?

I believe that the reason we don't have more young people in the church, but instead, they go to picture shows, to the theatre and to the dance in such large numbers night after night, is simply because there is so much gloom about our religion. How much gloom there is in our religious services! The preacher to be in fashion must wear black clothing, and you have got to put coloured glass in the windows to keep the light and the brightness out. But when you are going to the ballroom or some other place where you want to enjoy yourself, you get all the brightness and light you possibly can and put on the brightest garments and your brightest countenance and have the brightest conversation.

When you go to a religious service you put a long face on – as long as you can, and you will sigh and grumble and growl and you'll just be as miserable and wretched as can be, and some people think this is a mark of piety.

> God won't be offended by our happiness; in fact he's offended by
> sadness and demands joy.
> Martin Luther.

"Just like Grandpa"

But the fruit of the spirit is ...joy.
Galatians 5 vs. 22

I am reminded now of a little boy who lived with his gloomy old religious grandmother and grandfather, who were always moaning and groaning and sighing. He had a hard kind of life. They didn't believe in brightness and joy; it was all darkness and gloom, on the Sundays especially.

This little boy was just as full of life and brightness and energy as any boy, but he had a hard time of it; his Sundays seemed 72 hours long instead of 24. One Sunday he went out into the yard and when the dog saw him, he began to jump around and bark playfully. But the boy said, "Rover, you stop that; you are not a good Christian, or you wouldn't be going on like that on Sunday." Then he went down to the stable, and there stood the old donkey with his long, sleepy, gloomy face hanging over the half-door of his stable. The boy went to him and stroked his long face and said to him, "Donkey, you are a good Christian; you have a long face just like grandpa." That was the idea this boy got – if you have the religion of the Lord in your heart you must have a long face and be as miserable and wretched as you possibly can.

The Lord said I want you children of light to be filled with joy and peace and hope through the power of the Holy Ghost. Wouldn't we be a fine set of Christians if we were filled with this three-fold, this trinity of blessedness?

The late Gypsy Smith used to say that you could not get a 'hallelujah' out of some Christians if you squeezed them through a wringer.

Comfortable Christians

Great is my boldness of speech toward you, great is my glorying of you: I am filled with comfort, I am exceeding joyful in all our tribulation.
2 Corinthians 7 vs. 4

Paul does not say, "I am happy." Oh, no. That would be impossible under the circumstances. He couldn't be happy with his back all cut and bruised. Happiness is not joy. Happiness depends on what happens, but joy is independent of circumstances or disposition.

"I am exceeding joyful" – because I've got good health, because I've got a kind wife, or because I've got nice children and friends? No; but he said, "I am exceeding joyful in all our tribulation."

Say, friends, it seems to me we are only in the infant class, or in the primary department, in our religious life. If things don't go just the way we want them, we are just as miserable as we can be all the time. If anybody in the church gives us a snub, then we send in our resignation from our Sunday school class, and we leave the Board and will not come back to the church. Isn't that the way we do? Here's a man filled full of joy in his tribulations, a man filled with comfort in the midst of discomfort.

True joy glows in the dark.
John Blanchard

How Refreshing

I have learned in whatsoever state I am, therewith to be content.
Philippians 4 vs. 11

Isn't it refreshing to come across a comfortable Christian – a comforting Christian, but this is the exception, rather than the rule. You go into the homes of some of our Christian friends and sit down in a big chair, and in five or ten minutes they roll out upon you all their cares and troubles and tribulations and worries about things that never did happen nor ever will happen, until you are almost as comfortless as they are.

But it's fine to come across a comforting Christian, with a cheering and comforting word. How ready they are to comfort and how they know just the right word to say and just the right thing to do. The Word says we are to be filled with comfort, so that we may comfort our friends in this life.

> I would rather have the spiritual gift of bringing life to a broken heart than the ability to preach a thousand souls.
> Alan Redpath

23 JUNE

Filled with Knowledge

And I myself also am persuaded of you, my brethren, that ye also are full of goodness, filled with all knowledge, able also to admonish one another.
Romans 15 vs. 14

We are to be filled first of all with all knowledge. How ignorant we are of the things concerning the Lord? I have been greatly surprised since I have come to this country to find how little, compared with our Scotch people, you know about your Bible. I don't know why it should be, unless it is you don't love and read your Bibles. So few carry them with them to church. I will grant you there are depths in the Scriptures that the greatest intellects are unable to fathom, but the anointing you have received you need not that any man shall teach you. If you will only ask the Lord, His Spirit will guide you into all truth, and you will get the knowledge of God and of His will. I firmly believe that the reason for the failures today in the Christian life more than anything else is our ignorance of God and His Word. If we only knew God better we would trust Him better. They that know him will put their trust in Him, and the reason we are grumblers and murmurers when adversity comes, or when we lose our money, is that we don't know Him. If we would only be still and wait upon God and get His Word into our hearts, it would make a wonderful change in our lives.

If ignorance is your disease, knowledge must be your cure.
Richard Baxter

Ways and Acts

He made known His ways unto Moses, His acts unto the children of Israel.
Psalm 103 vs. 7

Because the children of Israel knew only the acts of God they misunderstood God, but Moses knew the ways of God and he never complained; he never misunderstood God.

If you don't know a person very well you may misjudge him by his actions, but if you know him very well you don't judge him by his actions, but you say, "I know his way; this is his way of doing things; there is no wrong intended; this is just his way." If you get the proper knowledge of God, then, although death comes into the home, although sorrow comes, although persecutions come, although poverty and adversity come, you just say, "I know God and this is God's way of doing things," and you don't begin to complain and whine, but you just praise Him for His great love, because you are filled with the knowledge of His will.

So the great apostle says, we are to be filled with knowledge.

God has no favourites but He does have His intimates.
Sidlow Baxter

Goodness and Beauty

And I myself also am persuaded of you, my brethren, that ye also are full of goodness, filled with all knowledge, able also to admonish one another.
Romans 15 vs. 14

We are also to be filled with goodness. There is a difference between a good man and a righteous man. This is an illustration of the difference: If a cabman's fare is fifty cents, a righteous man will give him fifty cents, but a good man will give him seventy-five cents. A righteous man is always just right. He's as cold and stiff as an icicle; he is so particular and precise. There is no allowance in his life or in his heart, but a good man will always go an extra mile. So many are filled with Greatness, an exaggerated estimation of themselves. We are to be filled with Goodness. There are two words rendered "good" in the New Testament and applied to works. The one means that which is inwardly intrinsically good. The other means that which is outwardly beautiful. The phrase rendered in the Pastoral Epistles, "Good works," might well be rendered "Beautiful works." We are intended to be at once ethical and beautiful. Now here is where our goodness often fails – it is not beautiful.

Oh, my, wouldn't it be grand if we would be emptied of all hatred and malice and envy and be filled with goodness and beauty? Wouldn't it be a grand thing to belong to a church where every member was filled with good works and beautiful works?

> Good in the heart works its way up into the face and prints its own beauty there.
> Anon.

Filled with God's Will

*For this cause we also, since the day we heard it, do not cease to pray
for you, and to desire that ye might be filled with the knowledge of
his will in all wisdom and spiritual understanding; "That ye might
walk worthy of the Lord unto all pleasing, being fruitful in every
good work, and increasing in the knowledge of God.*
Colossians 1 vs. 9-10

"That ye might be filled with the knowledge of his will", filled with the
will of God.

Did you ever notice that in the life of Christ He never questioned
God, except once, and that was when He was dying on the cross. He
said, "Father, why hast thou forsaken me?" All through His life He
never asked His Father a single other question. He was so filled with
the knowledge of His Father's will in everything He did; He never had
to say to Peter, "Do you think I am right?" or "Do you think this is
God's will?" He was filled with the knowledge of God's will and
didn't need to ask any questions.

We should be so well acquainted with the will of God concerning
our lives that we would not need to ask questions. Some are
continually asking questions: "What do you mean by this? What is the
cause of that? And I can't understand why this is so." Asking the why
and wherefore of things all through our lives. We are to be filled with
His will, so that we may know the will of God in all departments of
our life. It is by the study of God's Word that we get to know His will.

To understand the will of God is my problem. To undertake the will
of God is my privilege. To undercut the will of God is my peril.
Paul S Rees

Fruit of Righteousness

Being filled with the fruits of righteousness, which are by Jesus Christ, unto the glory and praise of God.
Philippians 1 vs. 11

"Being filled with the fruits of righteousness," or as your revised version has it "fruit of righteousness." It just means doing things right. The lady of a house said to her friend, "I am sure my maid is a converted girl." Her friend said, "What makes you think that?" "Because she sweeps under the hall mats now, instead of only around them."

If you show me a man who works with one eye on the ledger and the other on the clock, or if you will show me a man merely giving eight hours a day and so many days a month to his employer for the wages he gets, I'll show you a man who is not filled with the fruits of righteousness. If we are filled with the fruits of righteousness it means we are right in our relations to our employers; it means we are right in our relation to our children; it means we are right in our relation to our wives and our husbands and to our grocers, our milliners, our tailors, and everybody else.

If you are filled with the fruits of righteousness you are doing right deeds day by day.

Now mark you, it is not "Filled with the acts of righteousness." There is many a person filled with the acts of righteousness, but not the fruits of righteousness. Fruit is the outcome of life. Actions are merely doing right things because it is right, but the apostle says it is the fruit of life that is to be righteous; it is the outcome of our spiritual life that you and I have received.

Do right though the stars fall.
Bob Jones

The Enthronement of Christ

But this spake he of the Spirit which they that believe on him
should receive: for the Holy Ghost was not yet given;
because that Jesus was not yet glorified.
John 7 vs. 39

I know that in its historical application it refers to His ascension but in its spiritual application it refers to the enthronement of Christ in our hearts and lives. There is a difference between accession to the heart and being crowned in the life. King George of Great Britain ascended the throne and was King for a year before his coronation. If you are saved Jesus is in your heart, but has He been crowned Lord of all there? There are multitudes of lives in which Christ has gained accession, but if you are to know this overflowing life, there must be a coronation. Christ must be enthroned. He must be put on the throne of your life and your love and be crowned King. That fullness is not for my glorification, but it is to glorify Christ. It is the increase of Christ and the decrease of self.

Oh ye that are thirsting for fullness,
Make room by forsaking all sin,
Surrender to Him your whole nature,
By faith, let the Spirit come in.

He values not Christ at all who does not value Christ above all.
Augustine

The Light of the World

As long as I am in the world, I am the light of the world.
John 9 vs. 5

What a wonderful and beautiful thing light is. It brings cheer and gladness. It drives away our fears. It produces health and beauty, and kills germs. It is very difficult to keep it out and almost impossible to keep out of it.

We cannot become the light of the world and not know it. Jesus said, "He that followeth me shall not walk in darkness, but shall have the light of life." "Whosoever believeth on me shall not abide in darkness." "If we say that we have fellowship with him, and walk in darkness, we lie, and do not the truth." "He that believeth not God hath made him a liar; because he believeth not the record that God gave of His Son. And this is the record, that God hath given to us eternal life, and this life is His Son."

As the moon is the borrowed light of the sun, so are we borrowed light. Jesus said, "I am the light of the world." That is how it is that we may say we are the light of the world; therefore, let our light so shine that they may see our good works and glorify our Father which is in heaven.

If God lights the candle none can blow it out.
C H Spurgeon

Hiding your Light

That ye may be blameless and harmless, the sons of God, without rebuke,
in the midst of a crooked and perverse nation, among whom ye
shine as lights in the world;
Philippians 2 vs. 15

The Saviour said we must not hide our light under a bushel. "Neither do men light a candle and put it under a bushel, but on a candlestick; and it giveth light unto all that are in the house" (Matt. 5 vs. 15). This bushel may be, and very often is, a lovely, expensive, artistic and beautiful thing. It may be very attractive. If it were crude, vulgar and offensive, we would not have anything to do with it. Because it is attractive and rare, therein lies the danger. It may be a worldly bushel, commonly used by many but nonetheless hiding our light. Dancing, picture shows, card parties, Sunday picnics and bathing parties do not reveal the light that is in us. The world does not look at our words so much as our works.

The bushel may be a selfish one. A self-centred life will surely hide the light. Proud bushels are very common today. Pride of face, race, place and even grace, is the devil's pet sin and an abomination to God. Because you have made an alliance with some besetting, upsetting sin in which you are indulging, and are continually making an allowance for it, the light is hindered and dimmed. Some lights have lovely shades. These are beautiful and expensive, but they dim the light. If you want light, the shade must be removed.

The light of religion ought not to be carried in a dark lantern.
George Swinnock

JULY

1 ◆ A Lazy Man

2 ◆ Take Heed

3 ◆ Radiant Lives

4 ◆ Idols

5 ◆ Blood Guiltiness

6 ◆ Doubtful Things

7 ◆ Prayerless Lives

8 ◆ Worry

9 ◆ Praying about Everything

10 ◆ Be Thankful for All Things

11 ◆ True and False

12 ◆ The Peace of God

13 ◆ The Lord's Order

14 ◆ Reliance on Christ

15 ◆ Offended

16 ◆ Unanswered Yet

17 ◆ God's Knowledge

18 ◆ His Cross

19 ◆ Exaltation through Humility

20 ◆ Supernatural Power

21 ◆ No Reputation

22 ◆ His Companions

23 ◆ The Church

24 ◆ Christ's Reputation

25 ◆ Condescending Grace

26 ◆ Obedient

27 ◆ Common Folk

28 ◆ Reputation

29 ◆ The Servant's Place

30 ◆ Dependence

31 ◆ Confessions

A Lazy Man

And he said unto them, Is a candle brought to be put under a bushel, or under a bed? and not to be set on a candlestick?
Mark 4 vs. 21

Many a light is under the bed of laziness. It does not take much to tire some people in the work of the Lord. They are tireless in worldliness and pleasures, but shining for the Lord and seeking for souls tires them easily. A baseball or football game, a game of golf or a picnic does not tire them: but to see the lazy, slovenly way they teach a Sunday school class or go to church, one would think them very weary. They seem too tired to sing and they sleep through every sermon. If they acted like this at their work they would be fired and never succeed. Their light does not shine because it is covered by laziness. There is hope for any vile sinner, but little or no hope for a lazy man.

Must I be carried to the skies
On flowery beds of ease,
While others fought to win the prize,
And sailed through bloody seas?

If you can't shine at least twinkle.
Alastair Begg

Take Heed

No man, when he hath lighted a candle, putteth it in a secret place …
but on a candlestick, that they which come in may see the light.
Luke 11 vs. 33.

There are many today who call themselves "secret" disciples. They do not like an open confession. A testimony meeting shrivels them up and annoys them. They say they believe living the life is sufficient testimony. It would take a microscope to detect anything in their living that would betray the light. They are religious sneaks. Of course they do not call themselves that, and do not like to be called that by others. They say they are "shy" or "modest", but they are just hiding their light in a secret place or cellar. They fear public opinion. Since they are slaves to the fear of men they hide their light in a secret place. They fear lest they lose their reputations and be ostracized by their worldly friends or family for their testimony.

What solemn words the Lord spoke: "Take heed therefore that the light which is in thee be not darkness" (Luke 11: 35). The light or profession you make may be only a sham. You may have made a profession, been baptised and joined a church. You may be very active in the work and a generous supporter both of the church and of missions. You may be very sincere, devout and honest in your profession and still be all-wrong. Jesus said, "Take heed." We are told to examine ourselves, to give all diligence to make our calling sure. Jesus said, "Many (not a few) will say to me in that day, Lord, Lord, have we not prophesied in thy name? and in thy name done many wonderful works? And then I will profess unto them, I never knew you: depart from me." Even the light in many preachers and workers may be darkness. "If thy whole body therefore be full of light, having no part dark, the whole shall be full of light." Take heed. Make sure.

It costs to follow Jesus Christ; but it costs more not to.
Anon.

Radiant Lives

Let your light so shine before men, that they may see your good works, and glorify your Father which is in heaven.
Matthew 5 vs. 16

The Lord commands us, "Let your light ... shine." Do not hinder it by bushel, bed, cellar, or deception. A minister was preaching on the subject of letting our light shine. Afterward he asked an elder what he thought of the sermon. The elder replied, "All you said about the light was fine, but you never said a word about keeping the globe clean to let the light shine better." The minister was a smoking Christian. When a lamp smokes it becomes an offence to all in the house. Let it shine! Do not hinder it.

We are to shine clearly, constantly, collectively and conspicuously, not to show ourselves, but that our Father may be glorified.

> Study universal holiness of life. Your whole usefulness depends on this. Your sermons may last but for an hour or two. Your life preaches all the week.
> Robert Murray McCheyne

Idols

Son of man, these men have set up their idols in their heart,
and put the stumblingblock of their iniquity before their face:
should I be enquired of at all by them.
Ezekiel 14 vs. 3

How many idolaters there are today in our churches and amongst believers everywhere: for remember, these men mentioned here were "elders of Israel," not heathen. An idol is anything or anyone that takes God's place in our hearts or that would share our heart's throne with God. God is a jealous God and will not share His throne in our heart with anything or anyone else. He must be Lord of all or He will not be Lord at all. Our friends, family, church, denomination, sect, business or money may become an idol. Idols usually are right and proper and beautiful and artistic things, or very nice, kind and accomplished, religious people. The Lord is the Lover of our souls and demands the exclusive right to our love and devotion. He will never take any second place in our lives. Pride may usurp the throne and dethrone Christ. The pride of race; pride of place; pride of face; worst of all pride of grace. Until we crown him Lord of all and maintain His lordship, He will not be enquired of at all by us. Let us humble ourselves before God and ask Him to search our hearts and see if there is any rival there.

> Jesus Christ demands more complete allegiance than any dictator who ever lived. The difference is He has the right to.
> Vance Havner

Blood Guiltiness

And when ye spread forth your hands, I will hide mine eyes from you: yea,
when ye make many prayers, I will not hear: your hands are full of blood.
Isaiah 1 vs. 15

"When ye make many prayers, I will not hear: your hands are full of blood." "When I say unto the wicked, Thou shalt surely die: and thou givest him not warning, nor speakest to warn the wicked from his wicked way, to save his life; the same wicked man shall die in his iniquity; but his blood will I require at thine hand." (Ezek. 3 vs.18) The Lord said unto Cain – "Where is Abel thy brother… What hast thou done? The voice of thy brother's blood crieth unto me from the ground." (Gen. 4 vs. 9,10) Have we been convicted about confessing Christ to husband or wife, or son or daughter, or brother or sister, and not speaking to them about their soul's salvation and have stifled the conviction and disobeyed the call? You make many prayers for their salvation; God says, I will not hear you. Why? Your hands are full of blood. Maybe you are a Sunday-School teacher or teach a Bible class and you have felt the urge of the Spirit to speak to someone in the class about being saved. You have disobeyed. You can make all sorts of excuses, but you are disobedient. The Lord says, "You can make many prayers for their salvation but He will not hear. Your hands are full of blood. I wonder is there a minister reading this. What about ones in your congregation who are unsaved and you have felt you should speak to them about their interest in Christ and you haven't done it. You were frightened they might be offended, and you wonder your prayers for their conversion are not answered. The answer is - "Your hands are full of blood." No wonder David prayed to be delivered from blood guiltiness. We need to make it our prayer too.

> The great commission is not an option to be considered but a command to be obeyed.
> J. Hudson Taylor

6 JULY

Doubtful Things

...for whatsoever is not of faith is sin.
Romans 14 vs. 23

Every doubtful thing or doubtful pleasure or friendship is sin. Some ask – Can I smoke tobacco, or can I go to dances, or can I go to the theatre or cinema: can I belong to Lodges or secret societies, etc? Friend, your very question implies doubt, therefore as far as you are concerned, you can't do it. No matter what other Christians may do, you can't do it, for you have a question mark or doubt about it. Continue doing these doubtful things and the Lord will not hear you. Again, iniquity is: James 2 vs. 9- "But if ye have respect to persons, ye commit sin, and are convinced of the law as transgressors." Read the preceding eight verses and see the connection. God is no respecter of persons and neither should we be, especially when we gather together to worship God. There are those who will not allow anyone to worship with them unless they have received some ceremony or belong to their peculiar company. When we gather together in His Church or Assembly and around His table, we must never be guilty of being "a respecter of persons" or we are guilty of sin. When we meet around the common mercy seat or around His table and remember His dying and undying love, until He come, the Blood of Christ wipes out all social, denominational and national distinctions. We are all sinners saved by grace. There is neither Jew nor Gentile; Presbyterian nor Baptist; Methodist, Brethren or Episcopalian – Irish or Scotch – white or black. We are all one in Christ Jesus and there is no difference. When we make a difference and put one in a back seat and another in a front seat, we sin – and while we continue in sin the Lord will not hear us.

Unity is not something to be achieved, it is something to be recognised.
A W Tozer

7 JULY

Prayerless Lives

And he spake a parable unto them to this end, that men ought always to pray, and not to faint;
Luke 18 vs. 1

What prayerless lives so many who are born again live. They have time for everything else but prayer, then they are full of complaints because their lives are unsatisfying and unsatisfactory. "They have not because they ask not." This is God's answer to all their grumbling and complaining. "Ask and ye shall receive." "Thus saith the Lord, the Holy One of Israel, and His Maker, Ask me of things to come concerning my sons." (Isaiah 45 vs.11.) If we are to receive we must take the time and the bother to ask. If we haven't time to ask then we will have to do without. Taking things for granted is not God's way of dealing with us. Such a manner of life is pure presumption. There is no need too great or too small, secular or sacred, that we may not ask God about it

Beware of the barrenness of a busy life.
Anon.

8 JULY

Worry

Casting all your care upon him; for he careth for you.
I Peter 5 vs. 7

I believe this word of God just means what it says and says what it means, nothing less and nothing more. We are to be carefree always, under all circumstances. This is as truly a command as any other command of God. It is as great a sin to worry or to be careful or anxious, as it is to covet, steal or lie. Worry is charging God with folly. It is saying to God, "I doubt your love, wisdom and power." You are saying, "If I was God I would not have permitted what happened in my life. My child or loved one would not have died. My sickness or accident would never have been allowed, etc., etc." Such an attitude and language is bordering on blasphemy. To be careful or over-anxious is sinful. It is useless. It always brings bad results and worse than that, it brings reproach on God. How rarely, if ever, you have heard anyone confessing the sin of worry. I heard a woman say, "I am worrying in case I am not worried enough about a certain situation." Did you ever hear the like of it? And she called herself a Christian! Resist the tendency and temptation to worry, as you would resist the temptation to immorality and drunkenness. When we worry we don't trust: when we trust we don't worry.

> Worry is an indication that we think God cannot look after us.
> Oswald Chambers

9 JULY

Praying about Everything

Praying always with all prayer and supplication in the Spirit, and watching thereunto with all perseverance and supplication for all saints.
Ephesians 6 vs. 18

How simple and yet how all comprehensive these words are. We all believe in praying about some things. But how few pray about 'everything'. O what peace we often forfeit. O what needless pain we bear. Why? All because we do not carry everything to God in prayer. When we are really up against it, or some great sorrow or trial overtakes us, we are very prayerful then. But in the midst of our busy lives how little time we give to prayer about the seeming insignificant and unimportant things, and yet our lives are made up of these very things, and they are so essential to our peace, happiness and comfort. How sinfully foolish of us to live day and daily independent of God, who is all wise and all powerful, and desires to direct and guide us through each perplexing problem we meet in our daily lives. No wonder our lives are filled with regret and remorse because of the mistakes and blunders we have made and can never unmake. If we will be careful for nothing and prayerful for everything, we will revel and delight ourselves in God's own peace which passeth all understanding.

> I live in the Spirit of prayer. I pray as I walk about, when I lie down and when I rise up; and the answers are always coming.
> George Muller

Be Thankful for All Things

In everything give thanks: for this is the will of God
in Christ Jesus concerning you.
I Thessalonians 5 vs. 18

Recognising God's hand in every detail in our lives: not supposing or taking anything for granted, but seeing God working all things together for our good, our lives will be one unceasing poem of praise. There will truly be the absence of all care and worry, and the presence of a peace – God's peace – that passeth all understanding, and misunderstanding, and the possession of a joy unspeakable and full of glory. My peace I give unto you. Let us receive it and continue to revel in it by doing our part and God will do His.

I hear the words of love, I gaze upon the blood,
I see the mighty sacrifice and I have peace with God.
'Tis everlasting peace sure as Jehovah's name,
'Tis stable as His steadfast throne, forever more the same.
My love is oft-times low, my joy still ebbs and flows;
But peace with Him remains the same, no change Jehovah knows.

God is so pleased with gratitude; He gets so little of it.
William Tiptaft

True and False

There is no peace, saith the Lord, unto the wicked.
Isaiah 48 vs. 22

There are two kinds of peace – true and false. God's peace and the devil's peace. How are we to tell which is true and which is false? True peace is according to God's Word. False peace is contrary to God's Word. God's peace is the result of utter dependence on Christ, and on Christ alone, for salvation, sanctification and glorification. False peace rests, or depends, on good works and good times. False peace also depends on a faith that never produces godly living and doing.

Every truly saved man or woman has the peace of God. "Therefore, being justified by faith, we have (not will have, but have right now) peace with God through our Lord Jesus Christ." Peace, perfect peace in this dark world of sin! The blood of Jesus whispers peace within. Hallelujah! There is not a doubt about it. You couldn't accept Christ as your personal Saviour and not have peace with God. Just as sure as cause and effect, or daylight following sunrise, heat and fire. You can't have one without the other; neither can you have Christ as your personal Saviour and not have peace with God. If you are devoid of this peace, it is because you haven't Christ. Peace always accompanies salvation. It is the peace of assurance. Give all diligence, dear reader, to make your calling and election sure.

Peace is the smile of God reflected in the smile of the believer.
William Hendriksen

The Peace of God

And the peace of God, which passeth all understanding, shall keep your hearts and minds through Christ Jesus.
Philippians 4 vs. 7

There are days filled with sorrow, suffering, hunger and sickness, which abound on every hand, everywhere in the world today. The world is upside down, and the old devil working overtime, doing his deadly, dirty, peace wrecking and prosperity destroying work. No wonder men's hearts are failing them for fear of the things that are happening on every hand. The outlook is not very bright in spite of all their peace conferences and social schemes. And all this, years after peace has been declared, and the Second World War ended. Instead of peace and safety, which we were promised when the war ended, it has been strife, turmoil and distress. They are talking now of preparing for another war. Oh, the outlook is anything but peace producing. Yet, in spite of all this, and far more not mentioned, we have Christ's words to every born-again, blood-washed one, "Peace I leave with you. My peace I give unto you. Let not your heart be troubled, neither let it be afraid."

When we lack the peace of God, we should turn to our peace with God.
Robert M Horn

The Lord's Order

But ye shall receive power, after that the Holy Ghost is come upon you;
and ye shall be witnesses unto me both in all Judea, and in Samaria,
and unto the uttermost part of the earth.
Acts 1 vs. 8

Where are we to go? We must begin at our Jerusalem. Many are anxious about converting the heathen in China but neglect to convert those at home. "Go out quickly into the streets" (Luke 14 vs. 21). Many are afraid or ashamed to preach in their own streets, but are anxious to preach in church. "Go out into the highways" (Luke 14 vs. 23) – fairs, markets, shops, parks. "Go into the city" (Matt. 26 vs. 18), then "into all the world" (Mk. 16 vs.15). This is the Lord's order in our going. It is only as we obey fully that we may expect His support and blessing. The resources of God are promised only to those who undertake the programme of God.

Evangelism, like charity, begins at home.
Arthur Skevington Wood

Reliance on Christ

I am the vine, ye are the branches.
John 15 vs. 5

What use would the vine be without the branches? No vine ever gave grapes without branches. What use would the branch be without the vine? A branch cannot yield grapes unless it abides in the vine. How close is this union between my Lord and me? I need the Lord to represent me before a Holy God: so the Lord needs us to represent and present Him before an unholy world. Amazing condescension. I cannot do without Him, and He cannot do without me. He won't even be in heaven and leave me behind. "These things have I spoken unto you that ye might not be offended in me." May the Lord enable us to walk through life, because we know these things and believe them, unoffended and unoffending, and at last hear Him say: "Well done, good and faithful servant, enter thou into the joy of the Lord. One thing, dear friends, we may be sure of, and that is: when we see Him face to face we will wonder and be ashamed we ever were offended or annoyed or made angry with anything He ever did to us.

Then trust in God through all thy days:
Fear not, for He doth hold thy hand.
Though dark thy way, still sing and praise.
Sometime, sometime, we'll understand.

If I were fruitless it mattered not who commended me: but if I were fruitful I cared not who did condemn.
John Bunyan

Offended

And blessed is he, whosoever shall not be offended in me.
Matt. 11 vs. 6

Isn't it strange that anyone who knows Christ and has been saved by Him should be offended in Him? In Him we have eternal life. In Him we have pardon. In Him we have salvation. In Him we have peace with God and the peace of God. In Him we have joy unspeakable and full of glory. We sing with all our hearts at times: "O Christ, in Thee my soul has found, and found in Thee alone, the peace and joy I sought so long, the bliss till now unknown," and yet the Lord says that that man is blessed if he isn't offended or scandalized in Him.

I could understand being scandalized in the world or with the world. I could understand being scandalized with the devil, for the old hound of hell knows that we have broken friendship with him and yet he presumes on past friendship and butts in right along, so that one could understand being scandalized in him. I could understand being scandalized with Christians, for there are many things in the best and worst of us that must offend others. I could understand being scandalized in ourselves, for the better we know ourselves the more we marvel and wonder that the Lord could ever have loved us. There is much in every one of us that offends us all the time, but to be offended in Christ, or with Christ. This is what surprises us about these words of our Lord.

> Faith is the capacity to trust God while to being able to make sense out of everything.
> James Kok

Unanswered Yet

And let us not be weary in well doing: for in due season we shall reap,
if we faint not.
Galatians 6 vs. 9

How seemingly slow the Lord is in His work. We work and work; we toil and toil; and so very little to show for it all. How hardly any souls are won. I have sometimes felt as if the Lord was the most uninterested one in His work which one was trying to do. The devil seemed interested enough. The Christians were praying and sitting up nights in prayers and tears, but it just looked as if the Lord didn't care. How long you have taught in the Sunday school, and not one has come out for the Lord. How many sermons you have preached, and never a one to say they had come to the Lord. Oh it is easy to lose heart and feel annoyed with the Lord. I think if I were He and had all power in heaven and earth I would make things move more rapidly and more come out for Him. I know it is wrong to feel like this or even talk like this, but I am sure that many have felt just like this in His work. But the work is the Lord's and He knows best how it should be done, and He has never turned out a shoddy job or made a mistake, so that His work will be done in His time and His way. "Jesus shall reign where'er the sun does his successive journeys run." Hallelujah.

Unanswered yet, the prayer your lips have pleaded
In agony of heart these many years,
Doth faith begin to fail, is hope departing?
And think you all in vain those falling tears?
Say not, that Jesus hath not heard your prayer;
You shall have your prayer, sometime, somewhere.

Delays are not denials.
Anon.

God's Knowledge

But he knoweth the way that I take; when he hath tried me,
I shall come forth as gold.
Job 23 vs. 10

Although the way may be strange and mysterious to us, it is well known to Him. There isn't a foot of the way He hasn't been over and is not familiar with. There can be no surprises sprung on Him. There is no luck or chance or accident in our lives when we are in the centre of the circle of the will of God. We cannot always say we "understand" or "see" or "feel," but we know God is working together all things for our good. Let this grip our souls and we won't be offended in Christ. One day we will bless the hand that guided and bless the heart that planned when throned where glory dwelleth in Emmanuel's land.

Let us hug this to our hearts more and more as we move through the maze of interrogation marks in our lives and the perplexing paths of life.

No harm from Him can come to me on ocean or on shore.
I know not where His islands lift their fronded palms on air.
I only know I cannot drift beyond His love and care.

I know not the way God leads me, but well do I know my Guide.
Martin Luther

18 JULY

His Cross

And whosoever doth not bear his cross, and come after me,
cannot be my disciple.
Luke 14 vs. 27

We talk about our difficulties, sicknesses and troubles as crosses, but that isn't what the Lord means here. It isn't our cross, but His cross that we are to bear. What does His cross mean? What is represented by it? It represented the malignant, hostile hatred of the world. It was the worst they could do to Him. Now, says the Lord, if we are to be His disciples, then we must be willing to come right out from the world and share the shame and reproach with Him. The world may have changed in many ways, but it has never changed in its malicious and malignant hatred of Christ, and every man who will follow Him will share this with Him. It is so hard to be ostracised from friends and society. It is so hard to be looked upon as unfit for the company and shunned by them. Because of this many are offended in Christ and they cease from following Him or follow afar off.

> Christ's followers cannot expect better treatment in the world than their Master had.
> Matthew Henry

Exaltation through Humility

Humble yourselves therefore under the mighty hand of God,
that he may exalt you in due time.
I Peter 5 vs. 6

Because He emptied Himself of His reputation, His independence, His own life and will, the Lord exalted Him to His right hand. "The head that once was crowned with thorns is crowned with Glory now." The highest place that heaven affords is His by sovereign right; the King of Kings and Lord of Lords. He reigns in perfect light." He glorified Him and gave Him a name above every other name that at the name of Jesus, every knee should bow. What honour. What glory! You see, the emptied life God will and does honour. Tell me the names of the men whose names are fragrant and undying today and every one of them knew something of this emptied life. God has honoured them and their names will outshine the sun. This is the only pathway to usefulness here and glory and reward hereafter.

Exaltation is born out of the womb of humiliation.
Ian R.K. Paisley

Supernatural Power

*How much more shall the blood of Christ, who through the eternal Spirit
offered himself without spot to God, purge your conscience from
dead works to serve the living God?*
Hebrews 9 vs. 14

How was Christ enabled to do this? He was truly man, without sin.
It is not natural for us and was not natural for Him. It is and was
supernatural. "He through the eternal Spirit offered Himself without
spot to God." It is only through the same Spirit that we will be able to
have the mind of Christ. Such a mind is utterly beyond us, but we are
capable of it, if we are possessed by the Spirit and allow Him right of
way. May we be filled by Him daily, so that this emptied life may
become a reality to us.

O cross that liftest up my head,
I dare not ask to fly from thee,
I lay in dust life's glory dead
And from the ground there blossoms red
Life that shall endless be.

The higher a man is in grace, the lower he will be in his own esteem.
C H Spurgeon

No Reputation

For ye know the grace of our Lord Jesus Christ, that, though he was rich,
yet for your sakes he became poor, that ye through his poverty might be rich.
II Corinthians 8 vs. 9

How was it Jesus was born in a manger and not in a mansion? He was the Son of God and had every right to a mansion, but He was born in a manger that He might make Himself of no reputation. It was not chance that He was born in that stable or manger. It was the fulfilment of prophecy. It was the distinct object of His life to make Himself of no reputation, and therefore He was born in a manger instead of a mansion. We make a great deal of our birthplace today, and what a difference it makes if a man is born in a mansion. How we are puffed up with pride, and yet we had no choice in the matter. Jesus was the only one who ever had a choice of a birthplace, and yet he chose a manger rather than a mansion, because He would make Himself of no reputation in the eyes of the world. Then again, why was He born of a poor peasant instead of a prince of the land? He was the only one who had a choice of His mother. Why did he choose a workingwoman; why did He choose a peasant woman; why did He choose a woman so poor that she could not afford a better gift, but had to bring two little turtledoves? He made Himself of no reputation. He could have been born of wealthy parents. He could have been born of the best blood of the land, but He distinctly made Himself of no reputation by choosing His parents from among the peasants of His day. How many of us take pride to ourselves for the station in which we were born? That is no option of ours. You had no choice and nothing to say as to who your parents were to be. A man is proud of his parents and of the fact that they have done this or that. Jesus Christ had the choice of His parents and He made Himself of no reputation by choosing poor, peasant, working people. He became poor that we through His poverty might be made rich.

> Jesus Christ, the condescension of divinity and the exaltation of humanity.
> Philip Brooks

His Companions

For ye see your calling brethren, how that not many wise men after the
flesh, not many mighty, not many noble, are called:
I Corinthians 1 vs. 26

Then again, He made Himself of no reputation by taking fishermen to be His followers and friends. He could have selected the most learned and aristocratic of the land for His followers. When King George V of England went out to India some years ago he did not take common people to attend him. No indeed, they would not rank high enough. He took the dukes and the lords and the wealthiest and the highest in the land with him. King Jesus had common, ignorant, illiterate fishermen for His followers. He could have chosen the very greatest men of His day, and they would have been honoured by His choice, but He made Himself of no reputation and He took the common, ordinary fisher folk. Yes, these were His followers, and He said that on their testimony He was going to build His Church and carry on His purposes of Grace for the world. How often it is that we hear one preacher saying to another; "You know I have a very cultured congregation: I have a very conservative people; I have a very intelligent people, and a wealthy congregation." We pride ourselves because of this and speak disparagingly of others who have the "common people" for their congregations. How unlike Christ! He stooped to lift others up.

The church is a society of saved sinners.
Griffith Thomas

The Church

And they continued steadfastly in the apostles' doctrine and fellowship,
and in breaking of bread, and in prayers.
Acts 2 vs. 42

The church is God's earthly home for His heavenly bairns. Let your voice be heard in the church. Be sure and join the church and attend regularly and give liberally of your time, talents and money. The church may not be all we would like it to be and ought to be, but neither are we all we would like to be and ought to be, and the church is made up of just such erring and imperfect people as we are. There will never be a perfect church, and if ever you find one, whatever you do don't join it or immediately it will cease to be perfect. Thank God the day will come when He will present it to Himself a glorious Church, not having spot or wrinkle or any such thing; holy and without blemish. But be sure of the Church you join. If they are untrue to the Book and Blood, then you must not join them or you will become a partaker of their evil deeds.

Christians may not see eye to eye, but they should walk arm in arm.
Anon.

Christ's Reputation

Behold my servant, whom I uphold; mine elect, in whom my soul
delighteth; I have put my spirit upon him: he shall bring forth
judgment to the Gentiles.
Isaiah 42 vs. 1

Remember, Jesus had a reputation. He had a marvellous reputation
with God. God said, "My Beloved Son, in whom I am well pleased."
Everywhere, all the time, He had the smile of God's favour and the ear
of God to every cry. What a reputation He had with Angels! They
could not stay in heaven after He came to earth, but burst through the
clouds and broke the silence of the centuries as they sang, " Unto you
is born a Saviour which is Christ the Lord." Again and again they
minister unto Him. He had a reputation among men. Peter said,
"Thou art Christ the Son of the living God"; Nathaniel said, "Thou art
the Son of God; Thou art the King of Israel"; Thomas said, " My Lord
and my God"; Pontius Pilate could find no fault in Him; Judas said, "
I have betrayed innocent blood." The Chief Priests mocked Him and
Scribes and Elders said, "He trusted in God." What a wonderful
reputation to have before your enemies! I wonder if our enemies
could say such things about us?

He also had a wonderful reputation amongst the devils. When all
were denying and deriding His Deity and Divinity, they said, "We
know thee, thou art the Son of the Living God." What sort of a
reputation do we have amongst the devils? Does He need to concern
Himself about us, or are we so harmless ourselves that He doesn't
need to bother?

Until we have learned to set very little value upon our own
reputation, we will never be inflamed with true zeal in contending
for the preservation and advancement of the interest of Divine glory.
John Calvin

Condescending Grace

But made himself of no reputation, and took upon him the form of a servant,
and was made in the likeness of men:
Philippians 2 vs. 7

He emptied Himself of His independence. "He took upon Himself the form of a servant," Nothing in this passage, teaches that Christ emptied Himself of either His Divine nature or His attributes but only of the outward and visible manifestations of the Godhead, or, as Bishop Lightfoot said, "He emptied, stripped Himself of the insignia of Majesty." But when occasion demanded he exercised His Divine attributes. Notice the words, "He took". We read "He thought it not robbery to be equal with God" and yet He "took" the form of a servant, not the form of an angel or archangel or some glorified body, not even the form of a King or Priest or Aristocrat, but a servant. What condescending Grace! He stooped so low that He might reach all, from the lowest to the highest.

> He was like a king who temporarily put on the garments of a peasant
> while at the same time remaining king.
> John F Walvoord

Obedient

And being found in fashion as a man, he humbles himself, and became
obedient unto death, even the death of the cross.
Philippians 2 vs. 8

He emptied Himself of His will and life. "Became" obedient. How?
Paul tells us He learned it through suffering. His will was ever the will
of His Fathers. I "come to do thy will". "I delight to do thy will". It
was the supreme search of His life. "I seek to do thy will", He said.
How different all this is to us! We say, "It is God's will and we will
have to bear it." Christ said, "I delight to do it." He cried, "If it be
possible let this cup pass from me." When He was on the cross, He
cried, "Why did'st Thou forsake me?" His Father gave no answer, but
Christ drank the cup and yielded to the forsaking of God. All through
His earthly life how strangely the will of God led. What sorrow! What
persecutions!   What privations!   What loneliness!   What
misunderstanding!   What hostile hatred! He never wavered or
rebelled or questioned. His will was utterly given up to do God's will.
However hard or trying our circumstances may be or become, they
never can equal Christ's. Let us not be wearied and faint in our minds,
but consider Him who endureth such contradiction of sinners.

What is obedience? Giving up my will to the will of another.
Andrew Murray

Common Folk

...And the common people heard him gladly.
Mark 12 vs. 37

He made Himself of no reputation by choosing the common people to be His audience. Last year in Scotland I went to hear one of our aristocratic orators. I had a strenuous time securing a ticket to gain admittance to hear that man, but I think I could have done better myself. He made a fine humorous speech for twenty-five minutes. He did not say much. About all he did was to tell stories. As I looked around the audience I could see dukes and lords and men of letters and learning; I think I was the only common person in the audience. He would not talk to the common, illiterate folk, but when he came to talk he had to have the very best people for his audience. Jesus Christ spake as never man spake, and He spoke words of profound simplicity and simple profundity and yet He chose the common people to be His audience, and the common people heard Him gladly. Why? Could He not have addressed the College of Jerusalem? Could He not have spoken to the aristocrats? Why didn't He do it? He made Himself of no reputation, but He poured out all the loving wisdom of God upon the common people of His day.

God must love the common people. He made so many of them.
Abraham Lincoln

Reputation

But made himself of no reputation…
Philippians 2 vs. 7

He emptied Himself of His "reputation," verse 7, "He made Himself of
no reputation." It does not say that He made Himself of no character.
Oh, no, for He was very jealous of His character. He defied them to
find a flaw or fault in Him, but He made Himself of no reputation.
Reputation is not character. You may rob me of my reputation or ruin
it, but you cannot touch my character. The only one that can injure my
character is myself. My character is what I really am. My reputation
is what I appear to be or may be. Because you call me a grafter and
seek to destroy my reputation for honesty, that does not make me
dishonest or hurt my character. You may call me a liar, but that does
not make me one or rob me of my integrity. Isn't it strange we are so
touchy and jealous about our reputation and so careless about our
character. All the fights and factions in our Churches today are caused
by this very thing. May the Lord help us to regard not our reputation,
but be very careful about our character.

Lighter is the loss of money than of character.
John Calvin

The Servant's Place

*For even the Son of man came not to be ministered unto, but to minister,
and to gave His life a ransom for many.*
Mark 10 vs. 45

In His relation to man, He said, "I am among you as one that serveth."
He washed His disciples' feet. How approachable He was! No
bumptiousness about Him. Wherever He went He was serving,
always helping others. They flung it in His teeth when dying on the
cross. "He saved others, himself he cannot save." His only
consideration was for others and pleasing God. How different today
His followers are. We want to boss or lord it over others, but not to
serve! Ah, that goes against the grain. It's so easy to be the master; it's
so hard to be the servant. We are so fearful of being imposed upon and
we try to assert our independence and stand up for our rights, we
won't be taken advantage of, etc. How contrary it all is to "the mind
of Christ" who was equal with God and yet took the servant's place.
May God enable us to empty ourselves of our God-dishonouring, man
destroying, independence. We only win as we stoop.

> A servant of God is known by how many he serves, not by how many
> servants he has.
> D L Moody

Dependence

I can of my own self do nothing.
John 5 vs. 30

Notice how this was manifested all through His life in His relation first to God: He said He could do nothing of Himself. Every miracle He performed, He performed in dependence upon God. He raised the dead, He healed the sick, He stilled the storm, He fed the hungry, He gave sight to the blind, but all in dependence upon God. It was along this very line that Satan tried to get Him to fall. "If thou be the Son of God, command that these stones be made bread." If you are God's Son, you can do this, then why starve? Exercise your independence. It is not becoming Deity to starve. How can we believe you are God's Son, if you are so dependent. But Jesus "took" the form of a servant and would not help Himself until His God either provided for His need or gave the power to Him. He lived a hand to mouth existence – from God's hand to His mouth. Oh, how different this is amongst His followers today! You hear on every hand, "I am doing my best," How contrary to the mind of Christ! So many of us are independent Christian gentlemen. We don't like to be dependent on God. Our pride rebels against it. We would like to take credit for the victories won and progress made in our Christian lives and living. We forget it is not attainment, but an obtainment.

I was but a pen in God's hand and what praise is due to a pen?
John Bunyan

Confessions

Confess your faults one to another and pray one for another,
that ye may be healed.
James 5 vs. 16

Let me say a word about "confessing our faults one to another." You only confess to the one you have wronged, and him alone. This sort of promiscuous confession so popular today is of popery and the devil, and has no place in Scripture. We confess first to Christ and then to the one we have wronged or robbed, and we do it privately. These public confessions are unwarranted and harmful and degrading.

It won't be long, dear friends, until the Books will be opened and all will be revealed. What shame will be ours if there are things unrighted or unconfessed. Let us seek here and now, always to have a conscience void of offence toward God and man. Make Christ and your conscience close and constant companions and you will adorn the doctrine of our God and Saviour as well as defend it.

Search me, O Lord, my actions try,
And make my ways appear
As seen by Thine all-searching eye –
To me my ways make clear.
Thus, prostrate, I shall learn of Thee
What now I feebly prove:
That God alone in Christ can be
UNUTTERABLE LOVE!

Constantly keep up your confessing.
C H Spurgeon

AUGUST

1 ◆ The Unequal Yoke

2 ◆ The Call to Separation

3 ◆ Disloyalty to Christ

4 ◆ Are we Unequally Yoked in our Business?

5 ◆ Are we Unequally Yoked with Unbelievers in the Church?

6 ◆ Only in the Lord

7 ◆ God's Threefold Charge

8 ◆ God's Threefold Reason

9 ◆ The Joy of Jesus

10 ◆ Spiritual Indigestion

11 ◆ Joy in Service

12 ◆ A Joy Independent of Circumstances

13 ◆ An Abiding Joy

14 ◆ Joy Unspeakable

15 ◆ Joy Unstealable

16 ◆ The Joy of Living in God's Presence

17 ◆ The Shepherd's Voice

18 ◆ Suffering For and With Christ

19 ◆ Answered Prayer

20 ◆ Loving and Trusting God

21 ◆ Rejoicing in God's Word

22 ◆ Can our Joy be Restored?

23 ◆ The Mystery and the Ministry of Suffering

24 ◆ Suffering in the Will of God

25 ◆ Suffering is not Evidence of Lack of Faith

26 ◆ Thank God for Suffering

27 ◆ Spiritual Fruit

28 ◆ No Pain - No Gain

29 ◆ Job an Example

30 ◆ False Tenderness

31 ◆ Strange Instruments

1 AUGUST

The Unequal Yoke

Be ye not unequally yoked together with unbelievers:
for what fellowship hath righteousness with unrighteousness?
and what communion hath light with darkness?
II Corinthians 6 vs. 14

"Be ye not unequally yoked together with unbelievers" is a clear command of God, as definite a command as "Thou shalt not kill," or "Thou shalt not steal." If we fail to keep it, we are breaking a command of God and are living rebellious, disobedient lives. Don't let us quibble about it. Face it and ask yourselves, "Am I living as a Christian, unequally yoked?" If so, then you are breaking God's command: - "Be not unequally yoked." There is a lot of light flippant talk today about "we are not under law, but under grace." The impression is made that no command of God is binding on us because we are saved. When this error grips the life, the door is opened to all manner of loose living and worldly compromise. Do you mean to tell me, because I am saved I can steal and cheat and lie and murder and do as I like and not be found guilty? The Ten Commandments are for all men, in all times and under all circumstances and dispensations. They were given to a redeemed people - redeemed by blood and power - out of Egypt's bondage. They were written by the finger of God and they are for redeemed people ever since. Christ did not abrogate the law, He fulfilled it, and if we are in Christ and walking after the Spirit, the righteousness of the law is fulfilled in us.

> Before you venture away from this great moment, ask your King to take you wholly into his service, and ask Him to make and keep you ready to do just exactly what He appoints.
> Frances Ridley Havergal

2 AUGUST

The Call to Separation

And what agreement hath the temple of God with idols? for ye are the temple of the living God; as God hath said, I will dwell in them, and walk in them; and I will be their God, and they shall be my people. Wherefore come out from among them, and be ye separate, saith the Lord, and touch not the unclean thing; and I will receive you, and will be a Father unto you, and ye shall be my sons and daughters, saith the Lord Almighty.
II Corinthians 6 vs. 16 - 18

I like the reasonable and kind way God deals with us. He doesn't command us "not to be unequally yoked together" and give us no reason for doing so. He didn't need to reason with us about obeying Him. He could just have commanded us without any reason at all and punished us for disobedience, but instead of that He gives us good reason why we should obey this command.

What agreement hath the temple of God with idols? There can never be any agreement. There can only be constant and increasing disagreement between them. So is a believer's life that is unequally yoked! Surely you would think that any believer, after considering this God-given reason for a life of separation from the world unto God, would see the reasonableness of it, and refuse to have anything to do with a life of compromise. Friends! we are our worst enemies. God provides for us, and desires us to have a life of unalloyed joy and peace, and we do our best by wilful disobedience to His command, to make our lives the very reverse. Let us hear God say to us, "Come now and let us reason together," and let us be reasonable and obedient.

Man still wishes to be happy even when he so lives as to make happiness impossible.
Augustine

3 AUGUST

Disloyalty to Christ

I am a companion of all them that fear thee, and of them
that keep thy precepts.
Psalm 119 vs. 63

What is meant by the unequal yoke? The unequal yoke is anything that unites a believer to an unbeliever in a common purpose, no matter how legitimate or suitable it may be. Don't let us evade or explain away the issue, let us honestly face it. Let me apply this command closely to the various relationships of life and see if we are obedient or disobedient to the command. Are we unequally yoked together with unbelievers in our friendships?

Who are our friends in our everyday life? Who are we most intimate and friendly with as companions? Are they saved or unsaved? If we compromise here we will surely be the losers. We may argue about our keeping them as our companions, so that we may help them to come to Christ. A very plausible argument, but friend, the Lord never asks us to break His commands in trying to do His work. But supposing the object justifies the friendship, have you ever known it to succeed? It is usually the other way; instead of you leading the friend to Christ, he will lead you away from Christ. We never bless others by compromising. We bless by our difference, our separation. How can we be friends of the enemies of Christ?

Such conduct is pure disloyalty to Christ. I heard about a man who was a lover of birds, and kept an aviary filled with canaries. He thought one day he could catch some of the common sparrows and put them amongst his canaries. He soon found out that the canaries were chirping like sparrows instead of the sparrows singing like canaries. Make unbelievers your friends and you will soon and surely lose your love for Christ and His Word and the place of prayer and the friends of Christ and you will be found in the world and of the world of your own sorrow and reproach on Christ. "Friendship of the world is enmity with God."

Nothing is more dangerous than associating with the ungodly.
John Calvin

4 AUGUST

Are we Unequally Yoked in our Business?

Can two walk together, except they be agreed?
Amos 3 vs. 3

Are we in partnership with an unbeliever? I don't mean, are we serving an ungodly master or mistress, but are we in partnership with an unbeliever? What an unequal yoke this is and how many a true believer have had his testimony and inner life ruined by it. The standards and ethics of the world are not the standards and ethics of the believer. The unbeliever may keep out of gaol in his business transactions and yet be far from right. A deal may be legally right and morally wrong. If the believer is a partner of his, he becomes a partaker with him in his evil deeds. Many a Christian's life and testimony is ruined by an ungodly partner in business. His very name stinks in the nostrils of ungodly men because of his business transactions and relations. Of course it isn't his doing, it's his partner's: but he is unequally yoked with him and is a partaker with him in his evil deeds. How many leading members and officers of our Church today are hurting the cause of Christ in the Church and in the world by the unsavoury commercial reputation they have?

Honesty is not only the best policy it is the only policy for a Christian.
Anon.

Are we Unequally Yoked with Unbelievers in the Church?

...what communion hath light with darkness?
II Corinthians 6 vs. 14

I believe every true believer should belong to some Church and not forsake the assembling of themselves together. You may be a Christian and not be a Church member; but you won't be the kind of Christian the New Testament teaches us to be. But we must be careful of the kind of Church we join. If the minister denies or disbelieves the Book and the Blood, I become a partaker with him in his evil deeds if I become a member of that church. How many believers there are today who are members of such churches where Christ is denied. They defend their action on sentimental grounds. They say this is the church of our parents, I was born and baptised here. All very good, but are you to break God's commands because of sentimental or family reasons? These unbelieving rascals who have crept into our church boards and pulpits could never remain there unless you support them; your money keeps them preaching and God will hold you accountable for the use you make of your money as well as your talents. Come out from among them and get into another Church of the same denomination or some other denomination, where they are true to Christ and His Word. Don't sell out Christ for any sentimental or denominational reasons.

Division is better than agreement in evil.
George Hutchinson

6 AUGUST

Only in the Lord

The wife is bound by the law as long as her husband liveth;
but if her husband be dead, she is at liberty to be married
to whom she will; only in the Lord.
I Corinthians 7 vs. 39

Every unsaved man or woman is out of Christ. They may be decent, religious, and well to do and well behaved, rich or poor, but they are out of Christ and we are not to marry such a person. If we do we become unequally yoked together and break God's command. The minister and Church may bless such an unholy union; the curse of God rests upon it. Oh the matrimonial tragedies on every hand today because they have broken the command of God. I thank God I never married an unsaved and a saved person. No marriage fee would make me a partaker with them in their evil and unholy deed. There are many ministers today and they would marry archangel Gabriel and the Devil and never ask any questions as long as they receive their fee. Young people! Let me appeal to you and warn you, you must only marry a saved person, when you marry. Don't be unequally yoked together and bring sorrow and misery on your lives and on the lives of your children.

If we have become unequally yoked together with an unbeliever in any of these aspects, what are we to do? Just as clear and emphatic as the command of God not to be unequally yoked together with an unbeliever, so just as clear and emphatic God gives us a threefold charge to guide and direct us in what we are to do. He doesn't leave us in any uncertainty about it.

Don't look around for a life partner, look up. Any choice other than God's will mean disaster.
Anon.

God's Threefold Charge

Wherefore come out from among them, and be ye separate, saith the Lord,
and touch not the unclean thing; and I will receive you.
II Corinthians 6 vs. 17

Come out from among them. No half measures will satisfy God or meet your need. A clean and clear cut is what God demands and our condition demands. No compromise, no quibbling or trying to justify yourself. No excusing ourselves because of the difficulties involved or the consequence that would result from such an act of obedience. You may have fifty sensible reasons and quote great authorities, but God's charge makes no allowance for all such. "Come out" not half or part out - come out from among them. There is no other remedy. It may seem hard and it certainly isn't easy; the sacrifice and wrench will be great and painful, but it is the only way out of your bondage and misery. If there were some other way the Lord would have let us know about it.

Be ye separate. Not only "come out" but "stay out." Maintain your decision and action. We are to be in the world but not of the world. Live daily a separated life. A life separated from all compromise and uncleanness and worldliness and separated unto God.

Touch not the unclean. We are to have no compromising connection with anything in the world, which is alien to God. There is uncleanness of the flesh and also of the Spirit. We are to cleanse ourselves from these and keep clean by not touching, i.e. by not having anything to do with them in any shape or form. You cannot trifle or touch something unclean and remain pure or clean. Touch it and you are contaminated and polluted. There is only one safe rule-- - "Touch not."

> The tendency is strong to say, "Oh God won't be so stern as to expect me to give up that!" but He will.
> Oswald Chambers

God's Threefold Reason

Wherefore come out from among them, and be ye separate, saith the Lord,
and touch not the unclean thing, and I will receive you, and will be a Father
unto you, and ye shall be my sons and daughters, saith the Lord Almighty.
II Corinthians 6 vs. 17-18

This charge of God may seem harsh and severe and inconsiderate. Yes
it may seem so to us because of our ignorance and carnality, so the
Lord gives us three reasons why we should obey it.

"I will receive you." The Throne of Grace open to us at all times -
not only access, but acceptance. Received every time we draw near.
What a privilege! Surely we will not forfeit this privilege by our
disobedience and compromising living.

"I will be a Father unto you." God is the Father of every saved man
or woman, but if we are disobedient and wayward like the prodigal
Son, our Heavenly Father can't be all He desires to be and would be if
we were obedient to His commands and demands. If we are obedient
He will love us and educate, guard and provide for us every day and
all day long. Surely such blessedness should constrain us to be
obedient to His command and charge.

"Ye shall be my sons and daughters." Our relation to God our
Father will not be merely something abstract only, but concrete; a
living visible reality, not only in our own experience, but also before
the world. There will be a family likeness about us that will betray us
wherever we go. Men will take knowledge of us; we will not only
present Christ but also represent Him. Surely such a high and holy
calling is worth all the sacrifice we have to make in obedience to this
command. Remember His commands are our enabling. What He
demands, He provides. Give Him full obedience and He will carry
you through.

> Our heavenly Father never takes away anything from His children
> unless he means to give them something better.
> George Muller

The "Joy" of Jesus

These things have I spoken unto you, that my joy might remain in you, and that your joy might be full.
John 15 vs. 11

"My Joy." How startling and surprising, even almost shocking, such a statement as our text is. They are the very words of Christ, too; no wonder they startle and shock many today, when you consider their view of Christ and Christianity. How gloomy they are and how joyless. In fact, they have come to believe the gloomier they are and the less joy they have, the more truly Christian they are. They believe that sanctification and sourness are synonymous terms. If this is not their belief, then their looks belie them and they ought to take an action for defamation of character against their faces and actions; for their looks and actions are certainly lying about them. Their presence brings a chill - a real arctic chill - wherever they go. When they depart all breathe a sigh of relief and give themselves a shake to restore heat and comfort. This gloominess and funereal feeling is in our Churches and brought about by the architectural design of the buildings. They may be architecturally perfect and a wonder and a thing of beauty, from that standpoint, but they would never excite a feeling of joy and gladness. The subdued light, the arrangement of the furniture and its design, do not tend to make one joyful or feel that way. The music of the organ and the tunes of Psalms and hymns wouldn't give you the impression that religion was a very joyful thing to have anything to do with, unless you are dying or dead. The order of the service - so deadly orderly, decorous and dignified - does not give you the impression of joy and gladness. The minister, if he is to be looked up to as a cultured and refined and truly and fully trained one, must put on mannerisms of tone and action that would be absurd and ridiculous in any other department of life.

If you are not allowed to laugh in heaven, I do not want to go there.
Martin Luther

Spiritual Indigestion

..the joy of the Lord is your strength.
Nehemiah 8 vs. 10

A young fellow, full of life, laughter and vigour determines to become a minister. He enters a college or a ministerial factory, where they turn out ministers; the graduates from such a factory are entirely different creatures. He has become unnatural; he dresses different; he acts different; he speaks in accents different - his natural, joyous, laughing personality has been changed into a peculiar type of being, called a minister of religion.

I heard a story that illustrates this. A strange minister was to take the Sunday service in a country Church in the absence of the minister. One of the elders was deputed to meet him at the station on his arrival on the Saturday. The train arrived, the passengers alighted and departed, all except one man, who stood around as if he was waiting for someone. The elder approached him and asked him if he was the minister who was to conduct the service in the church. The man replied "No. I have indigestion and that makes me look like one." What a travesty and tragedy on the religion of Jesus Christ. The voice and tone of the voice become changed as soon as they enter the pulpit. They imagine a pious whine and an unnatural accent is the hallmark of an ambassador of the Christ who could speak about 'My Joy', and whose message is 'Good News of great joy.' If some minister were to speak to their wives in the tone of voice they speak to God in the pulpit, they would think they were crazy and feel insulted. The very book that contains the message of the "happy God" - the good news - the glorious life-giving, joy-begetting news - is bound with black covers inside and out. Who would ever imagine its message was "Good tidings of great joy."

If you have no joy in your religion, there is a leak in your Christianity somewhere.
Billy Sunday

Joy in Service

Serve the Lord with gladness: come before his presence with singing.
Psalm 100 vs.2

I remember preaching in a fine old church, and after the service one of the elders was asked by another what he thought of the preacher. He replied "I have been forty years an elder in this church and I never heard a minister laugh in the pulpit before." Oh the pathos of it! The tragedy of it! What a burlesquing of the Gospel and Christ. Doesn't it make your blood boil with indignations at it all? Thank God there are exceptions in the church's ministers, but they are rare and scarce. The birds sing; the flowers bloom and smell so sweetly; the sunrises and sunsets are glorious and thrilling. The very heavens declare His glory - not gloom, and the God who made and sustains all these is portrayed to the world by building, book, men and message, as a gloomy joyless, killjoy God. Every funeral Jesus attended He spoiled. Every life He touched, He blessed and beautified. He brought sunshine into the shady places of this sin-sick, sorrow-stricken, tear drenched world. Let us dear friends, not bring a false report of Christ our Saviour and His good news, by gloomy, morbid, sad lives. Let us enter into and possess His joy and "Brighten the corner where we are." Remember, "The joy of the Lord." "My joy is your strength." Mourning and sighing and sorrow weaken us and unfit us for life and service.

The Christian ought to be a living doxology.
Martin Luther

A Joy Independent of Circumstances

Although the fig tree shall not blossom, neither shall fruit be in the vines; the labour of the olive shall fail, and the fields shall yield no meat; the flock shall be cut off from the fold, and there shall be no herd in the stalls; Yet will I rejoice in the Lord, I will joy in the God of my salvation.
Habakkuk 3 vs. 17,18

Think of it? Rejoicing under such circumstances, and a farmer at that. Farmers are usually good growlers, even Christian ones. They growl when it's wet, they growl when it's dry; and they growl when crops are poor and even when they are good, for they might have been better. Their life is one long growl. What a different kind of farmer old Habakkuk was, and he lived hundreds of years before Christ. Christ's joy was independent of all circumstances too. How lonely a life He lived, what opposition and persecution He daily endured. What misunderstanding even from His disciples, He bore. What misrepresentation and misunderstanding He continually experienced. He died on a Cross between two thieves, jeered at, derided, insulted, God-forsaken and yet through it all He told his disciples "My Joy might remain in you." Was there ever a life like His? "He came to His own and His own received Him not." His own brothers and sisters didn't believe in Him. They said He was mad, and yet He lived a life of joy and desired His disciples to have the same joy. Whatever our circumstances may be, we can be joyful. We may not be happy and cannot always be, but we may be and can be and ought to be always joyful.

Happiness depends on what happens. Joy depends on our union with Christ and obedience to Him and is therefore independent of our circumstances. Paul could be joyful. It brought the jailer to Christ and founded the Church at Philippi. I am sure he didn't feel happy in jail or when scourged or stoned, but was joyful and commanded us to rejoice in the Lord always.

> Take a saint, and put him in any condition, and he knows how to rejoice in the Lord.
> Walter Cradock

13 AUGUST

An Abiding Joy

...that my joy might remain in you, and that your joy might be full.
John 15 vs. 11

How evanescent worldly joys are. They pass away like morning cloud and the early dew and leave ashes in the mouth. The least wee bit, or touch of adversity or sickness or sorrow and all worldly joy vanishes, but the joy of Jesus abides. Hallelujah! In fact, the very things that destroy the unconverted one's joy only intensifies and increases the joy of Jesus the converted one possesses. I received a letter from one of God's shut-in saints. She has her two legs cut off, her two arms, only a small stump left of the right arm. She endures torture day and night. The mutilation of her body was brought about by successive operations through the years. She has never left her wee room (10ft x 12ft.) for over forty years. I wish you saw her write, and her writing with an attachment to the right stump. She calls her room "Glad wish." She tells me her joy remains and deepens in spite of constant pain and no sleep without an opiate. What a joy! And it is ours, if we are in Christ.

When I am in the cellar of affliction, I look for the Lord's choicest wines.
Samuel Rutherford

Joy Unspeakable

Whom having not seen, ye love; in whom though now ye see Him not, yet believing, ye rejoice with joy unspeakable and full of glory.
I Peter 1 vs. 8

The world can give you a joy you can speak about, in fact, you can easily exaggerate about it and lie about it if you are not very careful, but the joy of Jesus is unspeakable and full of glory. You can never exaggerate when telling about it; in fact, we cannot tell it fully of half fully. The old Scotch woman said about it - "It was better felt than telt." This is our bother when we try to tell sinners about it and even when we very poorly tell about it, they think we are exaggerating. If we cannot adequately express it in word, let us express it by our lives. The world generally believes what it sees.

There is more joy in Jesus in twenty-four hours than there is in the world in 365 days. I have tried them both.
R A Torrey

Joy Unstealable

And ye now therefore have sorrow; but I will see you again and your heart shall rejoice and your joy no man taketh from you.
John 16 vs.22

They may take your money, they make take your loved ones and friends, they may take your reputation, they may take your happiness - but, Glory to God!- they can never take your joy. Isn't this something to possess and shout about? Hallelujah! The old devil with all his wiles and devices cannot rob us of this joy. Our worst enemies or best friends cannot deprive us of it. Glory to God it is unstealable. We may be stricken by disease and suffer torture; we may lose our money and friends, even our dearest - but all this cannot steal our joy. It is as safe, and maybe safer than any deposit in the vaults of the Bank of England. However clever the circumstances or incidents that may be brought to bear on our lives and succeed in robbing us of many precious things, here is something that cannot be taken from us – "Our Joy."

> Afflictions are blessings to us when we can bless God for our afflictions.
> William Dyer

The Joy of Living in God's Presence

*Thou hast made known to me the ways of life; thou shalt make me
full of joy with thy countenance.*
Acts 2 vs. 28

Jesus ever lived in conscious unclouded communion and fellowship with His Father in heaven. You hear some people when they begin to pray, say, "We come into Thy presence,"
Inferring that they were not there before. Jesus was continually in the Father's presence. No wonder He was joyful always and under all circumstances. If we will walk - not run or fly - but simply walk in the light as He is in the light, we shall have fellowship. You couldn't do this and not be joyful. It is as certain as cause and effect. You couldn't have sunrise without daylight and you couldn't have fire and no heat - two and two make four. So living in God's presence, moment by moment, you have fullness of joy and pleasure for evermore. God is the source of the believer's joy - it is His joy, and you couldn't live in His presence and not be joyful. You could not live without breathing, neither could you live in His presence and not be joyful. There is something wrong when you meet a mournful, sad believer. His sad face and mournful demeanour gives him away every time. There is sin in his life. Sin un-confessed, that mars his fellowship and makes God's presence painful to him. You remember when you were a child and living a life of obedience to your parents, what a source of joy their presence was. To be away from them or them to be absent, killed your joy, but when they returned, what joy there was. But if you had been living in disobedience or wrong, the thought of their presence, let alone their presence, produced misery and unhappiness. So it is with the believer. You cannot be joyful and not live in God's presence and you cannot be miserable and joyless and live in His presence. Jesus never had a cloud between Him and His Father - it was a sinless fellowship. Oh what exquisite joy must have been His continually! He can keep us walking in the light as He is in the light and the Blood will keep on cleansing us and our joy will be full and abiding. Hallelujah!

Communion with God is the beginning of Heaven.
William Booth

17 AUGUST

The Shepherd's Voice

He that hath the bride is the bridegroom; but the friend of the bridegroom,
which standeth and heareth him, rejoiceth greatly because of the
bridegroom's voice; this my joy therefore is fulfilled.
John 3 vs. 29

Have you ever heard his voice? There is no mistaking it. You may mistake His presence, because He has appeared " in another form." His "form" has bewildered you and perplexed you or even offended you but His voice will always betray Him to your heart. The hand may be the hand of Esau, but the voice is the voice of Jacob. So our Lord may appear strange to his own in His dealings, but when we hear His voice we detect His presence, for "The sheep hear his voice; and he calleth his own sheep by name, and leadeth them out. And when he putteth forth his own sheep he goeth before them and the sheep follow him, for they know his voice. And a stranger they will not follow, but flee from him. For they know not the voice of strangers."

Jesus also said; "My sheep hear my voice and I know them and they follow me." If we are truly born again, we are no longer goats, but sheep - and then we cannot help but hear His voice. It is the mark of His sheep - the earmark - "They hear His voice." There is also the foot mark - "They follow Me."

The two disciples on the road to Emmaus didn't know it was Jesus who drew near and joined them on their journey, but their hearts burned within them while He talked with them by the way. So it is today with every true disciple, as Jesus talks with them on their way, they rejoice greatly because of His voice. What exquisite joy must have been Jesus' joy. He always heard His Father's voice. "This is my beloved Son in whom I am well pleased." We too may have this joy when we hear His voice say: "This is the way, walk ye in it" as He leads us out and in.

Learn to recognise the Word of Christ to you through Holy Scripture.
Dr. Paul Rees

Suffering For and With Christ

Blessed (hilariously happy) are ye, when men shall revile you, and persecute
you, and shall say all manner of evil against you falsely, for my sake.
Rejoice, and be exceeding glad: for great is your reward in heaven…
Matthew 5 vs.11-12

If suffering and persecution is a source of joy to believers what an abundant source of joy it was to Jesus, for no one has ever suffered as He did or was so persecuted as He was -what joy must have been His. Paul tells us, "Who for the joy that was set before Him endured the Cross, despising the shame." Even the Cross and its shame was a source of joy to Jesus. It is queer how we deprive ourselves often of this source of joy by shirking the cross and the shame attached thereto, and bring misery and sorrow into our lives and sour sanctimonious looks on our faces. When vilified and reviled we get mad or sad, or maybe both, instead of rejoicing and being exceeding glad. No wonder the world has a wrong impression of what a Christian really is. "In this world ye shall have tribulation"-we cannot escape it, but "Be of good cheer," says Jesus. These last of the last days are days when every true born again one will have to suffer, but let us make our suffering and persecution a source of our joy, as it was a source of Jesus' joy. The oyster takes the injury it received and makes a pearl out if it, so may we make what seems to harm and hurt us into everlasting joy.

The Lord gets his best soldiers out of the highlands of affliction.
C H Spurgeon

Answered Prayer

Hitherto have ye asked nothing in my name; ask, and ye shall receive,
that your joy may be full.
John 16 vs. 24

Some loved one has decided for Christ and prayers of long years standing have been answered. What a joy comes to the heart. Some one has been raised from the dead in answer to prayer; what rejoicing and joy as a consequence. How many petitions offered and granted every day, and as we recall the answers, what a source of joy this becomes. Jesus could look up to heaven and before even He prayed, He could say, "I thank thee, Father, that thou hast heard me, and I know that thou hearest me always." He spent nights in prayer. He prayed without ceasing and always was answered - what peculiar joy this must have been in His life in the "days of His flesh." May we increasingly and unceasingly make use of this source of Jesus' joy.

> Four things let us ever keep in mind – God hears prayer; God heeds prayer; God answers prayer; and God delivers by prayer.
> E. M. Bounds

Loving and Trusting God

"But let all those that put their trust in thee rejoice;
let them ever shout for joy, because thou defendest them:
let them also that love thy name be joyful in thee."
Psalm 5 vs. 11

The Lord loved and trusted God perfectly. There never was any want of affection for or confidence in God in Jesus, therefore how full and complete His joy must have been. The more we love and trust God the more joy will be ours. You and I are the only ones who will be to blame if we lose our joy. Neither God; devil; man; circumstances; health; sickness; death; wealth nor the world, can rob us of this joy of Jesus. However bright or sad our lives may be, we can always be joyful and rejoice always. If we are not joyful there is a reason easily discovered. The devil will try to make us believe our joylessness and sadness is a sure sign of reverence and sanctity. Oh! So many believe this lie of the devil and go through life sour, cynical and sad. What a reproach on Christ and His salvation. What a source of joy to the old devil is a sad and mournful Christian. Remember, dear friends, the hallmark of a thoroughbred, pureblooded hypocrite is a long face. The longer the face the greater the hypocrite.

Joy ceases to be joy when it ceases to be in the Lord.
J A Motyer

Rejoicing in God's Word

Thy words were found, and I did eat them; and Thy word was unto me
the joy and rejoicing of mine heart...
Jeremiah 15 vs. 16

What an unfailing and abounding source of joy was God's Word to Jesus. Remember the many quotations He made from the Old Testament; when He would resist Satan He used the Word of God. Do you remember when the Word of God spoke to your heart for the first time and told you that you were saved by grace and you had peace with God and there was therefore now no condemnation, all your sins were forgiven, you were pardoned and possessed eternal life? How your heart sung that happy day – "Happy day! Happy day! When Jesus washed my sins away." Happy day! What a day! A day that will never see a sunset or know an end. Hallelujah! But tell me, have you heard His voice in His Word today? Do you find God's Word and receive joy and rejoicing in your heart? This is our privilege and portion. May we so read and digest His Word, so that daily we may be joyful and rejoicing Christians. You couldn't find His Word and not rejoice; you couldn't eat and not feel satisfied, so you couldn't eat His Word and not joy and rejoice. Neglect His Word and you cannot evade or escape the consequence; you will be a long - faced, sour - faced, mournful - faced Christian; so feed on His word Christian!

Leave not off reading the Bible till you find your hearts warmed...let
it not only inform you but inflame you.
Thomas Watson

Can Our Joy Be Restored?

Create in me a clean heart, O God; and renew a right spirit within me.
…Restore unto me the joy of thy salvation;
Psalm 51 vs. 10,12

If we are joyless Christians that is, back-slidden Christians, we can be restored and our joy returned.

Let us confess our sin or sins, and the sin of our joylessness, and He will forgive and cleanse our hearts.

Create in me a clean heart and then "restore." There must be confession and cleansing before there can be restored joy. In Isaiah 61 we read:

"The Spirit of the Lord God is upon me; because the Lord hath anointed me to preach good tidings unto the meek; he hath sent me to bind up the broken-hearted, to proclaim liberty to the captives, and the opening of the prison to them that are bound… To appoint unto them that mourn in Zion, to give unto them beauty for ashes, the oil of joy for mourning, the garment of praise for the spirit of heaviness…"

Remember, friends, a joyless Christian is like a piano out of tune, like a limb out of joint. It is said of Jesus, "Thou hast loved righteousness and hated iniquity; therefore God even Thy God, hath anointed Thee with the oil of gladness above Thy fellows." If we will love righteousness and hate iniquity, we too shall be anointed with the oil of gladness above our fellows.

He gives me joy in place of sorrow,
He gives me love that casts out fear,
He gives me sunshine for my shadow,
And beauty for ashes here.

The backslider is a man who because of his relationship to God can never really enjoy anything else.
Martin Lloyd Jones

The Mystery and the Ministry of Suffering

Beloved, think it not strange concerning the fiery trial which is to try you,
as though some strange thing happened unto you:
I Peter 4 vs. 12

If we are truly born again we are not to think it strange concerning the fiery trial, which is to try us as though some strange thing happened unto us. We are to rejoice inasmuch as we are partakers of Christ's sufferings, that when His glory shall be revealed we shall be glad also with exceeding joy.

Think it not strange! But it does seem strange. Strange that the waters of a full cup should be wrung out of the saints, while sinners walk on the sunny side of the hedge! Strange that the wicked should be permitted to plot so much and so successfully against the righteous! Strange that the profane should sit on the judgement seats at which the godly and devoted are arraigned for no other fault than their endeavours for the good of men. Strange to find some of the sweetest and noblest of God's children racked with agony, dying of cancer, beset with poverty, misunderstanding and hatred. It is hard not to think it strange. And yet it would be stranger still if it were not so. Let us now look into some considerations that rob suffering of its strangeness and help to explain its mystery.

> Scar not at suffering for Christ, for Christ hath a chair and cushion
> and sweet peace for a sufferer.
> Samuel Rutherford

Suffering in the Will of God

And his disciples asked him, Master, who did sin, this man, or his parents,
that he was born blind? Jesus answered, Neither hath this man sinned nor
his parents, but that the works of God should be made manifest in him.
John 9 vs. 2-3

All who suffer in the will of God are not necessarily suffering on account of sin or the consequence of sin. You remember the incident in the life of our Lord when He saw a man born blind. His disciples asked Him, "...Master, who did sin..."

Our suffering may be for the manifestation of God's works in us and for His glory. There are so many sufferers and they are robbed of the blessings they should experience as a consequence of their sufferings, because they have not realised this fact. We all know sickness and suffering is the result of sin. If man had never sinned, these evils would have been unknown in the world. That is only one side of this mystery of suffering. The others side is this; that we who are truly born again and living in the will of God daily, are assured by God that He is making all things work together for our good. We are not asked or expected to understand, or always feel this, but we know, and can therefore be like the kettle on the fire, which although up to the neck in boiling water, continues to sing. Happy are ye for the spirit of glory and of God resteth upon you and we are partakers of Christ's sufferings.

It is doubtful God can use any man greatly until He has hurt him deeply.
A W Tozer

Suffering is not Evidence of Lack of Faith

For unto you it is given in the behalf of Christ, not only to believe on him, but also to suffer for his sake;
Philippians 1 vs. 29

There are those who would rob the suffering saint of his comfort and consolation by telling him he hasn't faith. If he would only believe he would be healed. It is quite evident from Scripture and experience that there are multitudes of God's born again who are ordained to this ministry of suffering. Some of the choicest saints the Church has ever had have lived lives of excruciating pain and left behind them such a fragrance of Christ as to encourage and inspire those who follow in their steps. Do you mean to tell us these choice saints were lacking in faith? It isn't God's will to heal all who suffer; if that were so, there would be many who would charge God with their needless suffering. Away with all this rubbish so common in some circles today, that because all sickness and suffering is of the devil and sin, therefore God's suffering saints are living in sin or unbelief. God's word gives the lie to it, and the testimony of the suffering ones as they rejoiced in the furnace of affliction, loudly denies it. O ye suffering ones who are suffering in the will of God, don't permit the devil or some unwise saint to rob you of the comfort, joy and blessing that God has for you in suffering.

A little faith is faith as a spark of fire is fire.
Thomas Watson

Thank God for Suffering

...My son, despise not thou the chastening of the Lord, nor faint when thou art rebuked of him: For whom the Lord loveth he chasteneth, and scourgeth every son whom he receiveth. If ye endure chastening, God dealeth with you as with sons; for what son is he whom the father chasteneth not? But if ye be without chastisement, whereof all are partakers, then are ye bastards, and not sons.
Hebrews 12 vs. 5-8

The word chastisement here means "child-training;" "discipline." It is because we are His children that He deals with us and causes us suffering. It is for our good. It is never merely punitive; it is corrective. David could say before he was afflicted, "I went astray, but now I have kept thy word. It is good for me that I have been afflicted that I might learn thy statutes." There are many saints since then can say what David said about suffering. God doesn't make us suffer because He hates us or is angry with us, but because He loves us. What parent corrects his children merely because he is angry or has a grudge against them? If we being evil know how to correct our children, how much more our heavenly Father. How many of us can thank God for the suffering He permitted to enter our lives. How much sin and misery we were saved from and how much instruction we received as a consequence.

Suffering times are teaching times.
William Bridge

Spiritual Fruit

*Every branch in me that beareth not fruit he taketh away, and every branch
that beareth fruit, he purgeth it, that it may bring forth more fruit.*
John 15 vs. 2

Here is a garden filled with weeds and thorns - never cared for, never a spade or rake on it. Here is another garden well kept - filled with fruit and flowers, well cared for and attended to. Oh, how often the spade has painfully and roughly dug it up, and the rake ran roughshod over its back. Could you hear it speak it would tell you of much pain and suffering experienced. Could you imagine it desiring to be left alone and not cared for?

Our lives require as much care and attention if the fruits and flowers of grace are to appear. These cannot be produced without pain and suffering and constant correction.

This pruning process is always a painful one, but a very necessary one if we are to bear more fruit. Take notice that the branch that isn't bearing fruit is the one He doesn't prune; He just throws it away. It is useless and fruitless. But because the other branch bears fruit, He prunes it. Why? So that it may bring forth more fruit. If we are free from pruning - free from suffering - it is because we are useless and fruitless. Cheer up, suffering saint!

Not now, but in the coming years,
It may be in the better land,
We will read the meaning of our tears,
And there, sometime, we'll understand.

The one thing He commands us as His branches is to bear fruit.
Live to bless others, to testify of the life and the love of Jesus.
Andrew Murray

No Pain - No Gain

But the God of all grace, who hath called us unto his eternal glory by
Christ Jesus, after that ye have suffered a while, make you perfect,
stablish, strengthen, settle you.
I Peter 5 vs. 10

Another thing about suffering and its ministry and mystery that will help us is that it may be constructive.

The Lord not only prunes, He produces fruit that glorifies Himself and blesses mankind. How rich and strong and beautiful some lives are that we have known, and we wonder how they are so rich in the grace of the Spirit, but when we enquire we find they have been through fiery furnaces, deep waters and dark valleys. These are the places where strong, gentle, and tender character is produced. When you see a piece of wood in a home with unique and beautiful grain in it you will observe that the polishing has not added anything to it - it has only developed what was already there. Ask any lumberman to explain such grain in the wood. He will tell you that the tree has grown in some place where it was exposed to the storms and gales that hurled themselves through the mountains. The sheltered tree cannot produce such a grain. The life that has been free from suffering is not the life that can show the strength and traits of character we will admire. Oh no, these are only constructed in the school of adversity and pain. Suffering is God's constructive work operating in our lives. What an amount of patience is constructed in our lives through suffering. What floods of sympathy and unselfishness are let loose in our lives through suffering. You have known men and women who were hard, severe, selfish and unsympathetic in their relation with others. But after they had experienced or passed through some sore suffering, what a change was wrought in their lives. The experience of suffering constructed such traits of kindness and thoughtfulness and sacrificial service that we hardly knew them. Isn't it wonderful how God can and does take suffering and makes it constructive?

Praise God for the hammer, the file and the furnace.
Samuel Rutherford

29 AUGUST

Job an Example

...Naked came I out of my mother's womb, and naked shall I return
thither: the Lord gave, and the Lord hath taken away;
blessed be the name of the Lord.
Job 1 vs. 21

What an example Job has been to millions of suffering saints ever since! What God would have lost, and what God's saints would have lost, if Job hadn't suffered as he did and never charged God foolishly. What an example of suffering, affliction and patience Job has been and is today. But every sufferer today is an example, not only to other saints who suffer, but also to the world at large, of patience, faith, love and loyalty to God. I remember being asked one time to call on an invalid, one who had been confined to her bed and room for almost twenty years, and a great suferer. The room was small, so small that there was only room for a chair beside the bed. The outlook from the room was into a closed-in back yard. I wondered what word of comfort and cheer I might bring to her. What a surprise I got when I entered the room. She took my hand and thanked me for coming, and then began to tell me about her Saviour and how He had blessed her, and what peace and joy He gave her. Then she began to sing her favourite hymn of praise. Not a word of complaint or murmuring. She never charged God with folly. He had done only the best for her and her heart was filled with His praises. I came away more determined than ever to trust Him fully and serve Him more faithfully than ever before. The example of that dear suffering saint was such a blessing to me; instead of my helping and comforting her, she was the means of rich blessing to me. It isn't everyone God can trust with sorrow and suffering. He can trust almost anyone with joy, but to know the fellowship of His sufferings is only given to the few, and they are the Lord's choice ones. We often sing about trusting the Lord, but can the Lord trust us? Would we let Him down in the furnace of suffering? Oh ye suffering saints, take fresh courage. You are honoured of the Lord by being an example of suffering and patience. What a cloud of witnesses there is looking on, and as they look they are being blessed and encouraged to press on their upward way. Your life and sufferings are not in vain. Cheer up it won't be long until the day of review and reward will come. We'll see things in their true relation then. We'll know then as never before that all the way He led was good.

> We'll catch the broken threads again,
> And finish what we here began;
> Heaven will the mysteries explain,
> And then, ah then, we'll understand.
> We'll know why clouds instead of sun
> Were over many a cherished plan,
> Why song has ceased when scarce begun;
> 'Tis there, sometime, we'll understand.
> Why what we longed for most of all
> Eludes so oft our eager hand,
> Why hopes are crushed and castles fall,
> Up there, sometime, we'll understand.

Affliction may be lasting but it is not everlasting.
Thomas Watson

False Tenderness

For I reckon that the sufferings of this present time are not worthy to be compared with the glory which shall be revealed in us.
Romans 8 vs. 18

Let me give you an article, by an unknown author that I read some time ago; it has been such a blessing to my own soul; -

"I kept for nearly a year the flask-shaped cocoon of an Emperor moth. It is very peculiar in its construction. A narrow opening is left in the neck of the flask, through which the perfect insect forces its way, so that a forsaken cocoon is as entire as one still tenanted, no rupture of the interlacing fibres having taken place. The great disproportion between the means of egress and the size of the imprisoned insect makes one wonder how the exit is ever accomplished at all - and it never is without great difficulty and labour. It is supposed that the pressure to which the moth's body is subjected in passing through such a narrow opening is a provision of nature for forcing the juices into the vessels of the wings, these being less developed at the period of emerging from the chrysalis than they are in other insects. I happened to witness the first efforts of my imprisoned moth to escape from its long confinement. During a whole afternoon, from time to time, I watched it patiently striving and struggling to get out. It never seemed able to get beyond a certain point, and at last my patience was exhausted. Very probably the confining fibres were drier and less elastic than if the cocoon had been left to winter on its native heather, as nature meant it to be. At all events I thought I was wiser and more compassionate than its Maker, and I resolved to give it a helping hand. With the point of my scissors I snipped the confining threads to make the exit a little easier, and lo! immediately, and with perfect ease, out crawled my moth dragging a huge swollen body and little shrivelled wings. In vain I watched to see that marvellous process of expansion in which these silently and swiftly develop before one's eyes: and as I traced the exquisite spots and markings of divers colours that were all there in miniature, I longed to see these assume their due proportions and the creature to appear in all its perfect beauty, as it is, in truth, one of the loveliest of its kind. But I looked in vain. My false tenderness had proved its ruin. It never was anything but a stunted abortion, crawling painfully through that brief life which it should have spent flying through the air on rainbow wings. I have thought of it often, when watching with pitiful eyes those who were struggling with sorrow, suffering and distress; and I would fain cut short the discipline and give deliverance. Short sighted man! How know I that one of these pangs or groans could be spared? The far-sighted, perfect love that seeks the perfection of its object does not weakly shrink from present, transient suffering. Our Father's love is too true to be weak. Because He loves His children, He chastises them that they may be partakers of His holiness. With this glorious end in view, He spares not for their crying. Made perfect through sufferings, as the Elder Brother was, the sons of God are trained up to obedience and brought to Glory through much tribulation."

Suffering prepares us for glory.
David Kingdom

Strange Instruments

And we know that all things work together for good to them that love God,
to them who are the called according to his purpose.
Romans 8 vs. 28

The suffering may be caused by strange instruments - sickness, the sins of others, maligned, maliciously misrepresented, cheated, robbed, the devil, even our own mistakes and sin. Whatever the instrument, let us ever remember and hold tenaciously to this - God may allow the devil, or our enemies or friends, or circumstances to cause suffering in our lives, but they can only do so by God's permission, and they are under His supervision every moment; so we may rest assured that God is working them together for our good.

Then trust in God through all thy days,
Fear not, for He doth hold thy hand,
Though dark the way still sing and praise,
Sometime, sometime, we'll understand.

How soon you will find that everything in your history, except sin, has been for you. Every wave of trouble has been wafting you to the sunny shores of a sinless eternity.
Robert Murray McCheyne

SEPTEMBER

1 ◆ A Dog and a Sow

2 ◆ A Dupe of the Devil

3 ◆ Terrible Consequences

4 ◆ A Bitter Harvest

5 ◆ The Sins of the Saints

6 ◆ Words of Comfort

7 ◆ Troubles and How to Meet Them

8 ◆ Expect Trouble

9 ◆ Don't be a Quitter

10 ◆ Wit's End Corner

11 ◆ Believe in God

12 ◆ How are We to Know God

13 ◆ Heaven – Nearer and Dearer

14 ◆ Jesus is Coming Back Again

15 ◆ The Comforter – The Holy Ghost

16 ◆ Give Him a Chance

17 ◆ Unlike Other Men

18 ◆ Samson – A Warning to Us All

19 ◆ The Consequences of Compromise

20 ◆ Restoration

21 ◆ Union with Christ

22 ◆ A Living Union

23 ◆ An Indispensable Union

24 ◆ The Object of this Union I

25 ◆ The Object of this Union II

26 ◆ Following Afar Off

27 ◆ Peter's Weakest Hour

28 ◆ Coldness

29 ◆ A Strong Weakness

30 ◆ Dishonourable Conduct

A Dog and a Sow

But it is happened unto them according to the true proverb, The dog is turned to his own vomit again; and the sow that was washed to her wallowing in the mire.
II Peter 2 vs. 22

A genuine backslider cannot live in sin. He is of all men most miserable. You hear about someone who has lived for years a backslider. It is all a delusion, and a fatal one. You might as well expect a hen to live like a fish, or a fish to live like a hen, as expect a true believer to live as a backslider. He may backslide, but he neither enjoys nor continues in it. Like Lot, he vexes his righteous soul.

If you are content to continue living as you are now, imagining that you are a backslider, you are only "the dog turned to his own vomit again; and the sow that was washed, to her wallowing in the mire. Never anything but a dog. Never anything but a sow - even a washed one. You were never a sheep. I wonder do you know the difference between a sow and a sheep. A sow, even a pure-bred one, when it comes to a mud hole will wallow in it, a sheep even a poor mongrel sheep, when it comes to a mud hole, or even a puddle, will jump over it. He may fail and fall into it, but he will not wallow in it. Peter backslid and denied his Lord, but see him shortly after, weeping his heart out and soon saying: "Lord, Thou knowest all things. Thou knowest I love Thee." This is an example of a true backslider. I have taken up much space and time, and used plain, strong words, because I fear I might delude you into a false peace and carnal security by telling you how to be restored, and you needing regeneration and not restoration.

> As sheep can never become goats; as horses can never become cows; as cats can never become dogs; the children of God can never become the children of Satan. Christians can backslide, but they can never perish.
> Ivor Powell

A Dupe of the Devil

When the unclean spirit is gone out of a man, he walketh through dry places, seeking rest, and findeth none. Then he saith, I will return into my house from whence I came out; and when he is come, he findeth it empty, swept, and garnished. Then goeth he and taketh with himself seven other spirits more wicked than himself, and they enter in and dwell there: and the last state of the man is worse than the first.
Matthew 12 vs. 43- 45

I would a million times rather be a poor, genuine backslider than be the finest, happiest and loudest professing Christian who is only a dupe of the devil. The Lord gives us a word picture, a true description, of a sham backslider, or a man who is self-deceived and devil-deceived. "When the unclean spirit is gone out of a man" (the voluntary withdrawal of the devil is only a temporary one) what does the man do? "He walketh through dry places, seeking rest and finding none." That is, he is dissatisfied and distracted. The means of grace and house of God are "dry places" to him and he has no rest or inward peace. What does the devil say or do? "Then he sayeth, I will return into my house from whence I came out; and when he (the unclean spirit) is come he findeth it empty, swept and garnished. The dupe has cleaned up and furnished himself by reformation and good works, but remember, his heart and life are empty. Now see what the devil does to this poor make-believe backslider. "then goeth he (the devil) and taketh with him seven other spirits more wicked than himself, and they enter in and dwell there; and the last state of that man is worse than the first." What a true and graphic description of a devil-deluded sham backslider.

He falls deepest into hell who falls backwards.
Thomas Watson

Terrible Consequences

Be not deceived; God is not mocked: for whatsoever a man soweth
that shall he also reap.
Galatians 6 vs. 7

The consequences of backsliding are terrible and far-reaching. There is such a flippant, and false way of talking about sin. They tell you when "God forgives He forgets." Quite true, but He takes care you don't forget it or escape the consequences. "Whatsoever a man soweth that shall he also reap." You will reap if you sow, and you'll reap what you sow. You can never sow and not reap. The harvest is always sure and large. For you always reap more than you sow. To hear some talk they give you the impression that when you backslide all you have to do is to feel sorry for it and ask God to forgive you and that is all there is to it. 'The Lord God, merciful and gracious, long-suffering, and abundant in goodness and truth, keeping mercy for thousands, forgiving iniquity and transgression and sin, and that will by no means clear the guilty, visiting the iniquity of the fathers upon the children, and upon the children's children, unto the third and to the fourth generation.' Not only the guilty suffers, but the children's children unto the third and fourth generation. Then talk lightly of backsliding.

It is dangerous to backslide in any degree, for we know not to what it may lead.
C H Spurgeon

A Bitter Harvest

*Thine own wickedness shall correct thee, and thy backslidings shall
reprove thee: know therefore and see that it is an evil thing and bitter,
that thou hast forsaken the Lord thy God, and that my fear is not
in thee, saith the Lord God of hosts.*
Jeremiah 2 vs. 19

Let us ask Esau about it. He sold his birthright for a mess of pottage.
That was all. No vile, vulgar sin. Any hungry man might do it, and
like Esau say, "Behold, I am at the point to die: and what profit shall
this birthright do to me?" So he despised his birthright. Did he feel
sorry about it? Hear his lament, "he cried with a great and exceeding
bitter cry, and said unto his father, Bless me, even me also, O my
father." We are told: 'Ye know how that afterwards, when he would
have inherited the blessing, he was rejected; for he found no place of
repentance, though he sought it carefully with tears"

Consider Abraham, God's friend. God promised him a son and
heir. It seemed long in being fulfilled, so Abraham heeded his wife and
had a son by Hagar. Ishmael was the result. Did God forgive him?
Certainly, but what a harvest Abraham reaped. His family divided.
Hatred and bitterness between them. To this day the result of his
backsliding is seen and felt.

Moses spoke unadvisedly and in anger, although the meekest of
men. It was all over in a very short time, and God forgave him and
restored him to communion again, but he was not allowed to lead
God's people into Caanan or enter it himself. The children of Israel
backslid. They were forgiven, but their bones were bleached in the
desert, and they were not allowed to enter the promised land.

Sin will always take you farther than you want to go and make you
pay more than you want to pay.
Anon

The Sins of the Saints

Remember therefore from whence thou art fallen, and repent, and do the first works; or else I will come unto thee quickly, and will remove thy candlestick out of his place, except thou repent.
Revelation 2 vs. 5

The Ephesian church was born in a revival and was the means of evangelising the whole of Asia. John was a Bishop of that church. They began to slip and drift away from their first love. The Lord visited them 35 years after and said, 'I have somewhat against thee, thou hast left thy first love.' No great or vile sin. He commended them for their zeal and works but warned them and said: 'Remember therefore from whence thou art fallen and repent and do the first works, or else I will come unto thee quickly and remove thy candlestick out of thy place.' They did not repent and they were removed. The church was wiped out and even the ruins of it cannot be found. It is buried under the dust of antiquity, while the ruins of other churches and cities remain to this day. Paul said, "I keep my body under and bring it into subjection; lest that by any means when I have preached to others, I myself should be a castaway." Let me plead with you, my fellow believer, never play with sin, never trifle with it. The consequences are tragic and terrible here and hereafter. "For we must all appear before the judgement seat of Christ, that everyone may receive the things done in his body, according to that he hath done, whether it be good or bad." "Every man's work shall be made manifest; for the day shall declare it, because it shall be revealed by fire: and the fire shall try every man's work of what sort it is. If any man's work abide which he hath built there upon, he shall receive a reward. If any man's work shall be burned, he shall suffer loss, but he himself shall be saved; yet so as by fire." Whatever the loss the backslider has at the judgment seat of Christ, will be an eternal loss. O don't talk about the "sins of the saints," as if they were something to be lightly esteemed. Sin, whether in a believer or a sinner, never goes unpunished.

It may be hard going forward but it is worse going back.
C H Spurgeon

6 SEPTEMBER

Words of Comfort

If we confess our sins, he is faithful and just to forgive us our sins, and to cleanse us from all unrighteousness.
I John 1vs.9

If anyone reading these words is a backslider, that is, you are really a born-again, blood-washed soul and you have slipped and made a mess of your life and testimony and you feel ashamed to come back (and well you might), let me urge you here and now to get down before the Lord, confessing your sin. Be definite about it. Name it. He is, not was or will be, but is, this very minute, faithful and just to forgive us our sins and to cleanse us from all unrighteousness. Then make right, so far as possible, the wrong that was done. You openly backslide, then just as openly return. Don't delay. You will have a big enough harvest to reap without adding to it by continuing to backslide. Take the words of David when he returned from backsliding and make them yours. You will find them in Psalm 51. Get on your knees alone with God as you make David's prayer your prayer. It's a long and hard road back. Never mind how long or hard; you cannot afford not to take it. You may be sure when you sincerely and penitently return, the prodigal son's experience will be yours. "Take with you words, and turn to the Lord: say unto him, Take away all iniquity, and receive us graciously:" He says he will heal your backsliding and love you freely. Then what doth God require of thee? Do justly and love mercy, and walk humbly with thy God. Take Him at his word now!

However deep you fall, you are never out of God's reach.
Anon.

7 SEPTEMBER

Troubles and How to Meet Them

Let not your heart be troubled: ye believe in God believe also in me.
John 14 vs. 1

How different is Christ's teaching about our troubles and how to meet them. Let us consider His teaching here and follow it daily in the midst of our very real troubles. We will hear Him say, 'Let not your heart be troubled'. Be of good cheer! Why?

Twice over He says believe. Believe in God believe also in me. There is nothing we have that the old devil assails so constantly and viciously as our faith. If he can only get us and keep us doubting, well he knows we are 'down and out' and under our troubles instead of above them. Such living brings reproach on Christ and an evil report about Him to the world. The world says: 'If that is all Christ can do for us in trouble He isn't much use.' So we have maligned Christ before the world. Friends, whatever you do don't doubt. Believe and keep on believing. Remember, every doubt is devil born, the brood of hell. It has never solved a problem or helped a troubled one or eased a heavy burden. It is the very reverse. The troubles intensify and increase until the heart breaks and the burdens increase.

How readily and easily some believers let go their faith. The least trouble and they begin to doubt and worry and become melancholy, morbid and miserable, a disgust to all their friends, a disgrace to God and a delight to the old devil. 'Cast not away therefore your confidence which hath great recompense of reward, but hold fast the confidence and the rejoicing of the hope firm to the end.'

Faith in God is never out of season
Anon.

8 SEPTEMBER

Expect Trouble

These things I have spoken unto you, that in me ye might have peace.
In the world ye shall have tribulation: but be of good cheer;
I have overcome the world.
John 16 vs. 33

These words were Christ's farewell words to his disciples ere He died for us men and our sins. They were spoken in the upper room just a few hours before He was betrayed, condemned and crucified on Calvary's hill. Judas Iscariot had left the upper room and Jesus is now gathered with the eleven. Their hearts were sad and troubled as they had never been before. Jesus knew they were troubled. The disciples knew they were in trouble and felt troubled. Jesus never hid the fact of troubles being their portion in this life. He told them in this world ye shall have troubles. They were not to think it strange because they had troubles, and neither are we. There never has been a born again man or woman who has never had troubles and usually plenty of them. There never will be a born again person who will be without trouble. I am not now seeking to define the troubles. I am merely stating the fact, that we cannot evade or escape troubles in this world. Search the pages of history down through the ages and you will not find one who did not have troubles. Search the world over today and you couldn't find a Christian devoid of troubles. I want you to get this fact clearly before you, because you are apt to think we are the only ones who have troubles. No! They are common to all believers. They may be young Christians or old ones, sanctified or unsanctified, but they all have their troubles.

Jesus here did not specify any particular trouble or any particular class of people in trouble. He just recognised the fact and then said "Let not your heart be troubled' He didn't hide the fact from them nor from us. He recognised the fact of troubles being our portion down here.

The grace of God exempts no one from trouble.
J C Ryle

Don't be a Quitter

...and this is the victory that overcometh the world, even our faith.
I John 5 vs. 4

Fight man fight. Hold on to your faith. Don't let it go. It has great recompense of reward, here and hereafter. Earnestly contend for the faith once delivered to the saints. You prayed for faith and the Lord delivered it to you - didn't He? Faith is the gift of God. Well don't give it away by giving way to unbelief when in trouble. Earnestly contend for it. Fight the good fight of FAITH. Don't be a 'slacker' or a 'quitter'. Don't give up believing because of troubles. Any simpleton or fool or coward can do that. Be strong in faith, giving glory to God. Consider Abraham, he believed in hope, he staggered not at the promise of God through unbelief, but was strong in faith.

Faith is the victory that overcomes and if we lose that we are surely defeated, however much willpower we may have or however much we may stiffen our upper lip. You see, God allows troubles to come our way because it is the only way our faith is developed and strengthened. "We are shut up to faith". It is God's way with us still. God shuts us up to faith. Our natures, our circumstances, trials, disappointments, all serve to shut us up and keep us inward until we see that the only way out is Gods way of faith. Moses tried self-effort, by personal influence, even by violence, to bring about the deliverance of his people. God had to shut him up for 40 years in the wilderness before he was prepared for God's work. Paul and Silas were told to preach the Gospel in Europe. They landed and proceeded to Phillipi. They were flogged, they were shut up in prison, their feet were put in stocks. They were shut up to faith. They trusted God. They sang praises to Him in their darkest hour and God wrought deliverance and salvation. John was banished to the Isle of Patmos. He was shut up to faith. Had he not been so shut up to faith, he would never have seen such glorious visions of God.

Doubt breeds distress, but trust means joy in the long run.
C H Spurgeon

Wit's End Corner

They reel to and fro, and stagger like a drunken man,
and are at their wit's end.
Psalm 107 vs. 27

Tell me, friend, are you in trouble, some great trouble - you don't know which way to turn or what to do? You are at wits end corner. Cheer up! You are shut up to faith. Take your trouble in the right way. Commit it to God. Praise Him that He maketh all things work together for good to them that waiteth for Him. Give God a chance to prove His faithfulness in response to your believing.

You see we can never please God, only as we believe. We must believe that God is, not was or will be, but is. And He is a rewarder of them that diligently seek Him; and we can never have victory and peace and freedom from worry and anxiety and corroding care and joy unspeakable and full of glory unless we hold fast our faith. Let us therefore obey God's Word and believe.

Hold on my heart, in thy believing
The steadfast only win the crown,
He who, when stormy winds are heaving,
Parts with his anchor, shall go down;
Be he who Jesus holds through all
Shall stand though heaven and earth shall fall.

Hold out, there comes an end to sorrow;
Hope from the dust shall conquering rise;
The storm foretells a summer's morrow
The cross points on to Paradise.
The father reigneth; cease all doubt
Hold on, my heart hold on-hold out!

True faith is ever connected with hope.
John Calvin

Believe in God

…ye believe in God, believe also in me.
John 14 vs. 1

Isn't this fine? What a delusion and farce it would be if He had told us to believe in ourselves or our circumstances or friends or possessions, when we are in trouble. What use would it be or what good would it do or what comfort could it bring us? Suppose He had said, believe in our believing or prayers or faith or praying. It would have been just as useless and hopeless. Faith in itself is nothing; it is its object that determines its nature and character. Believe in God. What assurance and comfort this brings. God is from everlasting to everlasting the same. The same in His wisdom, love, power and ability to deliver His people out of their troubles, not from their troubles.

We will always have troubles, but He can and will deliver us out of them all. He hasn't changed. He says - 'I change not'. What a reputation He has built up along this line through the ages. Read about Abraham, Isaac, Jacob, Moses, Elijah, David and time would fail to tell about all the others who have been delivered. Let us consider our own past lives. How often He has come to our help and deliverance, Hallelujah! He is a very present help, not an absent one in the time of trouble.

Is there any trouble too great or peculiar that He cannot deliver us out of? What a long and varied experience He has had in dealing with His troubled children. He is an expert, a specialist, at this sort of work.

Let's keep our chins up and our knees down – we're on the victory side!
Alan Redpath

How are we to know God?

...he that hath seen me hath seen the Father...
John 14 vs. 9

How are we to know God? He seems so far away and above us - so great, so mysterious. Philip's cry is ours today: "Shew us the Father, and it sufficeth us." Listen to Jesus' answer to this cry of Philip. "Have I been so long time with you, and yet hast thou not known me, Philip? he that hath seen me hath seen the Father;" Do you want to know what God is like, how He acts and feels towards us? Look at Jesus as He is revealed in the Gospels. What did Jesus do? How did Jesus act? How did He feel? What was He like? Jesus is God. As you follow Him through His life, revealed in His word, you see God manifest in the flesh. Christ is the express image of God. What Jesus did, God is like that: What Jesus said, that is God speaking. Don't you see? God became flesh and dwelt amongst us. That is how and why we can know God and do know God. Doesn't this make it easy to believe in God? Believe in Me says Jesus. Believe in God. If Jesus is not God of very God, how could we ever know God or believe in Him in our troubles? So, dear troubled soul, make God your refuge and a present help in your time of trouble. He understands and feels for us. Nearer and dearer He could not be. He is nigh thee. Cast your care upon Him. What fools we are to try and weather our storms alone, when He is by our side. All wise, all loving, all-powerful and willing to deliver us in our troubles and out of them.

The characteristics of God Almighty are mirrored for us in Jesus Christ. Therefore if we want to know what God is like we must study Jesus Christ.
Oswald Chambers

13 SEPTEMBER

Heaven – Nearer and Dearer

In my Father's house are many mansions: if it were not so, I would have told you. I go to prepare a place for you.
John 14 vs. 2

If in this life only we have hope we are of all men most miserable. Glory to God! There is a land that is fairer than day. Our spirits will sorrow no more or sigh for the blessing of rest. Trouble, like sin, has never entered there. Life there is an untroubled sea. There are no furrowed brows or heavy hearts or troubled souls in that land of many mansions. It's our Father's house. This is the rest that remaineth for the people of God. Mind you, there are times when it is hard to believe in heaven. I remember sitting beside the body of a loved one, suddenly taken away. There in my sore sorrow, bewildered, stunned, numb, Satan whispered in the ear of my soul, "Where is your loved one now? Are you sure that there is a hereafter? Sure there is a heaven? Aye?" I was too numbed to answer. I could neither believe nor doubt, let alone answer his question. Right there and then Jesus spoke these words to my heart, 'If it were not so I would have told you." It was as real to me at that moment as if He had been visibly there and had audibly spoken. What deliverance out of my sore trouble was my believing in heaven. Don't doubt the fact. There is such a place prepared for every born again one and only for born again ones.

You are nearer Heaven right now dear troubled one, than you have ever been before. How soon we may be called to go there. Then all our troubles will be over and forever. Then we will understand why we were so sorely and constantly troubled. We will know then that all the way He led was good and we will sing with Samuel Rutherford:-

With mercy and with judgment my web of time He wove
And aye the dews of sorrow were lustered by His love.

All the places in heaven and hell are reserved.
Anon.

Jesus is Coming Back Again

...I will come again and receive you unto myself...
John 14 vs. 3

We are also to believe Jesus is coming back again. He said, "Let not your heart be troubled......I will come again" What a comforting hope this is to our troubled souls. Comfort one another with these words - what words? "The Lord Himself shall descend from heaven ... the dead in Christ shall rise first and we which are alive and remain shall be caught up together with them to meet our Lord in the air." When will this happen? "In a moment, in the twinkling of an eye." As sudden and as sure as that. Halleluujah! The Lord has had many ways of delivering us out of our troubles in the past, wonderful ways of deliverance this will be, and delivered forever. Just think as you read this, in a moment, in the twinkling of an eye, we shall be caught up. Tell me: could you get anything that should comfort our troubled hearts like this glorious fact, the fact of His return. Heaven may seem very far ahead of us. We are young, strong and healthy but in terrible trouble, and heaven seems far off, but when we consider that any moment, not year month or week, but moment - this moment, you may be caught up out of all your troubles and forever, surely we can obey His injunction, "Let not your be troubled" This is no quack remedy - it is a sure cure. Hold it fast troubled one, there is great recompense of reward in doing so. Believe He is coming again and coming again soon. Don't let Satan rob you of this comforting hope in the midst of your troubles.

Heaven will not fully be heaven to Christ till he has all His redeemed with Himself.
A W Pink

The Comforter - The Holy Ghost

And I will pray the Father, and he shall give you another Comforter, that he
may abide with you for ever;
John 14 vs. 16

How many comfortless believers there are today. Like the Ephesian converts, they can say, "we have not so much as heard whether there be any Holy Ghost." It is a wilful ignorance for this is the dispensation of the Holy Spirit. It is one thing to have the Holy Spirit, as all believers have, it is quite another thing for Him to have you. It is one thing to be born again of the Spirit, it is quite another thing to be baptised with the Spirit and continually being filled with the Spirit. Until we are fully yielded and receive by faith the Holy Spirit, troubles will overwhelm us and our hearts will be sorely troubled. But when we receive Him in His fullness, He makes God in Christ a blessed, living reality in our hearts. Heaven is near and dear; His coming again is a purifying, comforting hope. It is His work to make what is ours in Christ judicially ours in reality and experience. He conveys to us what is ours already in Christ. Have you received Him since you believed? There is no substitute for the Holy Ghost. You may try everything and anything to help you in your troubles, but you will remain comfortless. He alone is the Comforter. Believe in Him. Receive Him. Walk in the Spirit, day and daily and you will find comfort and sweet rest in the midst of your troubles and trials.

The Holy Spirit may be had for the asking.
R B Kuiper

16 SEPTEMBER

Give Him a Chance

...Let not your heart be troubled, neither let it be afraid.
John 14 vs. 27

Let us try this recipe of our Lord Jesus for troubles. Give Him a chance. It works and never fails. Believe in God, the God we see when we see Christ. Believe in heaven, the homeland of the soul and the home of rest. Believe He is coming again at any moment - this moment. Believe in the comforter - the comforting one, and see what will become of your troubles and what you will do with them and make of them. I am not going to try and show you why troubles are allowed and why we cannot escape them; maybe some future time I will do that. What I am at present concerned about is, that we may know and not think it strange because troubles come and that we may heed this exhortation of Christ and let not our hearts be troubled, by believing and keeping on believing what He taught.

> Faith in the heart of a Christian is like the salt that was thrown into the corrupt fountain, that made the waters good and the barren land fruitful.
> John Bunyan

Unlike other Men

…. I shall become weak, and be like any other man.
Judges 16 vs. 17

It's queer the notions people have about men and incidents in the Bible. Many think Absalom was hung in a tree by his hair. The Bible says '…his head caught hold of the oak…' Evidently when riding through the woods, he was caught in a fork of the tree. You hear about Elijah going up in a chariot of fire, whereas the Bible says, '…and Elijah went up by a whirlwind into heaven.' So about Samson. How often we see pictures of him with tremendous body and finely developed muscles, bearing the gates of Gaza on his shoulders or leaning on the pillars and destroying their temple at his death, until it is a common delusion that Samson's strength lay in his body and in it's development. So common in fact has this idea become, that when we say how strong someone is, we say, 'he is a veritable Samson'. We see wrestlers, heavy weight lifters, called by this name. Many Christians are carried away by the same delusion. Samson knew different to all this and when urged by Delilah to reveal the secret of his strength he told her. To her he was like any other man in his appearance and daily life but there were occasions when he became different and performed unusual deeds and this is what made him 'unlike any other man' in the Philistines' eyes and hers. When the secret was discovered by her and them, Samson became 'like any other man' and their plaything and object of their scorn. Notice how frequently, in the account of his life in Judges, we read such words as: '…and the Spirit of the Lord began to move him,' 13;25; 'And the Spirit of the Lord came mightily upon him,' 14:6; '…and the Spirit of the Lord came mightily upon him..' 15:14. Here is the open secret of his great strength and remarkable deeds. Apart from the Holy Spirits power 'he was weak like any other man'. It was when he became like any other man God's name was dishonoured and His cause hindered.

Christian friends, this is the danger of all our lives 'becoming like any other man'. We are 'chosen' people. We are to be 'peculiar' 'holy' 'separated' 'unblameable' 'jealous of good works'. Our lives are to be victorious and triumphant. We are to be famed for accomplishing possibilities, and doing wonders for God in our daily lives, showing to the world a life radiant with peace that passeth all understanding and a joy unspeakable and full of glory; freedom from all care and anxiety in the midst of distressing and disturbing circumstances and thronging duties; finding Christ a satisfying portion so that we can sing out of a glad experience -

O Christ in Thee my soul hath found,
And found in thee alone
The peace, the joy I sought so long,
The bliss till now unknown.

Such lives as these are what the Lord desires and requires, thank God that He can enable us to live such every day. The sad and God dishonouring thing is that so many are living lives 'like any other man'.

> If thou wilt fly from God, the devil will lend thee both spurs and a horse.
> Thomas Adams

Samson - A Warning to Us All

...And he wist not that the Lord was departed from him.
Judges 16 vs. 20

It is sad to read of how Samson came to the time and place where 'He wist not that the Lord was departed from him'. And how many are at the same plight today and are living like any other man. What was the cause of Samson's loss?

1. Presumtion

He thought because that he was saved and had been endued and used by God that he was safe and free to play with sin and temptation. Friends, hear me. It doesn't matter how long we have been saved or how wonderful the experience of our Spirit baptism has been, or how we may have been used of God; we can lose all, if we dare to trifle with the temptation of sin. The most common sin amongst Gods people today is the sin of presumption. There is no security for any believer except as he abides in Christ and Christ abides in him. There is no such thing as a 'once for all faith'. It is whosoever believeth keeps on believing. 'Simply trusting every day'. 'Trusting as the moments fly'. There is no such thing as a 'once for all' fullness of the Spirit. It is being filled. There is no such thing as a 'once for all cleansing'. It is only as we walk in the light that the blood keeps on cleansing – where there is no walking there is no cleansing Young man! Don't trifle with temptation and sin. The presumption will make you weak and like any other man.

2. Compromise

Samson entered into an unholy union with God's enemies. So many today are robbed of their spiritual power in the same way. Marrying an unconverted one, or joining lodges and clubs. Keeping company with ungodly worldlings, even though they are nominal Christians or church members. Joining a church, where the Book and Blood are denied or misinterpreted because it is the church of our family or for some social or business gain. Wherever there is compromise there is sure disaster. God's call is 'Wherefore come out from among them, and be ye separate' and where we fail to live uncompromising lives we lose our power and become 'like any other man.'

3. Sin

If ever there was a day when even Christians trifled with sin, excused sin, apologized for sin, it is today. And are we surprised they are powerless or 'like any other man?' God never forgives sin. God forgives sinners, but hates sin. God will destroy sin, but will never condone sin, whether in a believer or unbeliever. Let Samson be a warning to us all always to abhor evil, to flee youthful lusts, to forsake all sin.

Collapse in the Christian life is seldom a blow out. It is usually a slow leak.
Paul E Little

The Consequences of Compromise

But the Philistines took him, and put out his eyes, and brought him down to Gaza, and bound him with fetters of brass; and he did grind in the prison house.
Judges 16 vs. 21

Let us look briefly at the consequences of Samson's presumptuous compromise with sin. Some one has described the disastrous circumstances in these words.

Blind. The enemy put his eyes out. It is pathetic when you hear a Christian say "I don't see any harm in a dance or smoking tobacco". Why? They have been blinded by their own actions. Black is not black, and white is not white, they become grey when we allow presumption, compromise and sin. We lose the unsaved humanity. We see things 'as other men' and cease to live with eternity's values in view.

Bind. Samson lost his liberty and became their slave and plaything. So will we. We will become slaves to sin, to conventionality, to the fear of man, and become the plaything of the world, flesh and the devil, and earn the disgust and contempt of the ungodly.

Grind. O how many are on the devils treadmill. They go to church, but there is no joy or blessing. Ministers preaching with no enthusiasm or power. Sunday school teachers teaching, and feeling it such a tiresome drudgery. The faith of so many ceasing to fascinate, merely a bare fact. O the drudgery of it all. The salt has lost its savour. Life becomes uninteresting and monotonous as they grind out their existence. No song. No shout of triumph in their lives. No new conquests for Christ. Grind. Grind. Grind. Fruitless toil. Joyless service. Toiling on. Poor things. May the story of this man's life ever urge us on to "work out our salvation with fear and trembling"

If we know anything of true saving religion, let us ever beware of the beginning of backsliding.
J C Ryle

Restoration

Howbeit the hair of his head began to grow again after he was shaven.
Judges 16 vs. 22

If you have become like 'any other man' and lost out, is there any hope of recovery? Thank God there is. We read about Samson, "The hair of his head began to grow again". So may yours. God is able to restore you. But there must be honest dealing with God about the cause or causes of your sad experience. Confess humbly and fully. Renounce honestly and sincerely, and believe instantly and firmly that you are forgiven and cleansed, and receive His Holy Spirit to fill you to the uttermost, and you will again enjoy the experience of the blessedness you once had.

Come in, come in, Holy Spirit.
Thy work of great blessing begin
By faith I lay hold of the promise
And claim complete victory o'er sin.

You're probably more prepared to serve God after failure and restoration, than perhaps at any other time in your life.
Adrian Rogers

Union with Christ

I am the vine, ye are the branches…
John 15 vs. 5

When Christ would teach His disciples about their union with Him (and teach us today), He told them this parable or story of the vine and the branches. He didn't use some illustration they could not understand, or had never heard about. What a lesson here for preachers; Sunday school teachers; and Christian workers. His illustrations were plain and practical. When he would teach them about false doctrine He told them about leaven and bread. When He would teach humility, He placed a little child before them. When He would teach them about Gods care for His own, He told them about a common sparrow and how God attended the funeral of every dead sparrow. Also His care for His own was so wonderful that the very hairs of our head were all numbered - not counted, but numbered. He talked about sheep, fish, and flowers of the field. Also about the birds - not birds of the aviary, but birds of the air. So when He would teach them and us about union with Him, he illustrates it by the parable, or illustration of the vine and the branches. We have all heard about, and most of us seen, a vine and its branches. May we learn the lesson He teaches. If we learn this lesson and put it into practice, it will revolutionize our life and service. The parable is so simple, and yet so rich in its teaching that it gives us the best and most complete illustration of the meaning of our Lord's command and the union to which He invites us. This is the life of victorious rest and power. So many truly born again ones are living lives of struggle, resolution, and restlessness, instead of living as a branch in the vine.

What a simple thing it is to be the branch of the vine! The branch grows out of the vine, and there it lives and grows, and in due time bears fruit. It has no responsibility except to receive from the root system sap and nourishment. If we only by the Holy Spirit knew and realised our union with Christ, our lives and labours would be like a new experience, uniting us to Jesus as nothing else can.

Union with Christ is a unique emphasis among the world's religions.
John R W Scott

A Living Union

I am the vine, ye are the branches. He that abideth in me, and I in him, the
same bringeth forth much fruit: for without me ye can do nothing.
John 15 vs. 5

The connection between the vine and the branch is a living one. No
external or temporary union will suffice. No work of man can effect it.
The branch is such only by the Creator's own work, in virtue of which
the sap, the fatness, the fruitfulness of the vine communicate
themselves to the branch. And just so it is with the believer too. His
union with Christ is no work of human wisdom or human will, but an
act of God, by which the closest and most complete life-union is
effected between Christ and the believer. This is no structural union
merely. I may have lost a limb and medical skill may have provided
me with an artificial one. It may be a most ingenious device, but in
spite of all its ingenuity and usefulness it is not a living member of my
body. It is a dead union. The building and the foundation are united,
but it is a mere structural union. The one may, and can, exist without
the other. Separate a limb from the body and the limb dies, because it
is a living union. "Know ye not that your bodies are members of
Christ?"

"And hath put all things under his feet and gave him to be head
over all things to the church, which is his body, the fullness of him that
filleth all in all."

As the members of the human body are united in the head, the
source of their activity and the power that controls their movements,
so all believers are members of an invisible body, whose head is Christ.
The same Spirit that dwelt, and still dwells, in Christ, becomes the life
of the believer; in the unity of that one Spirit and the fellowship of the
same life that is in Christ, he is one with Him. As between the vine and
the branch, it is the life union that makes them one. O may this truth
lay hold of us. Christ is inside, not outside.

> Before there can be communion, there must be union. Union is the
> acceptance of Christ and communion continues by reliance on
> Christ.
> Stephen Olford

An Indispensible Union

I am the vine, ye are the branches. He that abideth in me, and I in him, the same bringeth forth much fruit: for without me ye can do nothing.
John 15 vs. 5

What good would a vine be without branches? What good would branches be without a vine? You must have a vine if you are to have fruit and you must have branches to bear the fruit. You never saw, or heard, of a vine without branches bearing fruit, and you never heard or saw branches bearing fruit and not joined to the vine. Such is the wonderful condescension of the grace of Christ, that just as His people are dependent on Him, He has made Himself dependent on them. Without His disciples He cannot bless the world. Marvel not. It is His own appointment: and this is the high honour to which He has called His redeemed ones, that as indispensable as He is to them in heaven, that from Him there fruit may be found. So indispensable are they to Him on earth, that through them His fruit may be found. As truly as we need Christ in Heaven to represent us before a Holy God, so He needs us on earth to represent and present Him before an ungodly world. There is another blessed truth here. As neither branch nor vine is anything without the other, that is, all the vine possesses belongs to the branch and all the branch possesses belongs to the vine, Christ has nothing that isn't ours, as born again ones. We are heirs and joint-heirs with Christ. There is no doubt about this and we have the right to draw on all Christ's resources for our every need. Yet how many of us are living like mendicants when we aught to be living like millionaires: living like paupers instead of princes. I believe this is so largely because of our ignorance of our union with Christ, and the consequences or blessings of the union. I wonder dear friend is all we have and are, wholly and unreservedly, yielded up to Him day and daily? Are we withholding anything from Him, and thus hindering His purposes of grace for us and for others through us? As He is wholly ours, let us be wholly His.

Unless you live in Christ you are dead to God.
Rowland Hill

The Object of this Union (I)

That ye might walk worthy of the Lord unto all pleasing, being
fruitful in every good work...
Colossians 1 vs. 10

The Lord clearly and repeatedly tells us the object of our union with Him. It is fruit (John 15 vs.2), more fruit (vs. 2) and much fruit (vs. 5,8). We are to be fruitful in three spheres:

1. The Sphere of Life

As we are filled and being filled with the Spirit we are to bear fruit; more fruit; and much fruit in love, joy peace, longsuffering, gentleness, goodness, faithfulness, meekness and temperance.   As these graces of the Spirit increase and abound in our lives what a representation Christ has in the midst of an evil and adulterous generation.

2. The Sphere of Labour

We are to bear fruit, more fruit, and much fruit in labours. It does not say we are to be successful in every good work. We may have success as well as fruit, but many a worker is successful and not fruitful. Success is determined by either genius, or circumstances or both, but fruit, more fruit and much fruit, is the outcome only of a life in union with Christ. This explains why some workers are very successful, but not fruitful. They may draw large crowds and win many souls, but their lives are anything but consistent. If we are really united to Christ and abide in Him, our lives as well as our labours will be fruitful.

It is deeply important for us to recognise that the fruit is the outflow
of our union with Christ.
A. W. Pink

The Object of this Union (II)

...ye shall ask what ye will, and it shall be done unto you. Herein is my father glorified, that ye bear much fruit; ...
John 15 vs. 7-8

Then we are to be fruitful in **The Sphere of Prayer**.

How many are in this sphere. They rarely, if ever, know of definite answers to prayer. They pray and pray but nothing happens, and yet we are to bear fruit, more fruit, much fruit, in our prayer life, and if we are really united to Christ and abiding in Him, we cannot help being fruitful in our prayer life. Let me close with these solemn words of Christ concerning a branch that is unfruitful. "Every branch that beareth not (i.e. does not keep on bearing) fruit he taketh away:" (15:2) "If a man abide not in me, he is cast forth as a branch, and is withered; and men gather them and cast them into the fire, and they are burned."(15:6). I do not attempt to explain these solemn words of our Lord. It surely shakes this flippant and carnal and presumptuous belief in a security that shows no evidence of a vital union with Christ in fruit, more fruit and much fruit in the spheres of life, labour and prayer. To those who are fruitful branches and yet are suffering in body through sickness, or far sorer suffering, of misunderstanding, misrepresentation, and persecution, let these comforting words of Christ bring you comfort and even joy in the midst of all the suffering. "Every branch that beareth (i.e. Keeps on bearing fruit) he purgeth it." Why? "that it may bring forth more fruit." (15:2) The pruning knife the Lord uses may be an enemy, sickness or sorrow, or Satan: never mind, the knife is in His hand and He uses it with loving, wise skill to produce more fruit in our lives. "Enemies may seek to injure, Satan all his arts employ. God will turn what seeks to harm me into everlasting joy" "...I live; yet not I, but Christ liveth in me" Let us maintain this union by continual surrender and obedience, so our lives will be fruitful and well pleasing to God.

> I live in the spirit of prayer. I pray as I walk about, when I lie down and when I rise up. And the answers are always coming.
> George Muller

26 SEPTEMBER

Following Afar Off

But Peter followed him afar off...
Matthew 26 vs. 58

There is one astounding peculiarity about the Bible's biography and that is, it not only tells the truth, but it tells all the truth about the men whose lives it portrays - their good qualities and their bad ones; the weaknesses as well as the strengths of their characters. Abraham is called the - not 'a' but the - friend of God. Yet we find him in a land other than the land of promise, lying to an ungodly king about his wife. Moses was the meekest of men, and we find him in anger, speaking and acting unadvisedly. David, a man after God's own heart, yet guilty of adultery and murder. Here we have Peter, one of Christ's most intimate disciples, cursing and swearing that he never knew Christ, and when Jesus needed a friend most we find him 'following afar off". How different man-written biographies are. They never mention the failures, weaknesses or wickedness of the characters; if they do make mention of them they do so in such a way as to either make light of their misdeeds or excuse them for being guilty of them. When God writes our biography He writes the truth, and all the truth and nothing but the truth about us. Our good qualities and evil propensities, our successes and our failures, will all be faithfully recorded. That is always the difference between a Divine biography and a human biography. So here we have this fact stated about Peter: "He followed him afar off". It is not only recorded by Matthew, but also by Mark, Luke and John. I am sure Peter could have wished it had been forgotten, but it is four times recorded to warn us about being guilty of the same disgraceful conduct, and if we are guilty of it, to encourage us to renounce it and return to close fellowship with Christ.

The pleasures of being forgiven are as superior to the pleasures of an unforgiven man as heaven is higher than hell.
Robert Murray McCheyne

Peter's Weakest Hour

But he began to curse and to swear, saying, I know not this
man of whom ye speak.
Mark 14 vs. 71

Here we have Peter, at his weakest hour. Set before us without a word of wonder, blame or excuse. They must surely have wondered why Peter was ever guilty of such conduct. He had so vehemently confessed Christ, and declared his love and loyalty to Christ. "Let all forsake Thee; I won't - I will die for Thee." Here he is a distant disciple following afar off. Let us not be too hard on Peter. How many of us have been guilty of the very same conduct; maybe the most of us at one time or another. "Those who live in glass houses shouldn't throw stones" is an old and wise proverb. Jesus said: "He that is without sin among you, let him cast the first stone" I don't wonder when I see one who once followed Christ closely and constantly, now following afar off, for I know my own heart and its deceitful nature, and the world we are living in with its subtle and alluring descriptions and attractions. What I do wonder at is such a one continuing following afar off. After all the experiences, so satisfying and sustaining, they had enjoyed in following Christ lovingly and closely, you would think they never could continue following afar off. Surely the memory of their own professions of love and loyalty to Christ, and now the loneliness of Jesus, should appeal to their heroism and loyalty, and constrain them to repent and return to close fellowship again. Surely friend if you, if you are following afar off, such memories must make you feel mean and despicable in your own eyes. When you consider His love for you and all He has done and is doing for you, doesn't He deserve better treatment at your hands. Did He ever wrong you? Did He ever forsake you or fail you? Did He ever not keep His word to you? What evil hath He done? You know He has always been loving and true. Why have you turned away from Him, and now follow Him afar off?

When is your life more fragrant than when the kiss of forgiveness is most fresh upon your cheek.
Al Martin

Coldness

And the Lord turned, and looked upon Peter. And Peter remembered the word of the Lord, how he had said unto him, Before the cock crow, thou shalt deny me thrice. And Peter went out, and wept bitterly. And the men that held Jesus mocked him, and smote him.
Luke 22 vs. 61-63

Surely He doesn't deserve such cruel coldness from you. They put a crown of thorns upon His head. They smote Him on the face until it was marred. They spat on His face. They scourged His back until it was one bruise. They did all this to Him. You never read about Him making any sign of hurt, but when Peter denied Him with oaths and cursing, He turned and looked at Peter. That act of Peter cut Him to the heart as nothing else did or could do.

Especially after all He has done for you and been to you. Let the memory of all this not only make you feel ashamed of yourself but constrain you with tears and words of confession to forsake such conduct here and now.

I love Thee because Thou hast first loved me,
And purchased my pardon on Calvary's tree.
I love Thee for wearing the thorns on thy brow,
If ever I loved Thee, my Jesus 'tis now.
William Ralph Featherston

A Strong Weakness

Watch and pray, that ye enter not into temptation: the spirit indeed is willing, but the flesh is weak.
Matthew 26 vs. 41

Let us remember that this following afar off is not an accident of a moment or some sudden crisis or experience. Oh no, it is the outcome of a gradual process It is caused by a variety of things before we settle down to a life of following afar off. Consider Peter's experience, as revealed in the Gospels, which resulted in his following afar off. There was first his "self confidence". Listen. Jesus said "All ye shall be offended because of me this night." But Peter said unto Him "Though all men shall be offended because of thee, yet will I never be offended". "Lord, I am ready to go with thee, both into prison and to death." Poor Peter! Ignorant of his weakness in spite of Christ's warnings. It was a strong weakness in Peter. He could understand every disciple being offended, but he was cocksure he would never be offended because of Christ. Christ's warning was unheeded. In fact, he felt so sure of himself that he was sure Christ was making a mistake when He said he would deny Him ere sunrise. It's a lesson we all must learn. "The arm of flesh will fail you. Ye dare not trust your own." Again there was "carelessness and prayerlessness" "And he cometh unto the disciples, and findeth them asleep, and saith unto Peter (he never mentioned any other disciple): "What, could ye not watch with me one hour?" Watch and pray! The very time he should have been on the alert and praying, he was asleep. His self-confidence led him to a careless, prayerless condition. He could do without constant watchfulness and prayer. Others might need care and prayer, but not him. Haven't we felt the same temptation regarding our early morning prayer and Bible reading, and our regular attendance on the means of grace every Sunday and careful endeavour to remember to keep the Lords Day holy? Take heed friend, the neglect of this will eventually lead to following afar off. You cannot escape the consequences.

A man that extols himself is a fool and an idiot.
John Calvin

Dishonourable Conduct

...Then all the disciples forsook him, and fled.
Matthew 26 vs. 56

Such conduct on the part of any true follower of Christ is not honourable. It is dishonourable. They vowed that they would follow Christ all the way. How often they sang, "I'll go with Him through the judgement" "I'll go with Him through the garden," "I'll go with Him all the way," "Where He may lead me I will go," etc., and now you find them following afar off. They don't want to suffer the offence of the cross. It may cost them too much. How unreasonable all this is. When you consider all they owe to Christ. Their salvation, forgiveness of their sins, peace with God, no condemnation, sanctification and satisfaction, eternal life, in fact, blessed with every spiritual blessing in Christ. How ridiculously foolish is it for them to forsake Christ. They have everything to loose and nothing worthwhile to gain by doing so. You never met, or heard of, or saw a contented, happy, comfortable follower of Christ, who was following afar off. Never! Once they have become a follower of Christ they are forever spoiled for following anyone or anything else. Look at their uncomfortable condition for a moment. They are despised by the ungodly; they know how contemptable their conduct is, and despise them accordingly, so they are uncomfortable in their company. They are a reproach to the cause of Christ. They are bringing His name and cause into disgrace. Worst of all, from their own personal consideration they are a disgust to themselves. However severe and hard another may treat them or speak about them, it is as nothing compared to all they say about and to themselves, concerning their treatment of Jesus. They secretly loathe and abhor themselves. They daily vex themselves. Like Peter they weep bitterly. You might as well expect to discover a truthful liar or an honest thief, or a sober drunkard, or a virtuous harlot, as find a happy, comfortable and contented follower of Christ who is following Him afar off.

Unsaintly saints are the tragedy of Christianity.
A W Tozer

OCTOBER

1 ◆ The Danger

2 ◆ You Cannot Hide It

3 ◆ A Healthy Christian

4 ◆ An Uncertain Sound

5 ◆ A Jealous God

6 ◆ What Are We To Do?

7 ◆ Prominent or Pre-eminent

8 ◆ The Snare of Success

9 ◆ Me First

10 ◆ The Cost of Discipleship

11 ◆ God is Jealous of His Word

12 ◆ Humour in the Pulpit

13 ◆ God's Glory

14 ◆ No Condemnation

15 ◆ Half-Baked Christians

16 ◆ Not an Imitation

17 ◆ Obedient Scholars

18 ◆ Satisfied

19 ◆ Set Free

20 ◆ Something to Glory In

21 ◆ The Means is not the End

22 ◆ The Payment of Debts

23 ◆ To Love Less

24 ◆ Unclaimed Deposits

25 ◆ We are a Gospel

26 ◆ An Uncommon Christian

27 ◆ Am I or Am I Not?

28 ◆ Assurance

29 ◆ Pentecost is Now

30 ◆ A Lamp and a Light

31 ◆ A Passion for Souls

The Danger

Blessed is the man that walketh not in the counsel of the ungodly, nor standeth in the way of sinners, nor sitteth in the seat of the scornful.
Psalm 1 vs. 1

Let us also consider the anger as well as the disgrace and discomfort, of one who is following Him afar off. "And when they had kindled a fire in the midst of the hall, and were set down together, Peter sat down among them." "And the servants and officers stood there, who had made a fire of coals; for it was cold: and they warmed themselves: and Peter stood with them, and warmed himself." "A damsel came unto him, saying, Thou also wast with Jesus of Galilee. But he denied before them all, saying, 'I know not, neither understand I what thou sayest." Another maid said unto him 'This man was also with him.' And again he denied with an oath, 'I do not know the man'. They that stood by said to Peter: "Surely thou art one of them: for thou art a Galilaean, and thy speech betrayeth thee' Then began he to curse and to swear saying 'I know not this man of whom ye speak'. One of the servants of the high priest, being his kinsman whose ear Peter cut off, saith: "Did not I see thee in the garden with Him?" Peter denied again. Friend! Don't you see what a dangerous thing it is for a follower of Christ to follow Him afar off? What a fix it got Peter in! What a set of circumstances Peter was brought into by following afar off! It was well nigh impossible for Peter to do anything else but deny Christ under such circumstances. This following afar off is truly a dangerous and disastrous thing. It is a costly thing. Talk about the cost of closely following Christ. It is as nothing compared to the cost of following afar off. See the company and circumstances you are brought into by following afar off. Why it makes it well nigh impossible for you to do anything else but deny Christ.

Keep such company as God keeps.
Anon.

2 OCTOBER

You Cannot Hide It

Nevertheless I have somewhat against thee,
because thou hast left thy first love.
Revelation 2 vs. 4

Try as you may you cannot hide the fact when you are following afar off. Your conduct and speech will betray you. You will forsake your "first love" Not forsake your love for Christ. Oh no. But you will forsake your "first love." Peter continued to follow, but he followed "afar off". You continue to love Christ, but all the warmth and emotion and enthusiasm are almost all gone. You can sing, "My Jesus I love Thee" as cold and correct as a sinner. No thrill, no tears or gratitude. You can partake of the Communion, and never a thrill or throb in the heart. You serve out of a sense of duty and not devotion. Everyone knows you are following Him afar off. You are ashamed of Christ. You are annoyed if someone almost compels you to confess Christ. You try to justify your attitude by saying you don't believe in testimony meetings or open and constant confession of Christ, but you are only confessing the fact that you are following him afar off. Your daily conduct is an indication. If anyone dares to rebuke you, you say it is nobody's business how you live; what you are really saying is " I am following Him afar off." You never lead a soul to Christ or even try to do so. We have become very orthodox and fundamental, very careful about order and decorum. Any breach of church order and ritual jars us severely. The fact that sinners are not converted in the service and by our preaching does not jar us. Why? Because we are following Him afar off. Friend! You cannot hide it. This following afar off will compel you to betray your condition before God and men. You cannot evade or escape the consequences of such following.

Though Christians be not kept altogether from falling, yet they are
kept from falling altogether.
William Secker

A Healthy Christian

Beloved, I wish above all things that thou mayest prosper and be in health,
even as thy soul prospereth.
III John vs. 2

Isn't it very strange how many delivered ones are frightened of holiness? The very mention of the word fills them with fear, and even anger. Many are frightened because they have been deceived by frauds and shams. Because you have been defrauded by a counterfeit £5 note, you don't turn down every £5 note. The very fact that there are counterfeits is proof that there is a genuine one somewhere, and it is worthwhile. You would not counterfeit something that is not worthwhile. So if you can show me a sham holiness believer, that is sure proof there is a genuine one somewhere. Others are frightened because of ignorance. They don't know the meaning of holiness. They never have searched their Bibles to see what is meant by holiness. The word is derived from a root, 'halig,' meaning health. So when we talk about the condition of our bodies, we say they are healthy. When we speak about the condition of the soul, we say it is holy. I am as correct in saying my body is holy and my soul healthy, as saying my soul is holy and my body healthy. So a holy Christian is a healthy Christian. Sin is a disease, and sinning is the manifestation of it. Are you afraid? Certainly not! We need not fear of being holy. In fact, we should fear not to be holy, for without holiness no man shall see the Lord. The pure of heart, the holy, they see God.

What health is to the heart, that holiness is to the soul.
John Flavel

An Uncertain Sound

For if the trumpet give an uncertain sound,
who shall prepare himself to the battle?
I Corinthians 14 vs. 8.

Proclaim God's word with boldness. William could say with Paul "For if the trumpet give an uncertain sound, who shall prepare himself to the battle." He made sure his message was not muted or misunderstood. He preached in the language of the farm labourer and the shipyard worker. His was the vocabulary of the street. No one needed a dictionary to understand his message. In the first nights of his missions William usually preached to the Christians, exposing the sins of pride, hypocrisy, prayerlessness, worldliness and defective consecration. He insisted upon Christians putting things right with one another and making restitution whenever possible. He had no time for half-baked believers. He was fully committed to the authority and infallibility of the word of God. At a time when the poison of modernism was making inroads, he spoke out faithfully and fervently in the defence of the Scriptures of Truth. George Whitefield wrote, "I love those that thunder out the word. The Christian world is in a deep sleep. Nothing but a loud voice can awaken them out of it." Truly Whitefield would have approved of William Patteson Nicholson's trumpet tones.

It is the mark of a prophet to make men face sin.
Vance Havner

5 OCTOBER

A Jealous God

For thou shalt worship no other god: for the Lord,
whose name is Jealous, is a jealous God:
Exodus 34 vs. 14

There is no more striking example of the anthropomorphic way of speaking of God so characteristic of the Old Testament, than this frequent ascription to Him of jealousy, associated as that word is in our minds with an evil meaning. But when we understand the meaning of the word, it will remove from our minds the notion of evil. There is a right and wrong jealousy. Whether it is a vice or a virtue depends on why we are boiling. Various meanings are given for virtuous jealousy. Jealousy is 'uneasiness which arises from fear that a rival may rob us of the affections of one whom we love.' Jealousy in a husband or wife is 'the energetic assertion of an exclusive right.' Jealousy is 'but the anger and pain of insulted love.' Jealousy is 'love on fire'.

In all these senses God is a jealous God. He is ever uneasy when He fears a rival in our hearts, and He energetically asserts himself and demands an exclusive right. He feels pained and angered because His love is being insulted. It takes all these meanings to give us an adequate conception of the meaning of our text, "The Lord, whose name is Jealous, is a jealous God".

> God as a jealous God, is filled with a burning desire for our holiness, for our righteousness, for our goodness.
> Donald Grey Barnhouse

6 OCTOBER

What are we to Do?

*Brethren, I count not myself to have apprehended: but this one thing
I do, forgetting those things which are behind, and reaching
forth unto those things which are before.*
Philippians 3 vs. 13

When, and how are we to do this one thing? Forgetting those things,
which are behind - not forsaking. We leave the alphabet as we learn,
we don't forsake it. The musician leaves the scales but does not forsake
them. The builder leaves the foundation but does not forsake it.
Therefore leaving, not forsaking, the principles of the doctrine of
Christ, let us go on to perfection, not laying again the foundation of
repentance from dead works etc. And this will we do says Paul. So
many are trying to live on a past experience. They testify to blessing
but never get any farther. Some live, or try to, on some past experience
of revival and stick there. They tell you what times they had and what
wonderful results etc. but they are now devoid of any such blessing.
We are to forget the things that are past.

Have you on the Lord believed?
Still there is more to follow
More and more always more to follow.

Let us not cease to do the utmost that we may incessantly go forward
in the way of the Lord.
John Calvin

7 OCTOBER

Prominent or Pre-eminent

...that in all things he might have the pre-eminence.
Colossians 1 vs. 18

There are many who are willing to give Jesus a place in their following. They recognise Him by praying and Bible reading and church going; and by more or less seeking to follow Him, as long as "ME first" is not interfered with. Just as soon as there is any conflict or disagreement, then the Lord is kept in His place and "ME first" exerts its authority, and so their following doesn't count for very much.

There are others who give Jesus a prominent position in their following. They really do sacrifice and suffer some for Christ. Their following involves the cross now and then. You don't have to be a detective to know they are followers, and their following is giving Christ prominence.

But how few there are who give the pre-eminent place in their following. It is this that Christ demands of every follower. And if we are to follow fully successfully, then it must no longer be "ME first". In all things He must have the pre-eminence. Let us all endeavour to give Jesus the pre-eminent place in everything always, and never let it be "ME first" again.

The first lesson in Christ's school is self-denial.
Matthew Henry

8 OCTOBER

The Snare of Success

And Jesus said unto him, No man, having put his hand to the plough,
and looking back, is fit for the kingdom of God.
Luke 9 vs. 62

Success might be long in coming, and prosperity always ahead of us, if we were not careful to consider "ME first". If you were seen in taking an active part in soul winning and attending open-air meetings, etc., well, orders might be lost and customers might cease their custom. So "ME first" tells us to be diplomatic and careful. When we hear the Lord's "Follow Me" we say: "Let ME first" see how this will affect my business, or my career, lest following fully should lead to serious consequences.

How much "ME first" following of Christ there is in business today? I've known men "follow fully" until they started business for themselves. Since then their following is very much "ME first". Their time and talents and money are all tied up and buried in their "ME first" following of Christ.

If the devil cannot use failure to drag you down, he will use success.
John Blanchard

Me First

And he said unto another, Follow me. But he said, Lord, suffer me first to
go and bury my father.
Luke 9 vs. 59

Following Christ in our social life is often hindered and marred by 'ME first, instead of Christ first. The Lord has prospered us since He saved us and we are apeing at being respectable and decent. What might have done when we were not so well to do and didn't live in quite so respectable a locality wouldn't do now? You see, we want to follow Christ, but decently, lest 'ME first' should suffer.

The open-air meeting and marches; the shouting, testifying, and singing for Jesus, would not help 'ME first' to rise in the social scale. It would spoil all your social scale. It would spoil all your social prospects in the church you have just joined, where there are so many nice people. It would be altogether out of place to be seen at an open-air meeting, or even attending such meetings, let alone testifying at them. Even going to evangelistic missions, although you were converted through one, would be entirely out of place with 'ME first'. You have been elected an elder of the church, and this has added to your social standing. It wouldn't at all seem proper for an elder to be out and out and enthusiastic in following Christ. It you were, 'ME first' would be hurt socially.

Some of you heard the call to follow Christ and you followed well for a while, but you felt He would have you enter the ministry, and you did so. But since you have entered college and mixed with the "wise and learned" your ardour has cooled down and your shouts of "Hallelujah" and "Praise the Lord" have died out. All this would hurt 'ME first's' future social life. You wouldn't get a call to a fashionable church and a good income. What a lot of 'ME first' followers there are today.

> There is a great difference between denying yourself things and
> denying yourself.
> Adrian Rogers

10 OCTOBER

The Cost of Discipleship

And he said unto another, Follow me. But he said,
Lord suffer me first to go and bury my father.
Luke 9 vs. 59

"ME first" hinders our following Christ in our domestic Life. Instead of hating father and mother, wife and children, sister and brother, and our own life also, we consider all these before Christ. "ME first" is always concerned about the effect following Christ fully would have on our relationship to our family, instead of considering only Him.

To follow fully might involve alienation and separation from our dearest and best, and "ME first" could never stand that. Many a young man and woman has said: "Jesus I will follow Thee to the mission field," but it would mean parting from my mother, father, brothers and sisters, and "ME first" couldn't stand that. It might to many a young man mean the cancelling of a loving, but unholy alliance with a young woman, for we must not be unequally yoked together with unbelievers. This would be more than "ME first" could stand, and so many a follower has begun to follow 'afar off'.

Some have been called to follow Christ to foreign lands, but "ME first" had to be considered on relation to wife or children, and because it didn't suit or wasn't convenient to "ME first" and family, the following was marred. "Let me first bid them farewell which are at home, at my house" unfits any man from following Christ and for the kingdom of God.

It costs to follow Jesus Christ, but it costs more not to.
Anon.

God is Jealous of His Word

…let God be true, but every man a liar;…
Romans 3 vs. 4

How flippantly and irreverently men handle God's Word today. What doesn't suit their pet theory is lightly denied and discarded, or if it 'criticises' their manner of life, it is ridiculed and rejected. If they only remember this name God gives Himself and it's solemn significance, they would surely write and speak differently regarding it. How keenly we feel when anyone doubts or calls in question our word. How much more God must feel these awful statements by our professors in colleges, and ministers in our churches. Fulfilled prophecy is a revelation of God's jealous regard for His Word. How careful He has been to see that every detail is carried out, and so moves holy men to prophesy in such a way that the miracle and wonder of it cannot be denied.

We need to go slow these days in the handling of God's Word, and it will help us do so when we remember the jealousy of God. When believers in Christ doubt their salvation and security, they are stirring God's jealousy. He that believeth not the record God gave of His Son maketh God a liar. And yet many imagine it is humility to doubt their salvation and safety, and even charge with presumption those who take God at His word and confess they are sure they are saved and safe. Is it any wonder such believers' lives are barren and unfruitful, joyless and powerless. God curses their blessings and blights the means of grace because they call Him a liar by doubting His word, and His jealousy is stirred and indignation moved against them. Let us ever remember God is a jealous God and very jealous where His word is concerned.

> Whatever contradicts the Word of God should be instantly resisted as diabolical.
> John Bunyan

Humour in the Pulpit

A time to laugh.
Ecclesiastes 3 vs. 4

The famous Baptist preacher, Charles Haddon Spurgeon, was once rebuked for introducing humour into his sermons. With a twinkle in his eye he replied, "If only you knew how much I hold back, you would commend me." Defending his use of humour in the pulpit, he wrote, "There are many things in these sermons that may produce smiles, but what then? The preacher is not quite sure about a smile being a sin, at any rate he thinks it less of a crime to cause a momentary laughter than half an hour of profound slumber."

Like Spurgeon, William knew the value of humour as a tool of evangelism. In justification of his use of humour he said, "Some say you should not make them laugh. But ninety percent of my audiences are babies. If I was to stand solemnly in the pulpit you would say, 'That is dry; it is dead,' so I have to tickle you and keep you in good humour, and all the time you are laughing and feeling good I am jagging at you and getting something down."

If you are not allowed to laugh in Heaven, I don't want to go there.
Martin Luther

God's Glory

...my glory I will not give to another...
Isaiah 42 vs. 8

He is jealous of His glory . His glory will He not give to another. His glory in redemption He will never share. He alone saves. Ceremonies and sacraments and our best endeavours He will never allow to share His glory in our redemption. There is no other name. There is no other foundation. There is salvation in none other but in Christ. His blood alone can cleanse from all sin. He is the guilty sinner's only refuge.

God will never share His redeeming glory with another. That is why so many religious people are still unsaved. They are unwilling to give God His place in their redemption, the place of solitary pre-eminence.

> God cannot allow another to be partaker of honours due to him without denying himself. It is as much his prerogative to be God alone as to be God at all.
> William S Plumer

No Condemnation

Who is he that condemneth? It is Christ that died, yea rather,
that is risen again, who is even at the right hand of God,
who also maketh intercession for us.
Romans 8 vs. 34

We are under the curse of a broken law. The wrath of God abides upon us. We are guilty before God. We are as sure of hell as if we are already in it, if we are not delivered. If we have accepted Jesus Christ as our Saviour and Deliverer, then, thank God there is therefore now no condemnation to them that are in Christ Jesus, who walk not after the flesh, but after the Spirit. Tell me friend, have you been delivered? Can you sing "Happy day when Jesus washed my sins away"? Free from the law, O happy condition! If you haven't had this experience, you can have it now just as you are, and where you are. If you are tired of your sin and bondage you can receive this deliverance. It is a gift. You do not, and never will, merit or deserve it. Cry out, "Out of my bondage, failure and fear, Jesus, I come." You have his word to assure you, "Him that cometh to me I will no wise cast out. By me, if any man enter in he shall be saved, and I give unto him eternal life and he shall never perish; neither shall man pluck them out of my hand." Deliverance has been purchased. Possess it. Then you will sing with Charles Wesley;

Long my imprisoned spirit lay
Fast bound in sin and natures night;
Thine eye diffused a quickening ray,
I wake, the dungeon flamed with light;
My chains fell off, my heart was free,
I rose, went forth, and followed Thee.

Justification is the very hinge and pillar of Christianity.
Thomas Watson

Half-Baked Christians

When He the Spirit of truth is come, He will guide you into all truth
John 16 vs. 13

When the Comforter comes He will guide us. Because we are sons, the Spirit of God leads us; we are guided day by day through each perplexing path of life. How does He guide us into all truth? He doesn't make sanctification crankification. He doesn't make us half-baked Christians. You know what half-baked soda bread is. One side of it is cooked, and the other side of it is dough. When you put your teeth into it you have a queer feeling. That is what some Christians are. They are kind of half-baked. But there is none of that half-baking about you. You are not a crank. You have Christian sanity. You are guided into all truth – all the truth about Salvation, all the truth about Sanctification, all the truth about the coming of Christ, all the truth about the work of the Holy Ghost, all the truth about this, that and the other. You are not a crank. You have a right division, a right proportion, in the word of God. When He comes He guides us in the will of God, and never outside the truth.

"What is truth?"

"Thy word is truth."

The Holy Spirit will never lead you and me outside the pages of the Bible, or get you and me to say anything or do anything derogatory to the inspiration and infallibility of that book.

> If the Holy Spirit guides us at all, he will do it according to the Scriptures, and never contrary to them.
> George Muller

Not an Imitation

I am crucified with Christ: nevertheless I live; yet not I, but Christ
liveth in me: and the life which I now live in the flesh
I live by the faith of the Son of God, who loved me,
and gave himself for me.
Galatians 2 vs. 20

Remember that this likeness to Christ is not an imitation; it is not doing your best to live as He lives; it is not doing your best to become like Him. I remember our little girl when I was going away, said, "Daddy, I will do my best to be like you by the time you get back." "Consider the lily how it grows." How does it grow? "It toils not, neither does it spin." And all your toiling and spinning, and mine, never made us one iota like the Lord Jesus Christ. It is not brought about that way. And yet how many there are to-day and they want to be like Christians but they do not want to be identified with Christ; they do not want it to be known that they belong to Christ; they do not want to take the reproach and the persecution and the suffering that is involved in that identification. Well friend, you cannot evade it. When you accepted Christ as your Saviour you immediately began to follow Christ. "Take my yoke upon you and learn of me." When you have rest to your soul you are in the yoke, walking with Christ and being conformed to the image of Christ.

The duty as well as the destiny of believers is to be conformed to the image of God's Son.
William Hendriksen

Obedient Scholars

His mother saith unto the servants, Whatsoever he saith unto you, do it.
John 2 vs. 5

A disciple is a "learner", a "scholar" a "taught one". He is in the school of Christ, and Christ is the teacher. He teaches him not only to be a loving loyal friend, but also the meaning and obligation of such friendship. Nothing in a disciple's life is unnecessary or accidental. God is working all things together for his good, according to His purpose. There are no errors, chance, luck nor accident in the grand eternal plan. In every disciple's life there are perplexing problems which may not all be solved here, but one day he will understand. In the meantime he is being educated as a student in the school of Christ. Many lessons are taught to us in the school of Christ. Many lessons are taught to us in school we could not fully explain or understand. So it is in Christ's school. Let us therefore be diligent, humble and obedient scholars; confident that Christ never makes mistakes and that He understands and loves us.

> As long as we live we must be scholars in Christ's school and sit at Christ's feet.
> Matthew Henry

Satisfied

He shall glorify me: for he shall receive of mine, and shall shew it unto you.
John 16.vs. 14

Oh what a Saviour he becomes: "Jesus, Jesus, Jesus, satisfies my every longing, keeps me singing as I go." Is that the Saviour you have got? Can you say with the Psalmist: "Whom have I in heaven but Thee? And there is none on earth that I desire beside thee"? Jesus, Jesus, wonderful Jesus, satisfying every longing. Have you entered into that experience? Have you been spoilt for the world? Are you like the children of Israel of old, who said that they were blessed by God, and that they would have nothing more to do with idols? Away you go with your worldly trash and your chaff, and your pigs' meat! I am back in the Father's home, there is music, and thank God, where there is bread enough and to spare, and where there are joy and satisfaction. Friend that is what the Comforter does. He glorifies Christ, makes Him all that He is in reality. He makes Christ all that your heart and mine desires, as we gaze upon Him we are changed into the same glory, from one radiant degree of glory to another, by the Spirit of the Lord, and men and women take knowledge of us that we have been with Jesus.

A wee girl was sitting at her mother's knee and old grandad was there sleeping, with the glory in his face. The mother was reading from the book of Revelation about: "His name shall be on their foreheads." The wee girl said to her: "Mamma, what does that mean?"

The mother whispered to her: "Dearie, look at your grandad's face." And the wee thing nodded her head. She said: "Yes I see."

As you and I walk with the Lord, and as the Spirit of God fills and possesses the glorified Christ in us, we are being transformed into His very likeness, and men and women see something and catch something of that wonderful Saviour.

It is not great talents that God blesses but likeness to Jesus.
Robert Murry McCheyne

Set Free

If the Son therefore shall set you free, ye shall be free indeed
John 8 vs. 36

We are set free to live and walk in newness of life. As we walk in the light, as he is in the light, we have fellowship one with the other, and the blood of Jesus cleanseth, (i.e., keeps on cleansing) us from all sin. When you are in Christ Jesus, Satan has no right to you any longer. The world has no right to you. Sin has no right to you. They are trespassers. You belong to Christ. He will take care of you, and by His Spirit, work in you to make you willing and able to do His will. He never sleeps or slumbers. He will perfect that which concerneth you. Don't fear to trust Him fully and always. The arm of flesh will fail you. Jesus never fails. This blessed deliverance from the practice of sin is yours. Don't fail to possess it. For the law of the Spirit of life in Christ Jesus has made you free from the law of sin and death. That the righteousness of the law might be fulfilled in you, who walk not after the flesh but after the Spirit. You are now the bond slave of Jesus Christ. No longer the slave of Satan, self, sin or the habits of sin. Don't remain in bondage any longer, step out and possess your freedom and maintain it by faith and obedience.

A Christian is the greatest freeman in the world.
Richard Sibbes

20 OCTOBER

Something to Glory In

And not only so, but we glory in tribulations also:
knowing that tribulation worketh patience;
Romans 5 vs. 3

I knew an old fellow who was a hypochondriac, with more money than sense, and he thought every disease and sickness was coming to him. One day he thought he was dying – and they would have been glad if he had! The doctor advised a trip to the Continent, but he came back just as bad as he was. The doctor said to him, - "You want to get out of yourself."

"Man, how could you get out of yourself?"

That's the rub. "The Lord....give you peace by all means." Sister, although your body may be racked with pain and suffering, you can have the peace of God. Although you may be living in a home that is a hell upon earth, with a drunken husband, you can have the peace of God. Although you may be working amongst the most ungodly gang, you can have peace. And, glory to God, it will be richer the harder your circumstances are. The easier your life and mine is, the less we know about it; but the harder the life is the richer it is. I have learned more on a sickbed than I ever I did in a pulpit. I have learned more when I was being kicked up and down the country than at any other time. We are wanting to get rid of the trouble, and the Lord says, "I will keep you in the trouble," and He will give you something to glory in while in it.

The anvil, the fire and the hammer are the making of us.
C H Spurgeon

21 OCTOBER

The Means is not the End

Christ in you, the hope of glory.
Colossians 1 vs. 2

All the beef steaks and the potatoes and bread and butter never made me a living man; they keep me living. All the means of grace God has provided never made a Christian man; they are the means to an end but they are not the end. The sad thing is that so many of us turn a thoroughfare into a terminus; turn a means into an end. And there are multitudes of God's people and they have not learned this lesson. You cannot make yourself like Christ any more than you could save yourself at the beginning. And all the energy of the flesh and training of men, with all the endowments God has given us could never fit us to serve God. We can never serve God in the energy of the flesh. Here is the lesson we have to learn, and that is the reason why so few people are being used of God today. We feel we are the whole cheese! I said about a friend of mine the other day, that if God were to bless that man, God would have to share His glory with that fellow 85 per cent. You just chew that over for a wee while. Say, where do you and I come in? Why, bless my heart, you think because you have gone to school or college and you have received degrees and had the hands of a Presbytery or Anglican Assembly on your head, that you are everything under God's heaven, that now you are equipped for service. Not on your life! This is a spiritual service. "It is not by might or by power, but by My Spirit," saith the Lord. And this victorious life is not the crown of an attainment on your part and mine. It is grace! grace! "Not of works, lest any man should boast."

God uses men who are weak and feeble enough to lean on Him.
J. Hudson Taylor

The Payment of Debts

Owe no man anything.
Romans 13 vs. 8

It is said that when William was conducting the mission in Newtownards, he went into a certain shop to make a purchase and in conversation asked the shopkeeper if he had been to any of the meetings. The shopkeeper said he wasn't impressed with that sort of religion. It was all very well for some people to hurry off to meetings, sing hymns and make a great fuss of their devotion, but he knew how many of them owed him money, which he never expected to collect. William was concerned and asked if he could borrow the shopkeeper's ledger.

That evening at the mission meeting he held the book aloft and explained that it was the accounts receivable ledger of a shop in town. He didn't say which shop it was, but he did say some things about honesty and the payment of debts, and added that he would read the names of the debtors and how much they owed.

Everybody was perfectly sure that he was capable of doing just that. Never was there such a rush in the town to settle debts! The shopkeeper who loaned William the book and a number of other shopkeepers as well were most impressed with Mr. Nicholson's brand of religion.

William preached powerfully upon honesty and the repaying of debts. In one service he said "If all the clothes that some of you are wearing and haven't paid for were to drop off, I would have to ask the ushers to put out the lights."

If faith does not make a man honest, it is not an honest faith.
C H Spurgeon

23 OCTOBER

To Love Less

If any man come to me and hate not his father, and mother, and wife,
and children, and brethren, and sisters, yea, and his own life also,
he cannot be my disciple.
Luke 14 vs. 26

Does this mean we are to break the fifth commandment? Matthew 10 vs.37 expressed it a little differently: "He that loveth father or mother more than me is not worthy of me." We understand then that the word "hate" means "to love less", and we can read the passage: He that comes after me and does not love his mother of father less than me cannot be my disciple. We are not at liberty to hate our parents but we are to love them less than we do Christ. We are to obey Christ rather than them. We are to be willing to forsake them if He calls us to go and preach the gospel, and we are to submit without murmuring when He takes them away from us. Jesus will not take any but the pre-eminent place in our affections.

> The church has no greater need today than to fall in love with Jesus
> all over again.
> Vance Havner

Unclaimed Deposits

Blessed be the God and Father of our Lord Jesus Christ, who hath blessed us with all spiritual blessings in heavenly places in Christ.
Ephesians 1 vs. 3

Why are so many not possessing their possessions? Because they are ignorant of their possessions in Christ. They are ignorant of this glorious fact that God hath blessed us with all spiritual blessings in Christ Jesus. We are already blessed, and the measure of the blessing is exceeding abundance above all we ask or think. We are multi-millionaires in the Grace of God, and yet so many are living like paupers and mendicants. They are bankrupt, barren and broken. In the banks of Scotland, they say, there are unclaimed deposits worth over forty million pounds. What amounts of unclaimed possessions are lying to our credit in Jesus Christ? Judicially we have everything. Experimentally we have only what we possess. What is mine judicially will save me from hell, but won't keep me from poverty and penury here. May we learn to possess our possessions, to use our talents, to enjoy our privileges, to rise to our dignity, to realise our standing, to pass through the length and breadth of our Canaan. Ours is a righteousness that is Divine, a peace that surpasseth understanding, a love which passeth knowledge, a kingdom that cannot be moved, a crown of glory that fadeth not away. Oh, let us go up and possess our possessions, so that we may show forth the virtues of Him who has called us out of darkness into light.

Learn to put your hand on all spiritual blessings in Christ and say, 'Mine'.
F B Meyer

We are a Gospel

*For if I make you sorry, who is he then that maketh me glad, but the same
which is made sorry by me?*
II Corinthians 2 vs. 2

Men and women in the world today do not read their Bibles but they read you and me. If they do read their Bible it is a closed book. The natural man cannot see the things of God, they are revealed by the Holy Spirit. But they can read your life and mine. And you will find that the conception they have of Christ and the conception they have of God is the conception that they have seen in your life and mine. How many of us are burlesquing the Lord. We talk about the Gospel according to Matthew, the Gospel according to Mark, the Gospel according to Luke, the Gospel according to John, and the Gospel according to Nicholson and the Gospel according to you. You are writing a Gospel everyday; just as truly as Matthew, Mark, Luke and John have given us a portrait of Christ, I am giving you a portrait of Christ and you are giving a portrait of Christ. You say, "Oh no, no, I will not take that." You cannot get salvation and escape the responsibility of likeness to your Lord.

Be walking Bibles.
C H Spurgeon

An Uncommon Christian

The thief cometh not, but for to steal, and to kill, and to destroy: I am come that they might have life, and that they might have it more adundantly.
John 10 vs.10

I came across a translation of the closing clause of this verse, by a very learned Greek scholar. Here it is, "I am come that they might have life and that they might have it above the common." An uncommon Christian. Tell me; are you a common Christian or an uncommon one? We read in Matthew 22 vs.14 "Many are called, but few are chosen" or "choice ones." Are you among the choice ones, or are you only a common Christian? There were two classes amongst Christ's disciples. There were Peter, James and John, three choice ones and eight common ones. There were disciples, followers, and the multitude. There are common and uncommon in every department of life, musicians, artists, scholars, businessmen, rulers, athletes, authors, and preachers. Many common, few uncommon. The sad thing is, we have the same amongst Christians. So many, oh so many, who are common. They are so common you can hardly tell one from the other or from those who are not Christian.

O Lord, make me an extraordinary Christian.
George Whitefield

Am I or am I Not?

And God said, Let the earth bring forth grass, the herb yielding seed, and the fruit tree yielding fruit after his kind, whose seed is in itself, upon the earth: and it was so.
Genesis 1 vs. 11

I can imagine some one saying, "I wonder am I a common or an uncommon Christian. You would be frightened to say you are an uncommon one, because your manner of life would be an open and loud contradiction of your confession. You need not be in doubt about the matter. Every effect must have an adequate cause. A tree is known by its flower or fruit. Every animal is known by its nature. At the beginning of creation we are taught, "Every thing after its own kind." The cow has always been a cow; the horse always a horse; the elephant always an elephant. A human being is never anything else but a human being, and all this in spite of the ridiculous theory of evolution. It is queer if evolution is true that we haven't some animals, say, half horse and cow or half sheep and pig. So if you want to know, and to be sure, whether you are a common or an uncommon Christian, you can easily find out. Jesus said that a good tree cannot bring forth evil fruit and a corrupt tree cannot bring forth good fruit. Therefore by their fruits ye shall know them. When a child has scarlet fever, mumps or measles there are evidences or symptoms, universal and everlasting, which reveal the nature of the disease. It doesn't matter whether the child is black, white, red or yellow; whether it is born rich or poor; or born a heathen, or born of Godly parents. It makes no difference; the evidences are the same in every case, everywhere, and at every time. So it is the same in the matter of whether we are common or uncommon Christians.

Nothing locks the lips like the life.
D L Moody

Assurance

He that believeth on the Son hath everlasting life...
John 3 vs. 36

A first evidence of the uncommon Christian is one who is born again (John 3 vs.7), and knows it. He doesn't think, or hope, or trust, or believe - he knows for sure. He has the witness. The Spirit answers to the blood and tells him he is born of God. He has the assurance - blessed assurance. He can tell you when and where it happened. This is a "know so" religion and experience. Friend, if you are not sure whether you are born again or not, you may be dead sure you are not and never have been. You couldn't be born again and not know it - Hallelujah! There are many things you don't know, and never will know, but if you are really blood washed and Spirit born, you can say with assurance, "One thing I know, whereas I was blind, Hallelujah! now I see." Have you this blessed assurance? If you have you may be sure you are an uncommon Christian.

It is so common, these Laodicean days we are living in, to hear so-called Christians, when cornered about confessing whether they are born again or not, say, "I never knew a day I didn't love the Lord." "I have always tried to live the Christian life." "I do all the good I can." "I pray and read my Bible and go to church regularly, as a member." "I teach in Sunday School." "I sing in the choir," "I am an officer in the church." "I follow the light of my conscience," etc., etc. Oh, how common all this is these days everywhere. Friend, if this is the way you talk and live, you may be sure you are a very common Christian, even if you are one. This is neither the language nor life of an uncommon Christian.

Faith will make us walk, but assurance will make us run.
Thomas Watson

Pentecost is Now

For by one Spirit are we all baptized into one body...
I Corinthians 12 vs. 13

A second evidence is that he is baptized with the Holy Ghost and fire (Matt.3 vs. 11). This is the blessed and second experience every uncommon Christian has. He has not only been to Calvary for the cleansing blood, but he has been to the upper room - to Pentecost - for the sanctifying, purifying enduement of power - the promise of the Father. He has received the Lord Jesus as his Justification at Calvary. He has gone on to Pentecost and received the baptism of the Holy Ghost for his sanctification and power. He knows the Lord Jesus as his personal Saviour, and also as the Baptiser with the Holy Ghost. A common Christian is one who is stuck between Calvary and Pentecost. He is one who has begun in the Spirit and is now trying to be sanctified by ceremonies and his best efforts. What an up and down life this is. More down than up. What a life of constant defeat, dissatisfaction, frustration, discontent and failure. No constant joy or peace or victory.

Once I thought I walked with Jesus,
Yet such changeful feelings had:
Sometimes trusting, sometimes doubting,
Sometimes joyful, sometimes sad.

This is always the language and life of a common Christian but when he receives the Baptism of the Holy Ghost and fire, all the chaff is burned up and he begins to sing

Now I'm trusting every moment less than this is not enough
And my Saviour leads me gently o'er the places once so rough.
Oh, what peace my Saviour gives, peace I never knew before!
How my way has brighter grown, since I learned to trust Him more.

I was baptized with the Holy Spirit when I took Him by simple faith
in the Word of God.
R A Torrey

A Lamp and a Light

Thy word is a lamp unto my feet, and a light unto my path.
Psalm 119 vs. 105

A third evidence of the uncommon Christian is, "The Bible is his one and only rule for faith and practice." He is not carried away by every wind of doctrine. He is not controlled and guarded by public opinion, his own opinion, or the opinion of others. He is being delivered from a man - fearing spirit and guided by "Thus saith the Lord." He is not dominated by the fashions of this world. The Bible is manna to his soul, light to his path, the norm of his counsel. It is sweeter than honey from the honeycomb. Because he believes it is the very Word of God, absolutely perfect without mistake or error, inerrant and infallible, unchanging and unchangeable. He has no fear for the future. The world may be upside down or wrong side up. Evil may be abounding, rioting, unhindered. Evil men may wax worse and worse. He has a peace that passeth all understanding. He knows for sure, "The Lord God Omnipotent reigneth." He is on the Throne and is working out His will and ruling among the armies of heaven and the inhabitants of the earth and none can stay His hand or say what doest Thou?

Peace perfect peace in this dark world of sin.
The blood of Jesus whispers peace within.

The Bible is his daily companion and constant guide.

My conscience is captive to the Word of God.
Martin Luther

A Passion for Souls

Where there is no vision, the people perish…
Proverbs 29 vs. 18

A fourth evidence of the uncommon Christian is that he has a passion for souls. He just can't help seeing men as fallen and falling creatures, lost, ruined, weak and helpless, blinded by the god of this world and on the road to hell. The thud of their Christless feet on the road to hell sounds constantly in his ears. He is moved with compassion as he sees them like sheep without a shepherd. He can't get used to them going to hell but seeks by all means, all the time, everywhere, to save some. He is careful about what he does, and where he goes, and who he goes with, in case he might hinder some one from coming to Christ. He seeks by life and lip to warn and woo them. He is continually in prayer for them. By all means he seeks to save some. How many Christians there are and they have little or no concern for the lost. Their children can go to hell, as long as they go decently and religiously. Their Sunday school class can be lost eternally, but they don't seem or feel concerned as long as they can instruct and amuse them. This is the mark or evidence of a true common Christian. They always detest and deride those who are seeking the lost. Ministers denounce missions and yet never see a convert, or by their preaching never move a sinner. The uncommon Christian is the very reverse. He is a hound of heaven on the track of sinners and seeking to win them for and to Christ.

Go for souls - and go for the worst.
William Booth

NOVEMBER

1 ♦ The Family Altar

2 ♦ A Week of Content

3 ♦ God's Tithe

4 ♦ The Example of Job

5 ♦ God is Working

6 ♦ It is Worth Fighting For

7 ♦ Pleasing God

8 ♦ True to God

9 ♦ Thanksgiving

10 ♦ Sudden Sorrow

11 ♦ Nicholson's Prophetic
    Prayer for Revival

12 ♦ A Monument of Souls

13 ♦ The Day of Pentecost

14 ♦ A Necessary Blessing

15 ♦ History or Experience

16 ♦ A Red Letter Day

17 ♦ Making God a Liar

18 ♦ Eve's Sin

19 ♦ False Teachers

20 ♦ The Sin of Worry

21 ♦ Dumps and Depression

22 ♦ Assurance of Salvation

23 ♦ Jesus Saves Completely

24 ♦ It Pays to Accept

25 ♦ Hard to Accept

26 ♦ Present your Bodies

27 ♦ Worldly Conformity

28 ♦ Be Ye Transformed

29 ♦ Your Reasonable Service

30 ♦ A Battlefield not a
    Playground

The Family Altar

And Noah builded an altar unto the Lord.
Genesis 8 vs. 20

A fifth evidence of an uncommon Christian is this. He erects a family altar in the home, and keeps it erected. At least once a day he gathers the family together and the Bible is read and all kneel in prayer. The children hear their parents' voices in prayer. They not only pray for them, but they pray with them. They hear their names in their prayers. When God started the human race, He didn't start a nation but a family. When they pitched their tents, we read, they erected their tent, but they built their altar. The transitory thing was the tent - the permanent thing was the altar. It is the reverse today everywhere amongst common Christians, but the uncommon one erects and establishes the family altar. It is like oil to the domestic machinery and what a blessing to the household.

The family altar would alter many a family.
Anon.

A Week of Content

...And he gave him tithes of all.
Genesis 14 vs. 20

A sixth evidence of an uncommon Christian is that a seventh of his time is given wholly to the Lord. One day - the first day - of the week is the Lord's. Every hour of the 24 is His for worship and work. He doesn't keep back part of the day for his business or pleasure. It is wholly given to the Lord, for he reckons it is the Lord's Day. You don't get him joy-riding or visiting friends or conducting his business. You find him in the House of God. You will find him engaged in service for the Lord and souls. Sunday papers and worldly literature are out of sight. Religious literature is conspicuous in the home. Like David he says "I joyed when to the house of God, go up they said to me." He didn't endure it, he enjoyed it. "A Sunday well spent brings a week of content and health for the toils of tomorrow; but a Sunday profaned, whate'er may be gained, is a certain forerunner of sorrow." It is a day of rest and gladness - the day of all the week the best, emblem of eternal rest.

We are to redeem the time because we ourselves are redeemed.
Richard Chester

God's Tithe

Bring ye all the tithes into the storehouse, that there may be meat in mine house, and prove me now herewith, saith the Lord of hosts, if I will not open you the windows of heaven, and pour you out a blessing, that thee shall not be room enough to receive it.
Malachi 3 vs. 10

A seventh evidence of an uncommon Christian is that he lays aside one-tenth of his money for the Lord. He is a tither, as God commands. Will a man rob God? God says, "Ye have robbed me of tithes." The common Christian has turned the Church into a den of thieves, instead of a house of prayer. A Christian who is not a tither is a thief and a robber. " Ye have robbed me," says God. But the uncommon Christian is not guilty of such a crime. He sets aside a tenth (2/- in £). This is done not after every other obligation has been met, and then taking one-tenth of what is left. Oh, no. God first - before ever another bill has been paid, God's tithe is sacredly set aside. In doing this he recognises he is not doing God a favour. "The silver and the gold is mine," saith the Lord, "and the cattle on a thousand hills." He is only doing his duty. He is recognising he is not the proprietor but the trustee of his money. He gives a seventh of his time and one-tenth of his money. You will usually find he doesn't stop at the tenth; he gives a fifth or even one half of his income. An uncommon Christian is neither a thief nor a miser. This isn't legal, it is gospel. Four hundred years before ever the law was given the tithe was recognised.

If you are not a tither you are a robber.
Stephen Olford

4 NOVEMBER

The Example of Job

There was a man in the land of Uz, whose name was Job, and that man was
perfect and upright, and one that feared God, and eschewed evil.
Job 1 vs. 1

As a final evidence of the uncommon Christian let us take Job for an example. He lived in Ur at the same time as Abram. I wonder did they know each other. Hundreds of years before Moses, God said he was perfect and upright, and one that feared God and eschewed evil. Satan said he was only all this because God had made an hedge about him and about his house and about all he had on every side. He said, "doth Job fear God for nought?" God turned him loose on Job's possessions to prove Job was all this because he trusted God. There came a day, what a day, when Job lost all his property: 7,000 sheep, 3,000 camels, 500 asses, 8,000 oxen; all his family, 7 sons and 3 daughters, his health; the sympathy of his wife and friends and even his good name. What did Job do? How did he feel about it? "Job arose, and rent his mantle, and shaved his head, and fell down upon the ground, and worshipped, and said, Naked came I out of my mother's womb, and naked shall I return thither: the Lord gave, and the Lord hath taken away; blessed be the name of the Lord. In all this Job sinned not, nor charged God foolishly." In all this Job did not sin with his lips. What an example of trust in God. Job said "Though he slay me, yet will I trust Him." If we are truly an uncommon Christian, we will in some measure and degree act and believe and say as Job did. We will give God a chance to boast about us as He did about Job. He said to Satan, "Hast thou considered my servant Job, that there is none like him in the earth, a perfect and upright man, one that feareth God and escheweth evil?" Can the Lord depend on you? Does He find you ever true?

Faith tries God and God tries the faith He gives.
Mary Winslow

God is Working

What shall we then say to these things? If God be for us,
who can be against us?
Romans 8 vs. 31

While we live in the will of God, He is working all things together for our good. We know this, we don't always see it, or understand it, or feel it, but, glory to God we know it. Therefore there is no whining, grumbling or rebelling. Even if Satan is at work on us he can only go so far and no farther. He is under the permission and supervision of God. The Lord allows queer instruments to refine and develop our faith in Him and love for Him. He never makes any mistakes. He never leaves anything to chance, accident or luck. He is working all things together for our good. We cannot see how it can be, but one day here or hereafter we will bless the hand that guided, we'll bless the heart that planned. So there is no mourning or complaining - nothing but peace, perfect peace, Hallelujah!

> God is working out His eternal purpose not only in spite of human
> and satanic opposition, but by means of them.
> A W Pink

6 NOVEMBER

It is Worth Fighting For

Fight the good fight of faith...
I Timothy 6 vs. 12

Let us hold the beginning of our confidence steadfast unto the end. Man! don't hand over your faith cheaply and easily to the devil. There is nothing would delight him more. Fight the good fight of faith - it's worth fighting for, and it takes constant and hard fighting to keep our faith in God. Any fool or weak-kneed believer, can give up their faith in God, but it takes a red-blooded, stiff, back-boned believer to have faith in God when the world is turned upside down and all hell let loose. You be that sort of a believer.

Look up Hebrews eleven, and walk through God's Westminster Gallery and have a good look at them. Abel; Enoch; Noah; Abraham; Isaac; Jacob; Joseph; and Moses, and take courage. They were all men of like passions as ourselves. You will notice we are not told about their Faith in God. That's the big thing with God. Not one of these men had an easy time of it, not one! Read their lives and see, and yet they believed God in spite of adverse circumstances, persecution and imprisonment, poverty and even death.

Faith in Jesus laughs at impossibilities.
C T Studd

Pleasing God

But without faith it is impossible to please him:...
Hebrews 11 vs. 6

There is nothing pleases God like our faith in Him. In fact, without faith it is impossible to please Him. That's sensible and logical. Supposing you gave your wife every good gift and rendered her every service and yet withheld your faith or confidence. Would your gifts and service substitute for faith or please her? You know right well it wouldn't. So it is with God. You may give your money, your time, your health, your loved ones, your body to be burned, but if you withheld your faith, all the other things would never satisfy or please God, for it is impossible to please God without faith. So let us see to it that we have faith in God

> You can do a great deal without faith, but nothing that is pleasing to God.
> John Blanchard

True to God

But made himself of no reputation...
Philippians 2 vs. 7

Why did He do that? Make Himself of no reputation? My friends, here is the curse in your life and mine. Isn't it the fear of our reputations? What would so and so think about us? We would lose our social reputation if we happened to try to get downtrodden sinners won to Jesus. What would they think of you? You would lose caste and you would be ostracised from their society. They would not invite you to their card parties and to their afternoon teas. You would lose your reputation. This applies not only to you, but also to teachers and preachers. If we preachers talked about sin and about hell and about damnation and the blood of Christ and that we need to be saved, it would not be popular and we would not be recognized in ecclesiastical society. They would say; "He is only an ignorant, tough-tongued blustering kind of preacher." The minister that I was reared under left his Church and large salary and went down into the slums and commenced work without the guarantee of a cent. He was slandered and misrepresented by his brethren, but he continued seeking and saving the lost. He felt that they could get someone to take his pulpit, but they could not so easily get one to work amongst the outcast and fallen. Today they have highly honoured him, but he had to go through the deep waters and empty himself of his reputation.

God can do little with those who love their lives or reputations.
C T Studd

Thanksgiving

Rooted and built up in him, and stablished in the faith, as ye have been taught, abounding therein with thanksgiving.
Colossians 2 vs. 7

Abounding – overflowing - therein with thanksgiving. It is a grand thing to live with a person overflowing with gratitude, but there are some of us just grumbling and growling and whining all the time. You meet them and say, "Well, how are you getting along?" and they'll say, "Oh, I have no reason to complain" as if they were looking for something to complain about. Why, the Lord says we are to abound – overflow - in thanksgiving. I don't care however poor you may be, there is always a great deal to be thankful for. An acquaintance of mine had a Sunday school class of girls who worked in the factory from six in the morning to six at night for a comparative pittance, and the conditions under which they worked were extremely trying. However, one Sunday when they were in the Sunday school class, he said to them. "Now, look here girls, I'm going to show that all you girls are millionaires". Their eyes all brightened at this. Just about a few pence would cover the value of the poor dress they had on their backs. He said to one of them "What would you sell your health of body for? How many hundreds of pounds would you sell it for?" "Oh" she said, "I wouldn't do that at all; nobody would do that". Then to another he said, "How much would you sell your sight for? How many hundreds of pounds"? "Oh" she said, "I wouldn't do that. I couldn't do without my sight". "Jeannie", said he "What would you sell your hearing for"? And she replied "Oh, I wouldn't sell it at all, and be deaf all the days of my life", Some of these girls had what money cannot buy, and if every one of us will count our blessings over and over, we will see that we all ought to be overflowing with thanksgiving.

Christians should have a gratitude attitude.
Stuart Briscoe

Sudden Sorrow

...ye shall be sorrowful, but your sorrow shall be turned into joy.
John 16 vs. 20

Some great, sudden sorrow may have come into your life and left life so empty and sad. Your constant cry unuttered is "O for the touch of a vanished hand, the sound of a voice that is stilled." Life has never been the same since. Why should they have been taken? And maybe taken under fearful circumstances. You have tried to explain it or understand it and you are baffled and defeated. There is constantly wrung from your heart the cry, "Why?" There is no answer. If only God would take you into His confidence and explain it all - as He will some day - but, if He would only do so now, it would help you to hold fast your confidence in God, firm unto the end.

It is so hard under these circumstances to "Have faith in God." I know it is so easy saying "Have faith in God" no matter what has happened or is happening; but friend, you will lose far more by disobeying the command; your joy, song, peace of mind, the smile of God, will all vanish. Be one who will please God by having faith in Him even amidst such sorrow.

It is the trial of our faith that makes us healthy in God's sight.
Oswald Chambers

Nicholson's Prophetic Prayer for Revival

...O Lord, revive thy work in the midst of the years...
Habakkuk 3 vs. 2

"The revival which ought to come to our churches is a revival that will make preachers forget their manuscripts and burst out and weep in their pulpits; a cyclone of mysterious omnipotence that, when it strikes a church or community, will make people awfully mad or gloriously happy.

"I declare, in the presence of God and His Church I am ready for just such a spiritual scene. Nothing is so alarming as the absence of alarm in the churches. Nothing is so dreadfully terrific, to my mind, as that, sinners have no terror. Oh that God would so baptise with power and fire five thousand people, as to render them incomprehensible amazements of power! Oh for men so dead to all things but God, and so filled with Him, as to make them more than a match for the rest of mankind! Oh, Thou God of Sinai, Calvary and Pentecost, art Thou not now nursing, under the horizon, the lightning and thunder and rain of an amazing holiness revival?

"Lord, let it strike Ireland, though it blow our abominable church pride in the dust, though it thrust our philanthropic fairs and festivals in the gutter, though it should confound all the wise ones, and be understood by none but Thy DIVINE Self, LET IT COME! Oh, send us the storm of the Holy Ghost before Thou sendest the storm of judgment!

"May God so consume us with an intolerable craving for just such a revival of genuine old-fashioned, Holy Ghost religion, something unparalleled and unprecedented in the history of the Church - a revival in such measure that man will be wiped out and God be everything, a revival that will fill hell with consternation and make heaven delirious with joy, and fill the heart of every true saint of God with wonder, love and praise, a revival that neither ministers nor churches nor the devil will be able to stop." Let us cry to God night and day for this.

A revival is from God or it is no revival at all.
Wilbur M Smith

A Monument of Souls

For what is our hope, or joy, or crown of rejoicing?
Are not even ye in the presence of our Lord Jesus Christ at his coming?
For ye are our glory and joy.
I Thessalonians 2 vs. 29-30

Someone once said of Sir Christopher Wren, the architect of St. Paul's Cathedral in London, "If you want to see his monument, look around you!" This could also be said of William P. Nicholson. His monument is the lives and ministries of those whom he won for Christ. He once paid a tribute to the Old Testament shipbuilder Noah when he said that Noah was God's evangelist for 120 years, and his text was always the same - Genesis 6 vs.3, "My Spirit will not always strive with man." He pointed out that Noah never got a convert outside his own family: William then admitted that, as an evangelist, he could not have carried on without seeing some results.

Give me souls or take away my soul.
George Whitefield

The Day of Pentecost

And when the day of Pentecost was fully come…
Acts 2 vs. 1

What a day! The baptism with the Holy Ghost and fire was no longer a mere promise. It was a promise fulfilled - a blessed, glorious experience in the lives of the 120 converted men and women. Cowards were suddenly changed into heroes. Deniers of Christ suddenly became bold, courageous confessors of Christ. Doubters suddenly became shouters - loudspeakers for Christ. Weakness was suddenly changed into Herculean strength. Failure was suddenly changed into phenomenal success.

The Comforter had come. The promise had been fulfilled. They were all - women as well as men - the rank and file as well as the apostles - "filled with the Holy Ghost, and began to speak with other tongues…" The bars on the doors were removed - and doors were blown open. The noise went abroad. The multitudes were gathered together. Thousands were converted - mostly men. The day of Pentecost had fully come. "Hallelujah!"

> There I one thing we cannot imitate; we cannot imitate being full of the Holy Ghost.
> Oswald Chambers

A Necessary Blessing

...Not by might, nor by power, but by my spirit, saith the Lord of hosts.
Zechariah 4 vs. 6

This blessing was necessary to meet the problems in the lives of these early disciples. It was an absolute necessity in their case. They were told they were to be lights in the world, the salt of the earth, to preach the Gospel to every creature and make disciples of all nations. In fact, they were to do greater works than Jesus ever did, because He went to the Father. How ridiculous all this seemed. They were a bunch of devoted but defeated disciples. They all forsook Him and fled when He was taken to trial and Calvary. Even now, after they had seen Him and talked with Him for 40 days, and seen Him ascend on high, we find them shut in the upper room. The doors were barred for fear of the Jews. Surely something had to happen if they were to fulfil their commission. Glory to God! it did happen that day of Pentecost, when they were all baptized with the Holy Ghost and fire and they were all filled with the Holy Ghost. God never sends us at our own charges. He provides us with all we need for the performance of His programme. You couldn't expect the Lord to do otherwise, could you? This was God's only solution for their problem. He had no other. Have we been able to provide a better solution?

> The Spirit filled life is not a special, deluxe edition of Christianity.
> It is part and parcel of the total plan of God for His people.
> A W Tozer

History or Experience

And they were all filled with the Holy Ghost…
Acts 2 vs. 4

What a day and what a change! Let me ask you, dear friend, do you know anything about it, not merely historically, but experimentally? There are many who can sing "Happy day that fixed my choice on Thee my Saviour and my God," but they are entirely ignorant - experimentally - of this day - the day of Pentecost. They think it was necessary for that day and the 120 disciples, but not for our day and for us believers. They forget the first disciples serve as examples for all time and for all believers everywhere, showing us the necessity for the same blessing and the disposition of heart necessary for receiving it. As a result they are living on the wrong side of Pentecost experimentally. As post-Pentecostal believers, they are living a pre-Pentecostal experience. They have got stuck between Calvary and Pentecost. The sad thing about it is - they seem satisfied with a pre-Pentecostal experience, with its defeat, dissatisfaction and failure. What a reproach they are to Christ and what a hindrance to the work of the church. There are others who are bitterly antagonistic to such an experience. They are blinded and prejudiced by preconceived unscriptural notions. Their Christian life is an open confession of the fact they need this very experience and blessing. Surely if the early disciples needed it, we need it. When you read the Gospel story of the disciples and turn to the Acts of the Apostles and read about them there, you would not think you were reading about the same people. Would you? They had lived with Jesus; they heard His teaching; they saw His miraculous works for almost three years. Surely, if any class of believers might have been exempt from such a blessing they were of that class. What a privileged crowd they were. And yet, to these very disciples Jesus said "Tarry until ye be endued with power from on high." We need the very same baptism as they did, for without it we may be devoted disciples of Christ, but we will be disobedient and defeated disciples.

> God commands us to be filled with the Spirit and if we are not filled
> it is because we are living beneath our privileges.
> D L Moody

A Red Letter Day

...but wait for the promise of the Father, which, saith he, ye have heard of me. For John truly baptized with water; but ye shall be baptized with he Holy Ghost not many days hence.
Acts 1 vs. 4-5

The tarrying is necessary for us. How long have we to tarry? Ten days? No! How long? Until your all is on the altar. Until you are fully yielded and have a conscience void of offence to God and man. How long have we to tarry? Until we are "endued with power from on high". We are to tarry until we get the blessing. When we are fully yielded and wrongs are righted, and debts paid, we can receive the Holy Ghost by faith to fill us to the uttermost. Then the day of Pentecost will become a red-letter day in our experience.

Let me plead with you dear friends, don't despise your birthright. Don't resist the Holy Ghost. Yield fully and believingly. Don't be afraid. Jesus in not a policeman or enemy. He is the lover of your soul. Surely you can trust Him fully and unafraid, seeing He loved you enough to die for you. At any cost or cross, seek the blessing until you find it. "Seek and ye shall find," Jesus says. Say to Him and to yourself, "Jesus I am going through." Leave the consequences and evidences with Him. You take and He will undertake. Then walk in the light as He is in the light, and the blood of Jesus Christ, God's Son, will keep cleansing you from all sin, and the Holy Spirit will keep on filling you with all the fullness of God

Speak Lord, before Thy throne we wait, Thy promise we believe,
And will not let Thee go until the blessing we receive.
Lord, send the old-time power - the Pentecostal power,
Thy flood-gates of blessing on us throw open wide.
Lord, send the old-time power - the Pentecostal power
That sinners be converted and Thy saints sanctified

There is no substitute for the baptism with the Holy Ghost.
W P Nicholson

Making God a Liar

He that believeth on the Son of God hath the witness in himself; he that believeth not God hath made him a liar; because he believeth not the record that God gave of his Son. And this is the record, that God hath given to us eternal life, and this life is in his Son. He that hath the Son hath life; and he that hath not the Son of God hath not life.
1 John 5 vs. 10- 12

"God is not a man, that he should lie; neither the son of man, that he should repent: hath he said, and shall he not do it? or hath he spoken, and shall he not make it good?" (Numbers 23 vs.19). I wonder, dear friend, has this awful sin ever been committed by you? Have you ever thought it possible for you to commit it? Have you ever recognised there was such a sin as this against God? May the Lord burn this truth in our hearts as never before, and warn us of the possibility of committing it. Thus being forewarned, we will be forearmed against it. This is a terrible thing for anybody to do, 'Make God a liar.' In other words, 'Call God a liar.' To call anybody a liar is as great an insult as one can give. We vehemently and vigorously repudiate and deny it. It is looked upon as no ordinary charge in parliament. One member is not allowed to use that word about another member. You are not permitted to call a fellow member a liar. It is unparliamentary and therefore forbidden. If it is such a serious and dreadful thing to call your fellowman a liar, what a horrible and hellish thing it is to call God a liar. What depth of depravity must there be in a man, or what full possession the devil must have of a man that inclines and enables him to call God a liar. And yet how many there are today on every hand who are dong this very thing. I believe there are many doing it that are doing it ignorantly

> Unbelief is not simply an infirmity of fallen human nature; it is a heinous crime.
> A W Pink

Eve's Sin

Now the serpent was more subtil than any best of the field which the Lord God had made. And he said unto the woman, yea, hath God said, Ye shall not eat of every tree of the garden.
Genesis 3 vs. 1

To doubt or deny God's Word, is "making God a liar." This was the sin Eve committed in the Garden of Eden. "The Lord God commanded the man saying "Of every tree of the garden thou mayest freely eat, but of the tree of the knowledge of good and evil thou shalt not eat of it; for in the day thou eatest thereof thou shalt surely die." The serpent said unto Eve "Yea, hath God said, ye shall not eat of every tree of the garden?" The woman said "God hath said, Ye shall not eat of it lest ye die." The serpent said "Ye shall not surely die."" Satan cast a doubt on God's Word when he said, "Hath God said?" That is, are you sure God said it? When she doubted, she believed the devil's lie when he said, "Thou shalt not surely die." She called God a liar by doubting His Word, and by her sin brought misery and sorrow upon the whole world. It's a terrible and tragic thing to make God a liar, not only the consequences in your own life, but also in the lives of others.

The teachers of doubt are doubtful teachers.
C H Spurgeon

False Teachers

All scripture is given by inspiration of God, and is profitable for doctrine,
for reproof, for correction, for instruction in righteousness.
II Timothy 3 vs. 16

This blasphemous sin is being committed openly and blatantly in our colleges and churches today. Of course it is not called "making God a liar." It is done in the name and guise of scholarship. The Church and character of God is not suffering at the hands of infidels and unbelievers outside the church. Oh no, but by the hands of many of our theological professors in our colleges and ministers in our pulpits. Every professor, no matter how learned he may be or however upright and clean in his character or religious in his profession, who denies or doubts the verbal, plenary inspiration of the Bible is calling God a liar. They do this when they proclaim that the Bible contains the Word of God, just as quartz contains the gold, and begin to tear it to pieces by teaching and preaching man was evolved, not created; that Moses never wrote the first five books of the Bible; that David never wrote the 110th Psalm or Jonah was never swallowed by a giant fish. In fact they deny the reality and historicity of the Book of Jonah altogether. They are committing this terrible blasphemy of calling God a liar. Jesus said man was created. That Moses wrote the first five books. That David wrote the 110th Psalm. That Jonah was a real person and his Book is the very Word of God. When they deny His Virgin birth, His vicarious death, His victorious resurrection and His personal return, they are calling God a liar. They believe not the record God gave of His Son.

God cannot endure the contempt of His Word.
John Calvin

The Sin of Worry

Commit they way unto the Lord; trust also in him;
and he shall bring it to pass.
Psalm 37 vs. 5

There are many rank and file believers who are daily committing the sin of worrying. There are multitudes of real believers who are daily living lives of fret and worry and anxiety. They live by worry not by faith. Worry in a child of God is calling God a liar or making God a liar. I heard a dear man of God - he had been over 50 years in the ministry - say "He would as soon get drunk as worry." He said drunkenness might be more vulgar, but worry was pure blasphemy. In other words, making "God a liar" You see, when you worry, you are charging God with folly. You are sinning against God's love and care by worrying. God loves you and God cares for you, but when you worry you are doubting His Word that tells you how dearly He loves you and how concerned He is about your welfare. Why even the very hairs of your head are numbered, not counted, but numbered. When you worry you disbelieve the record of God and therefore make Him a liar. When you worry you don't trust, and when you trust you don't worry.

There is a living God. He has spoken in the Bible. He means what He says, and will do all that He has promised.
J Hudson Taylor

Dumps and Depression

Casting all your care upon him; for he careth for you.
I Peter 5 vs. 7

Other believers give place to depression and discouragement and live lives of sorrow and sighing, instead of songs and everlasting joy. They are affected with mental malaria and ingrown thoughts of gloom and morbid introspection. They are continually in the Blues and Dumps. You would think God was dead, or had to vacate His throne and Satan was a conqueror, the way they mourn and mope and murmur through life. They are religious hypochondriacs. What a travesty on the character of God and His salvation. They are calling God a liar every breath they draw and every day they live. God has promised to care for them, to never leave or forsake them, to withhold no good thing from them. He tells them to cast their burdens upon the Lord and He will carry them through, and in failing to do this they are giving the lie to every promise of God. They believe not the record. They are making God a liar. Oh ye mourners in Zion cease your mourning and sighing and doubting and fearing and thus maligning the character of God by making Him a liar. God is not a man that He should lie, neither the son of man that He should repent. Hath He said and shall He not do it, or hath He spoken and shall He not make it good.

Believing prayer takes its stand upon the faithfulness of God.
D Edmund Herbert

Assurance of Salvation

These things have I written unto you that believe on the name of the Son of God; that ye may know that ye have eternal life, and that ye may believe on the name of the Son of God.
I John 5 vs. 13

You will notice in the text from John's epistle that this sin of making God a liar is in connection with the assurance of our salvation. "He that believeth on the Son hath (is in possession of) everlasting life." He that believeth not the record God gives of His Son makes God a liar, that is, he calls God a liar. I firmly believe that if this solemn and awful truth was clearly declared and taught there wouldn't be so many believers lacking the full assurance of their saving, justifying and sanctifying interest in Christ. We have coddled them by unscripturally allowing that a man can be saved and not be sure about it, and that it is pure presumption for any believer to say that he is sure of his salvation. So, as a result we have in our churches and halls many who say they truly believe, but cannot, or will not say they are sure they are saved. They say, "I hope so" "I think so" "I trust" "I believe" but they are unable, or unwilling, to confess they know Him whom they have believed and are sure. If they were told that such an attitude was making God a liar, instead of sympathizing with them in their unbelief, they would flee from such an awful sin as calling God a liar.

Faith rests on the naked Word of God; that Word believed gives full assurance.
H A Ironside

Jesus Saves Completely

As far as the east is from the west, so far hath he removed our
transgressions from us.
Psalm 103 vs. 12

Jesus saves complete sinners completely. He not only forgives us and pardons us, but He justifies us. That is, we are made in Christ as if we never sinned. Supposing I was being tried for theft. The judge had the power to forgive me. He took pity on me and loved me and forgave me. It would be wonderful, but he could never make me anything else but a thief, although a pardoned one. All the rest of my life they would say, there goes W.P.N., a pardoned man, but still a thief. But when Jesus saves us we are justified from all things. Who shall lay anything to the charge of God's elect? It is God that justifieth. Hallelujah! God not only forgives, He forgets. Suppose you were before God and you said, "God, my sins are many and scarlet," He would say, "Your sins? I don't remember any sins against you." He has cast them behind His back. They are in the depths of the sea. They are removed from you as far as the east is from the west. Why didn't He say, "As far as the north is from the south"? That would mean you could calculate how far He had removed them from you. But as far as east is from the west that is an incalculable distance. Truly Jesus saves completely. He is a wonderful Saviour. You are completely and eternally saved. Thou shalt never perish but have everlasting life. I give unto them eternal life and they shall never perish and no man shall pluck them out of my hand. They are the means God has provided to help us to enjoy our salvation. When I was born of my mother many years ago, I became her son. All I have done to her and for her has not made me one whit more her son. They have helped me to enjoy the fact of being her son. So when you accepted Christ, by faith, as your personal Saviour you become that very moment a son, or child of God. All you may do, or have done for Him can never make you any more or any less a son or child of God. So completely does Jesus save complete sinners.

God does not wish us to remember what He is willing to forget.
George A Buttrick

It Pays to Accept

I beseech you therefore, brethren, by the mercies of God, that ye present your bodies a living sacrifice, holy, acceptable unto God, which is your reasonable service. And be not conformed to this world: but be ye transformed by the renewing of your mind, that ye may prove what is that good, and acceptable, and perfect, will of God.
Romans 12 vs. 1- 2

Oh! Dear child of God, it pays to believe God's will to be good and perfect and to accept it. It doesn't pay to refuse it and rebel at it. Your rebellion only leads to vexation of spirit and misery of life. Civil war is a terrible thing in any country. To doubt or deny God's will to be good and perfect and acceptable, is civil war in your life, and what misery and sorrow follows in its train. Say it to your heart over and over again, "God's will is good, acceptable and perfect. I cannot understand it or explain it, or even feel it is so, but I believe it is so. God says it. I believe it and that settles it." It will bring such a peace that passeth all understanding and joy unspeakable and full of glory into your heart and life and you will radiate the joy of the Lord and His sweet beloved will to all around you, and show forth the virtues of Him who has called you out of darkness into an ungodly and gainsaying world. You will become like a kettle, which, when up to the brim with boiling water, sings. What a testimony for God a Christian is who can believe and rejoice and praise the Lord, even when sickness or death or trial or tribulation and persecution are his portion, because he believes it is the good and acceptable and perfect will of God for him. Will you be or become such a Christian, child of sorrow or of woe.

The will of God is the place of blessed, painful, fruitful trouble.
A W Tozer

Hard to Accept

And be not conformed to this world: but be ye transformed by the
renewing of your mind, that ye may prove what is that good,
and acceptable, and perfect, will of God.
Romans 12 vs. 2

Why is it so hard to accept the good and perfect will of God and why is it so easy to think and feel it isn't good or perfect and therefore not acceptable? I believe it is because we don't know our God and His ways. God has strange ways and we are apt to be offended because we are ignorant of His ways. When we know a person intimately and well, we get to know his ways. Others who don't know your friend as you do, are apt to be offended, shocked, and stumble at his ways. But you excuse you friend by saying: "Oh! It's all right, it is only his way." Tell me dear friend, do you know God so well and intimately that you know His ways and are not offended? They who know their God will put their trust in Him.

He made known his ways unto Moses, His acts unto the children of Israel. Therefore the children of Israel rebelled, grumbled, and murmured at God for 40 years. You never read of Moses rebelling or grumbling. Why? Because he knew God's ways. Tell me friend, do you know God's ways? You live so intimately and constantly with Him, that you know Him so well, you get to know His ways and therefore accept the will of God as good and perfect; or are you like the children of Israel, only knowing God by His acts and therefore rebel and murmur? Let your prayer be the Psalmists: - "Show me Thy ways."   Moses prayed like that too: "Show me thy way that I may know Thee".

God's heavenly plan does not always make earthly sense.
Charles R Swindoll

Present Your Bodies

I beseech you therefore, brethren, by the mercies of God, that ye present
your bodies a living sacrifice, holy, acceptable unto God,
which is your reasonable service.
Romans 12 vs. 1

"Present your bodies a living sacrifice." You do this and God will make his will good and perfect and acceptable to you. This is your part of the bargain.

No withholding, full confession,
Riches, pleasures - all must flee.
Holy Spirit take possession,
No longer I, but Christ in me.

God does not ask for a perfect surrender, but he demands an honest one. All includes everything and excludes nothing. There must be no reservation or evasion. A whole burnt offering is required; no one can do it for you - you must do it fully and freely and forever - your whole body, soul and spirit. Mind, it is a big thing to do, but it is a safe thing to do. It is a terribly dangerous thing not to do.

You remember Ananias and Sapphira who kept back part of the price; they surrendered some, but not all. Their surrender was partial. What swift and terrible judgement fell on them! Tell God you do present your all - all you know and don't know, without any reservation. "All to Jesus I surrender. All to Him I freely bring". Are you afraid to do this? Surely you can trust the One who loves you enough to die for you?

Consecration is handing God a blank sheet to fill in with your name
signed at the bottom.
M H Miller

Worldy Conformity

And be not conformed to this world: but be ye transformed by the
renewing of your mind, that ye may prove what is that good,
and acceptable, and perfect, will of God.
Romans 12 vs. 2

There never was a day in the history of the Church when this command is more openly ignored and disobeyed than today. Worldly conformity is so widely practiced on every hand that it is looked upon as the wise and sensible thing to do and be. To obey the command is looked on as old fashioned; narrow minded; having zeal without knowledge; bigoted; fanatical; etc., etc. It is looked upon as the right thing to do to belong to several secret societies; to be hail-fellow well met; to be mixed up in politics and hold municipal or government positions. This broadmindedness is highly esteemed on every hand today. To act and live as one who is a "peculiar people," "a chosen generation," "a royal priesthood," or "a holy nation" is considered very much out of date and unnecessary by many Christians. Then they can give a fine reason for adopting this worldly compromising policy. They tell you they will be able to do good and bring better times, or bring them to the Church, etc. How many ministers have adopted this policy and have introduced Badminton Clubs, Table Tennis, Dramatic Societies, Tennis and Golf Clubs, Football and Cricket Clubs, Sales of Work, Bazaars, Jumble Sales, and Teas of all kinds. This all pleases the world and carnal Christians. They argue that it succeeds in bringing in funds and filling the Church. It may all be true, but remember! It is willful disobedience of God's command. "Be not conformed".

"Come out from among them; be separate" is the only wise and safe course.

> Worldliness is rampant in the Church. The devil is not fighting Churches; he is joining them! He is not persecuting Christianity; he is professing it.
> Vance Havner

Be Ye Transformed

And be not conformed to this world: but be ye transformed by the
renewing of your mind, that ye may prove what is that good,
and acceptable, and perfect, will of God.
Romans 12 vs. 2

The first command was positive, "Present your bodies." The second command was a negative one "Be not conformed." This third and last command is a positive one, "Be ye transformed." There are many and their lives are all negative; they give up this and the other, but they never go in for the transforming of their lives. Like the monks they deny themselves and shut themselves in their monasteries, but their lives are not being changed from one radiant degree of glory to another into the image Christ. They will leave their church and separate themselves with some company and congratulate themselves in their smug complacency and self-righteousness. They are zealous for the Word and earnestly contend for the faith, but become contentious and hard and harsh and censorious. They forget that grace and truth come by Jesus Christ – they leave out the grace and graciousness. This is not being conformed into the image of Christ. How are we to be transformed? "By the renewing of your mind." Fill your minds with the Word of God, and the ways of God.

The secret of holy living is in the mind.
John R W Stott

Your Reasonable Service

I beseech you therefore, brethren, by the mercies of God, that ye present
your bodies a living sacrifice, holy, acceptable unto God,
which is your reasonable service.
Romans 12 vs. 1

"Your reasonable service." There is nothing unreasonable about all this. We are not our own; we are bought with a price and surely it isn't unreasonable of the Lord to possess His own property? He has a right to you. The devil has no right to any believer - he is a trespasser, an interloper. You are the Lord's by creation and redemption; you are twice His.

Let me unite my pleading with the Apostles; I specially plead with you young people. Keep nothing back – make a full and complete surrender of your all and always maintain the surrender.

High heaven that heard my solemn vow,
This vow renewed shall daily hear,
Till in life's latest hour I bow,
And bless in death a bond so dear.

We may never meet again - until we meet to part and sin and sorrow or sigh no more - at Jesus' feet. Let me plead with you. My day is almost run; my work is almost finished; I have had 40 years in His service and revelling in His sweet, beloved will. You are at the beginning of your life, take an old man's advice and heed his pleading.

Present your body a living sacrifice and DO IT NOW and never revoke it!

Rid me, good Lord, of every diverting thing.
Amy Carmichael

A Battlefield not a Playground

Wherefore take unto you the whole armour of God that ye may be able to withstand in the evil day, and having done all, to stand.
Ephesians 6 vs. 13

We have turned our churches into a kind of hospital filled with weak and sickly patients. We have turned it into a kind of hydropathic, where life has to be carefully nurtured. The church is filled with sickly, anaemic, crippled spiritual lives instead of Christians full of health and vigour, warriors on the battlefield. And we have turned the minister into a kind of spiritual doctor instead of a fighter or general in the army. The church is an army, not a hospital. It should abound in soldiers and not abound in cripples and hospital patients. The minister is a fighter, a leader of soldiers, not a hospital attendant caring for sickly patients. My friends, there are to be no exceptions. We are every one to be fighters. We are every one to be soldiers "enduring hardness as good soldiers of Jesus" but the sad thing about it is that so few of us are willing to stand up against the enemy. The least bit of temptation, or the least bit of persecution, and we are all down in the dumps and our feelings are hurt, and we go to the minister and tell him we are not feeling just right, and the poor man, he's a doctor, instead of a general. This is altogether contrary to the Lord's idea of the thing. He wants His people to have overflowing, abounding lives.

God wants us to be victors, not victims; to grow, not grovel; to soar, not sink; to overcome, not to be overwhelmed.
William A Ward

DECEMBER

1 ◆ Fertile Soil

2 ◆ The Need of Revival

3 ◆ Revival

4 ◆ Quit Quibbling

5 ◆ Hindrances to Revival

6 ◆ Prejudice Against Revival

7 ◆ Don't Keep Bad Company

8 ◆ No Cheap Road to Revival

9 ◆ Preparation for Blessing

10 ◆ Take Care

11 ◆ Seen and Heard

12 ◆ First Hand Evidence

13 ◆ A Personal Pentecost

14 ◆ Unlimited Zeal

15 ◆ Filled with the Holy Spirit

16 ◆ Our Relationship with Others

17 ◆ Lasting Joy

18 ◆ Examining the Evidence

19 ◆ Keep His Commandments

20 ◆ Righteousness

21 ◆ The Habit of Holiness

22 ◆ Forgetting not Forsaking

23 ◆ Must We Believe Only What we can Understand

24 ◆ Confessing Christ

25 ◆ Robbing God

26 ◆ God's Acid Tests

27 ◆ Our Talents

28 ◆ Passion for Souls

29 ◆ A Great Privilege

30 ◆ Essentials

31 ◆ Go Forward

Fertile Soil

… that ye may prove what is that good, and acceptable,
and perfect, will of God.
Romans 12 vs. 2

You see, while you have this question about God's will you are fertile soil for the old devil to work on! And mind you, he isn't idle tilling it. He knows how to do it, and oh, what a crop he will raise in your lives – sooner or later – and sooner than later, if you don't get rid of the question about God's will.

How many are backsliders today because of this? We think and speak of backsliding as if it were the act or accident of a moment. Oh no, dear friends, it is the result of some hidden, secret questioning of the will of God. The old devil can work havoc in our lives when he can keep us questioning God's will for us. Sure that was the way he wrecked Eve's life. "Hath God said?" said the devil. That is, "Are you sure God said it, and if He did, is His will fair and kind? He won't let you eat a certain fruit. Ay? Is that kind and good of God to treat you like that?" Poor Eve believed the devil - the old serpent –and questioned God's will, and oh what a mess he made of her life and husband and home, and succeeding generations. Friend, it is a terrible harvest, not only for yourself but to untold multitudes.

So you see what a serious thing it is to question God's will for your life, however strange and staggering and mysterious it may be.

Seek neither more or less than God's will for you.
Vance Havner

2 DECEMBER

The Need of Revival

Wilt thou no revive us again: that thy people may rejoice in thee?
Psalm 85 vs. 6.

"O Lord, revive thy work in the midst of the years, in the midst of the years make known; in wrath remember mercy." Habakkuk 3 vs.2.

God is the only Author and source of real heaven-sent revival in all ages and today. There is nothing He and heaven delight more in than revivals. There is rejoicing in the presence of the angels of God over one soul repenting. Then what rejoicing there must be over hundreds and thousands repenting, as they do during a revival? Was there ever a time when a revival was more needed than today? These terrible war days when moral and religious bars are being let down and all hell let loose and Satan working overtime and the world upside down and the end is not yet. For when peace comes there will be conditions and problems that only a real Holy Ghost revival can meet and solve. We hear it on every hand, "If we don't get a revival there will be a revolution." Rulers, Statesmen, Politicians, Editors, Ministers and the rank and file of the people everywhere feel and say the same thing. There seems to be a general agreement about the fact of revival and the necessity for one. Our desperate condition - worldwide condition - has driven us out of wondering whether there is such a thing as a revival and whether a revival is possible in our day and age. It has largely driven us out of our fear of a revival. For mind you, there were many ministers and church members who were dead scared of a revival coming to their church. They would a million times rather have a decent respectable dignified but dead church and services, than a revival. There may be some such today, but they are scarce, for if they have any love for God's work and Church and even their country, they are forced to recognise a revival from heaven is the only thing that can meet our present need.

Revival is a sad necessity.
Arthur Skevington Wood

Revival

O Lord, revive thy work in the midst of the years...
Habakkuk 3:2.

The church began in a revival. Every evangelical denomination had its birth in a revival. Just as the church has kept this spirit aflame has she been successful in winning the lost to Christ. No dead body can carry a living head. No dead branches can be suffered on the Living Vine. The dead bodies belong to the grave. There must be something pungent and vitalising about the life of a true Church. Savourless salt is only fit for the footpath and rubbish heap. Leaven that has lost its power is disgusting. Seed that has lost its fertility means barren lands and starving populations. A church without enthusiasm is a church without God. A lukewarm Christian or Church is a disgust to Christ and He says He will spue them out of His mouth.

> Revival is God rending the heavens and coming down among His people.
> Vance Havner

Quit Quibbling

If my people, which are called by my name, shall humble themselves, and pray, and seek my face, and turn from their wicked ways; then will I hear from heaven, and will forgive their sin, and will heal their land.
II Chronicles 7 vs. 14

Let us quit quibbling and questioning about revival, let us try and find out why we haven't one and how we may obtain one. There is one thing we may be sure about and that is, God is willing and able to give us a revival. It is never God's fault if we are not in the throes of a personal, congregational, and national revival constantly. Let us humbly and honestly try and discover any and every hindrance to a revival. Let us examine ourselves. Don't let us say or imagine because we are doing nothing wrong or making no trouble we are alright and therefore we are not hindering a revival. This revival business is like pulling a chariot along. Some don't pull; they don't block the wheels, but because they are doing nothing they are making it all the harder for those who are pulling. When you do not help to pull you are increasing the weight that has to be drawn. If my leg does not help me in walking it certainly hinders me and hampers me. So does the Christian hinder and hamper revival if he is not doing all he can to further it. There is something every born-again, blood-washed one can do and must do if the revival is not to be hindered.

> Whenever self-effort, self-glory, self-seeking or self-promotion enters into the work of revival, then God leaves us to ourselves.
> Ted S Rendall

Hindrances to Revival

For I will pour water upon him that is thirsty, and floods upon
the dry ground: I will pour my spirit upon they seed,
and my blessing upon thine offspring:
Isaiah 44 vs. 3

Let me mention some hindrances and if we are guilty of any of them, let us put them away from us. It is awful to think we could be a hindrance to our own soul's growth. That is bad enough but that I should hinder a revival and deprive sinners of the means of their salvation and maybe be the cause, directly or indirectly, of their damnation: what a terrible crime that would be.

The first hindrance is frequently lack of desire. The Lord will never come where He is not wanted or welcomed. He will never cast His pearls before swine. "I will pour water upon him that is thirsty and floods upon the dry ground." You must be thirsty and like dry ground. "Blessed are they which do hunger and thirst". Says Jesus. "Whatsoever things ye desire when ye pray". Some seem more concerned about the condition of the building and the order of service and so-called classical music of the choir and eloquence and learning of the preacher, than they are about a revival in the midst. Some are more concerned about the "jot and tittle" of the service and order of service, while all the time they are devoid of revival as a desert is of water. And worse than all, they are satisfied with themselves and their churches and wee meetings in their hall. May the Lord deliver us from such a state of soul and mind as this and fill us with a consuming divine desire for times of refreshing from His presence that will constrain us to do all we can and pray all we can, until revival comes down from heaven.

Waiting for general revival is no excuse for not enjoying personal revival.
Stephen Olford

Prejudice against Revival

And he marvelled because of their unbelief...
Mark 6 vs. 6

Another common hindrance is prejudice against revivals. They can tell you all about the dangers and doubtful things in revival. You would think to hear them opposing a revival that a revival was a curse instead of a blessing. God is the Source and Author of revivals, but they will have nothing to do with them, except denounce and hinder them. They charge God with folly by their attitude. They forget there is only one way of knowing whether the revival is of God or not and that is "By their fruits". Whatever movement issues in regenerated lives, whatever makes sinners into saints and changes drunkards into sober, godly men and women, whatever changes white-washed proud Pharisees into blood-washed, humble, loving, followers of Christ, is surely not a work of the devil but of God the Holy Ghost. The devil doesn't save souls and further God's cause among men. It is the very reverse. The devil is prejudiced against and hates a revival. Every publican, every swearing, gambling, Sabbath-breaking sinner, every wicked, God hating, self-righteous Pharisee is prejudiced against and hates a revival.

They tell me a revival is only temporary; so is a bath, but it does you good.
Billy Sunday

Don't Keep Bad Company

And he did not many mighty works there because of their unbelief.
Matthew 13 vs. 58

Some of you professing Christians who are prejudiced against revivals are in bad company and you should be ashamed of yourselves. What the old devil is for, I am against, and I am for all he is against. Don't let your prejudice make you do the devil's dirty work and hinder God's work. Away with prejudice and let us desire and love and work for a mighty revival. Certainly there will be a lot about a revival we can't agree with, and won't like, because of the ignorance and idiosyncrasies of Christians, but this should not prejudice us against revival. Look at the blessing that has come to Church and community. See the number of believers who are on fire for God and souls, who were once cold, decent and unconcerned about the salvation of the lost. Also the number of all sorts of sinners powerfully converted and living Godly lives. Surely your prejudice will die and you will become an enthusiastic believer in revivals and begin praying and working for one.

> It may seem mysterious that God should permit a work of His own
> holy and blessed Spirit to be accompanied, marred and perverted by
> errors and abuses. But so it has been from the beginning.
> Ashbel Green

No Cheap Road to Revival

They that sow in tears shall reap in joy.
Psalm 126 vs. 5

Another very common and common–place hindrance is lack of sacrifice. We must bleed if we would bless. There is no revival without sweat, blood and toil. It is a costly thing. We must prepare if we would participate in a revival. Everything worthwhile in life is costly and the more worthwhile it is the costlier it is. Jesus said, "Virtue is gone out of me" as He blessed others. There is no cheap road to revival. There is no cheap price to pay for one. Revival is a precious and costly thing. It cost God dearly to make revivals possible. "He gave His only begotten Son". It cost the Lord Jesus a lot. Bearing shame and scoffing rude, lifted up was He to die. But Jesus paid it all. It costs today the Holy Spirit a great price. How He works in spite of insult, resisting, striving and unbelief. Never resting, never ceasing, never wearying until we are willing to suffer and sacrifice too, for a revival. How many men and women have become nervous wrecks, broken in mind and body as they livingly, sacrificially, unceasingly laboured for revival. It is because it is so costly so many shirk the cross. It is a costly thing. Many are praying for revival but not willing to pay the price. Is the cost and sacrifice too great? It may seem so now, but when we stand around the judgement seat of Christ and give an account of the deeds done in the body, whether they are good or bad, and be accused of hindering a revival by our want of self sacrifice and the blood of souls laid to our charge, will it seem too great a sacrifice?

There is no revival possible in any fellowship without a price being paid.
Alan Redpath

Preparation for Blessing

Jesus said, take ye away the stone…
John 11 vs. 39

There is an unwillingness to let the Holy Spirit have His own way. So many want to manage His operations. If the Lord would only send a revival that would suit them they would gladly receive it and revel in it. They are scared that the Lord would do something that would shock them or outrage their sense of order and decency. What presumption! As if the Lord didn't know how to behave Himself or do His own work. If the Lord would only give a revival consistent with Presbyterianism, or one that would be agreeable to the Baptists, Methodists, Church of Ireland, they would all go for it, but because the Lord won't pledge Himself to their denomination or sect and their way of doing His work, they wont have anything to do with it. It must have their brand or imprimatur before they will condescend to have anything to do with it - unless condemn it. Friends! let us get this thing fixed in our minds, you cannot make a Presbyterian, Baptist, Methodist, or Episcopalian out of the Lord. He is inter-denominational. He is sovereign in His operations. The Spirit breatheth where He willeth so is everyone that is born of the Spirit. Oh may we be so desperate for a revival from heaven that we will pray, "Lord send us your own revival anyhow, and by whatever method or man or woman you choose. We wont criticise or complain, only send us a mighty revival." It wouldn't be long until there was a holy epidemic of revival everywhere. We and our petty notions and our inconsistencies are the hindrances to its coming. If we would only roll away the stone we would soon see Lazarus' coming out of their graves to live and walk in newness of life ever after.

When we cease to bleed we cease to bless.
A. Jowatt

Take Care

Not forsaking the assembling of ourselves together, as the manner of some is; but exhorting one another...
Hebrew 10 vs. 25

The Church is God's earthly home for His heavenly bairns. It is the only institution He started. He knows we need it and therefore He provided it for us. We need it more than it needs us. We are not to forsake the assembling of ourselves together. When we join church after our conversion, never before, we witness before all that we are His. Take care what sort of church you join. If the minister denies or doubts the Book or the Blood have no fellowship with him, or you become a partaker with him in his evil deeds. When you take your Communion you are witnessing to the Blood and to the coming again of Christ. If you teach a Sunday school class, be sure and try and win it for Christ. Don't be content to merely teach a lesson, but to win every scholar for Christ. Let all our organisations and societies be an opportunity for witnessing and delivering souls.

The church is not a yachting club but a fleet of fishing boats.
Anon

Seen and Heard

...we are all witnesses.
Acts 2 vs. 32

A witness is not a dummy. Yet how many there are today and they say they don't believe in people giving their testimony or speaking about their soul's salvation. They believe, they say, in living it. Well, are we to follow our own notions, or other people's notions or the Word of Jesus? We won't be judged on that day by what others thought or even by our own thought; but by His Word. Just imagine a man being subpoenaed as a witness in a court case and after being sworn in he said, "Judge, I don't believe in talking about the case; I believe in living it." They would think such a man was more fit for a lunatic asylum than a witness box in court. It is just as ridiculous for a Christian to say, "He believes in living it, not speaking about it." The high priest had bells and pomegranates hung alternatively on the hem of his priestly robes. A bell and a seed. That is not only life but also testimony; not only seen but heard. So the Lord would have our lives not only the "Light of the world," but witnessing; not only shining as lights in the midst of a crooked and perverse nation, but also holding forth the Word of Life. You will generally find where there is opposition to witnessing on the part of Christians, it is because they are not living right. Where the life is lived for Him the witnessing is a natural outcome and delight.

God has no dumb children.
J C Ryle

First Hand Evidence

I believed, and therefore have I spoken; we also believe, and therefore speak;
II Corinthians 4 vs. 13

A witness is one who gives first-hand evidence not second-hand. He speaks of the things that he has seen and heard and which are most surely believed among us. He has been saved and washed in the blood of Christ and brought to know Christ as his own personal Saviour. His isn't second-hand religion, but first hand. His is a "know so" religion. He has the full assurance of faith in the dead certainty that he is born again and now is a child of God. So when he begins to speak he doesn't tell what someone told him or what he read. No he tells what he knows, experimentally. Christ's virgin birth and sinless life and substitutionary death and victorious resurrection are no mere theories to him, but personal realities. How could a mere man, however good or great, save his soul? God alone can forgive sinners and Jesus is God to him and none other. You may confound him in argument, but he will still sing out of his heart and experience.

I want no other argument,
I want no other plea;
It is enough that Jesus died,
And that He died for me.

One thing I know – that whereas I was blind, now I can see, Any minister or Christian who gives mere second-hand testimony is a fraud and a farce.

One man with a glowing experience of God is worth a library full of arguments.
Vance Havner

A Personal Pentecost

But truly I am full of power by the spirit of the Lord...
Micah 3 vs. 8

In the Gospel, according to Luke, our Lord says, "Ye are my witnesses." In Acts 1 vs. 8, we read, "Ye shall be." Is this a contradiction? No it isn't contradictory but complimentary. Luke was written before Acts. We are witnesses now; but we never can become what we are until after the Holy Ghost is come upon us; then we shall be. The Lord provides the dynamic for the demand, the power for the programme. Let us "tarry until we be endued with power." "Wait for the promise of the Father." Then when we are filled with the Holy Ghost we shall begin to witness in the home, in the church, and in the world by prayer, going and giving. Without this Power we will never succeed. The work of witnessing is the duty of the whole church. The field of witnessing is the territory of the whole world. The power for witnessing is a personal Pentecost.
Ye are...Ye shall be...After.

Stir me, Oh! Stir me, Lord;
Thy heart was stirred
By love's intensest fire-
Till Thou did'st give Thine only Son,
Thy best beloved One!
Even to the dreadful Cross.
That I might live;
Stir me to give myself so back to Thee.
That Thou can't give Thyself again through me

The message of the infilling of the Holy Spirit in many evangelical centres is looked upon as a form of fanaticism, if not of heresy. As a result, many churches are sound, yes, but sound asleep.
Ian R K Paisley

Unlimited Zeal

Whatsoever thy hand findeth to do, do it with thy might...
Ecclesiastes 9 vs. 10

Remember, it is always 'the little farther' in every walk of life that counts. The musical genius has only gone 'a little farther' than the ordinary musician. The painter who paints for all time has only gone 'a little farther' than the ordinary artist. The difference between the successful business man and the man who can barely make a living is just this – 'he went a little farther'; the student at college who passes his exams with honours and the one who barely gets through is just this – 'he went a little farther.' It is true in the Christian life also. One is eminent for holiness and soul winning, while the other is just a nominal Christian. The one has gone 'a little farther' than the other. We have the historic incident in the lives of Luther and Erasmus. The one's name is a household word and his memory beloved. The other name barely known and when known, not very highly respected. Why is this? Our text explains it. Luther went 'a little farther' than Erasmus. You remember the incident. Erasmus said: 'I intend to be true to the truth as far as the times will allow.' While Luther said, 'Here I take my stand, so help me God. I cannot retract.' So Luther's name will outshine the sun.

We never test the resources of God until we attempt the impossible.
F B Meyer

Filled with the Holy Spirit

Wherefore be ye not unwise, but understanding what the will of the Lord is.
And be not drunk with wine, wherein is excess, but be filled with the Spirit.
Ephesians 5 vs. 17,18

It is only when we are emptied that we are filled with the Holy Spirit. To be filled with the Holy Spirit is the open secret of this life of fullness. You have noticed in the life of Christ how this is clearly manifested. He said "My joy I give unto you," and He said "My peace I leave with you". So much of hope was in His life. You never found Him discouraged. We are told in the book of Isaiah "My servant shall not fail or be discouraged". What comfort was in His life! He brought sunshine into the shady places wherever He went. What goodness He had! Peter says He was filled with the Holy Ghost and went about doing good. His life was a continual benediction. He spoiled every funeral He attended. He knew God's will perfectly. How righteous His life was! He said, "which of you convinceth me of sin". He was filled with righteousness, and He was filled unto all the fullness of God. But my Christian friends, will you not let the Lord fill you in His loving way with His fullness? Just say to Him, "Lord, I come, I yield, I believe," and He will fill you unto all fullness, and as He fills you He will empty you of other things, so gently, surely and lovingly. He empties us of these other things that we might know and enjoy His fullness and also that our lives may be a channel of blessing to others continually. "Be not drunk with wine, but be filled with the Spirit".

Fill me with thy fullness, Lord,
Until my every heart o'erflow
With kindling thought and glowing word
Thy love to tell Thy praise to show.

The Holy Spirit may be had for the asking.
R B Kuiper

Our Relationship with Others

Ye are the salt of the earth
Matthew 5 vs. 13

Jesus was referring to our relationship with others. The world is in a rotting condition all around. It is not getting better and never will. Many talk about making the world a better place in which to live. If the salt were withdrawn it soon would be seen whether the world is getting better or not. Christians arrest in some degree its total corruption. History reveals the corruption of nations as the salt was withdrawn from them. The influence of the salt is sometimes unpleasant. When salt is applied to a corrupting sore it smarts and stings. This is why we are told, "ye shall be hated of all men for my name's sake". But even when the salt is unpleasant it still is beneficent. What a blessing it is today everywhere it exists. Every country that is worthwhile and fit to live in is so because of the beneficent influence of Christians. Men who have been a blessing even in generations past still have an influence on the present day. What a blessing a godly mother and father have over their children. The presence of good men hinders the old devil from having elbowroom to do his dirty work. Every Christian has an influence upon public opinion. To be effective salt must be in contact with the substance to be seasoned or preserved. As Christians we cannot stay aloof from our family circle or refuse to mingle with men in business connections. Worldly people of the circles in which we mingle may hate us, but they cannot prevent Christians from being a blessing.

We are not saltcellars but saltshakers to scatter our blessings everywhere we go.
Vance Havner

Lasting Joy

Thou wilt shew me the path of life; in thou presence is fullness of joy; at thy right hand there are pleasures for evermore.
Psalms 16 vs. 11

Oh, what a wonderful Saviour Jesus becomes when we are yielded and filled! There are lots of God's dear people, and they have the root of the matter in them, they have Christ in them - there is no doubt of that - but it is a root out of dry ground. There is no form or comeliness, and no beauty in Him that they should desire Him, so they have to go to the world for satisfaction; they have to go to a dirty piece of tobacco to get a wee bit of comfort, to gratify their appetites; they have to go to dances and picture-shows to get a wee bit of fun. They have a Jesus who doesn't satisfy them. They are roots out of dry ground. But when the Comforter comes He glorifies Christ; the root becomes the rose of Sharon, the Lily of the Valley, the fairest among ten thousand, the altogether lovely One to your soul, and you begin to say, out of the depth of your experience; "I am satisfied with Jesus. This vain world is nought to me. All its pleasures are forgotten in remembering Calvary." and you sing with all your heart.

Oh, Christ, in Thee my soul hath found,
And found in Thee alone,
The peace, the joy, I sought so long,
The bliss till now unknown.
Now none but Christ .

Not your old picture-show, not your old theatre, or your dances, but Christ.

Now none but Christ can satisfy,
None other name for me.
There's love, and life, and lasting joy,
Lord Jesus, found in Thee

Joy in God is the happiest of all joys.
C H Spurgeon

Examining the Evidence

Examine yourselves, whether ye be in the faith;...
II Corinthians 13 vs. 5

I want to take you to the Word of God and see the evidence given there whereby we may be scripturally sure we are really and truly saved. Thank God for our Bible. We don't need to accept our own notions or the notion of others however scholarly and religious they may be. We have God's simple sublime words to comfort and assure us or to convict us if we are deceived. In the first Epistle of John we have several clear unmistakable evidences whereby we may find out whether we have any right to say we are born again - we are saved. Remember, this Epistle was written for this very reason. "This then is the message which we have heard of Him and declare unto you, that God is light and in Him is no darkness at all. If we say that we have fellowship with Him and walk in darkness, we lie, and do not the truth, but if we walk in the light, as he is in the light we have fellowship one with another". So let us consider some of these evidences and if in the light they reveal we are assured we are born again then we have a scriptural foundation for our faith and will not be easily carried about by our changing circumstances and fluctuating feelings or notions of others.

> The most important point is where you are today in terms of holiness.
> George Verver

Keep His Commandments

And hereby we do know that we know him, if we keep his commandments.
1 John 2 vs. 3

"Whatsoever we ask we receive of him, because we keep his commandments. And he that keepeth his commandments dwelleth in him and he in him" (1 John 3 vs. 22,24) By this we know that we love the children of God when we love God, and keep his commandments. For this is the love of God, that we keep his commandments: and his commandments are not grievous. (1 John 5 vs. 2,3) What are some of His commandments? "Except we repent ye shall perish". Have you really repented of your self-righteousness and sin, your good works and bad works! Have you come to the place where you confess the absence of all good and the presence of all evil in your heart. Have you changed your mind about God, Christ, Salvation, Heaven, Hell, Sin and Guilt? Are you sorry for sin and sinning, and have you ceased from it. Here is another commandment. "Except ye be converted ye shall not enter the kingdom of heaven". Have you been converted? When? Where? Have you turned unto the Lord from your own thoughts and ways? Another commandment. "Except a man be born again he cannot see the kingdom of God". Are you born again? Are you a new creature? The new birth is just as real and necessary as the natural birth. These are some of His commandments. Have you kept them? It is only those who do so have any right to say they are born again, for He that saith I know Him and keep not His commandments is a liar and the truth is not in him.

Holiness is not an experience you have; holiness is keeping the law of God.
D Martin Lloyd Jones

Righteousness

...everyone that doeth righteousness is born of Him
1 John 2 vs. 29

"Little children, let no man deceive you; he that doeth righteousness is righteous, even as he is righteous"..."Whosoever doeth not righteousness is not of God". (1 John 3 vs. 7) Jesus said "By their fruits ye shall know them". When we are truly saved, then our outward actions will betray and reveal the reality of our conversion. Holiness deals with character. Righteousness deals with conduct. A righteous man is one who is right with God and his fellowman. He isn't a cheat, thief or liar. In all his actions he is all-right, up-right, down-right and out-right. His word is as good as his bond and he pays his debts. "Owe no man anything but love". Some would give you the impression that when you are saved you can live and do as you please. They would have you believe that salvation was a cloak for their rascality and meanness. This is turning the grace of God into lasciviousness. You get apples from a tree because it is an apple tree. You can tell a tree by its fruit, a flower by its scent, and a bird by its song. So you can tell a born again man by his life. He is a righteous man in Christ and this is manifested by righteousness. You will notice it is continuous - doeth. It isn't sometimes, some-places but all the time, everywhere, not merely on Sundays or at home, but every day of the week and all day long. Holidays as well as at home. Summer as well as winter. He doeth righteousness.

> Do all the good you can, in all the ways you can, to all the people you can, as long as you can.
> John Wesley

The Habit of Holiness

*Whosoever is born of God doth not commit sin; for his seed remaineth in
him: and he cannot sin, because he is born of God. In this the children of
God are manifest, and the children of the devil...
We know that whosoever is born of God sinneth not...*
1 John 3 vs. 9,10;   5 vs. 18

This verse does not say "A born again man is a sinless man, a man who
never sins" Oh, no, it does mean a born again man does not make a
habit of sinning. The habit of his life is holiness. Whosoever keeps on
sinning hath not seen Him or known Him. He that keeps on
committing sin is of the devil. We are sheep not sows. A sheep may be
a poor scraggy creature but it will jump over every mud hole; it may
jump short and fall into it but it will not lie in it. A sow may be a
pedigree sow, but when it comes to a mud hole it will wallow in it
because it is a sow. "The sow wallowing in the mire" Because we are
sheep we cannot wallow in the mire. It isn't a sheep's nature to do so.
If an honest man is tempted to be dishonest he says, "I cannot because
I am an honest man". A truthful man cannot lie. A righteous man
cannot be immoral. A born again man cannot sin, that is, he cannot
live in sin. He may through weakness or ignorance fall into sin, but he
does not live in it. This is the way you can tell a child of God. Holiness
is the habit of his life not wickedness.

A holy life is the eye of God.
William Gurnall

Forgetting not Forsaking

Brethren I count not myself to have apprehended, but this one thing I do,
forgetting those things which are behind, and reaching forth
unto those things which are before.
Philippians 3 vs. 13

I press toward the mark for the prize of the high calling of God in Christ Jesus. God is calling us day by day to be like Jesus. To love Him better, to resemble Him more completely, to strike off from our character a little more of the encompassing stone and to bring out some new line and lineament of the perfect statue. It is a "high calling" because it comes from above. Men strive to get money forgetting that the pleasures of this world are like snow upon the river. One moment, white, then gone forever. They strive after fame, forgetting there must be a moment when their remains will lie beneath the pall on which the crown and sceptre rest to be assumed by another. Paul said, "This one thing I do". He was determined to be like Christ and win men for Christ. What a passion he had. He said "I could wish myself accursed from Christ for my brethren. My heart's desire and prayer is that they might be saved." One thing I do that by all means I might save some. His one concern was to save the lost and win the prize – the crown of life.

May we never get used to the thud of Christless feet on the road to hell, but by all means save some. What a prize to go in for. Some one that day of review and reward, to stand and confess that we led him to Christ. God save us from being delivered from this soul-saving work.

I have one passion only: It is he! It is he!
Nicolas von Zinzendorf

Must We Believe Only What We Can Understand?

The wind bloweth where it listeth, and thou hearest the sound thereof,
but canst not tell whence it cometh, and whither it goeth:
so is every one that is born of the Spirit.
John 3 vs 8

A minister was preaching one Sunday in his church in a country village. The local doctor used to come in now and then, just to patronise the minister. They used to sit and chat together at times after the services of the Sunday were over. This Sunday evening the minister was preaching on "Ye must be born again." Among other things he said was this, "He couldn't understand being born again, although he believed it." After he got home the doctor called on him, and after some chatting the doctor said, "I was surprised at what you said to-night. I always thought you were a man of some intelligence. You said you believe in what you could not and did not understand." "That is true," said the minister. The doctor said, "How absurd. Did you ever see regeneration? No. Did you ever taste it? No. Did you ever smell it? No. Did you ever hear it? No. Did you ever feel it?" "Oh, yes I have," said the minister. "Well," said the doctor, "will you believe what four out of your five senses are against?" "Let me answer that," said the minister, "by asking you a question. Do you believe in pain?" "Certainly I do." "Have you ever seen it? No. Have you ever tasted it? No. Have you ever heard it? No. Have you ever smelt it? No. Have you ever felt it?" "Certainly I have." "Yet you believe in what four out of five of your senses are against." The doctor saw how absurd his position was. Your position is just as absurd as his, if you believe only what you can understand.

"The wind bloweth where it listeth, and thou hearest the sound thereof, but canst not tell whence it cometh, and whither it goeth: so is every one that is born of the Spirit"

Faith is greater than our learning.
Martin Luther

Confessing Christ

*Whosoever therefore shall confess me before men, Him will I confess also
before my Father which is in heaven. But whosoever shall deny me before
men, him will I also deny before my Father which is in heaven.*
Matthew 10 vs. 32-33

Isn't it strange how many believers (so called) there are today who
live, daily disobeying these solemn words of Jesus? They never
confess Christ before men, unless maybe they are caught in a corner
and cannot very well do otherwise. They fight shy of it wherever
possible. If a meeting is turned into a testimony meeting, they are
greatly annoyed and irritated and make all sorts of excuses for not
feeling at home in such a service and confessing Christ. If the preacher
"tests" a meeting and asks all who are really saved and know it, to
stand to their feet and thus confess Christ, they are so angry they sit
still or get up and clear out, or maybe they are ashamed to do either,
so they sort of half stand up, feeling very awkward and very angry.
Yet they believe they are saved and take the place of a saved person by
joining Church and sitting around the Lord's Table and partaking of
the sacrament. They say "They don't believe in confessing Christ by
making a public display of themselves or their faith." Well friend, how
can you say such a thing, and take such a stand, in the light of such
solemn words of our Lord Jesus? Remember this: If you deny Him, He
will deny you; if you are ashamed of Him, He will be ashamed of you.
He will do with you what you do with Him. Deny Him before men,
in this adulterous generation and He will deny you before His Father
and the holy angels. This is only fair, isn't it? Deny Him down here
and He will deny you up there. Be ashamed of Him down here and
He will be ashamed of you up there.

Be not ashamed of your faith; remember it is the ancient gospel of
martyrs, confessors, reformers and saints. Above all, it is "the truth
of God", against which the gates of hell cannot prevail.
C H Spurgeon

Robbing God

Will a man rob God? Yet ye have robbed me. But ye say, Wherein have we robbed thee? In tithes and offerings.
Malachi 3 vs. 8

We will deal today with the sin of "Robbing God." Malachi asks with astonishment, "Will a man rob God?" God says, "Ye have robbed me." But ye say, "Wherein have we robbed thee?" God says, "In tithes and offerings, " and because of this, "Ye are cursed." What a terrible thing for a child of God to be cursed – even his blessings to be cursed by God. Friend! You cannot get away with robbing God and not suffer for it. "Be not deceived. God is not mocked – whatever a man soweth that shall he reap. You can't sow and not reap." You can't cheat and rob God, and not be cursed. If we are not tithers we are robbing God and living under His curse. You can neither evade nor avoid it. We are either living under His curse or His blessing. If we are robbing God by not tithing we are under His curse. The tithe and tithing is God's method of dealing with us about money. It is not of man, neither did it originate by man, but of God.

God can rain money into farmers' pockets and He can rain it out.
He can shine it in and He can shine it out.
William Tiptaft

God's Acid Tests

*...remember the words of the Lord Jesus, how he said, It is more blessed
to give than to receive.*
Acts 20 vs. 35

God tests every man. These tests reveal what is in him. Because of
this, we are taught in the Bible a great deal about money and tithing.
One in every six verses of the entire Bible relates to the subject of
giving. Of Christ's 38 parables, 16 have reference to man's attitude
towards money. In the four Gospels, one verse in every seven deals
with this subject. Christ summed it all up in the great statement.
"Render unto God the things that are God's." Someone says, "As a
Christian we are no longer bound to a tenth." No, certainly not. Many
give more than the tenth. But if the objector means that God will be
satisfied with less than the very minimum prescribed to beginners in
His kingdom, he is disregarding the limit God sets as the least margin
of safety to guard men from the pitfalls of covetousness. We must not
forget that Christian stewardship does not stop with the tithe but
begins with it. When a man has learned to tithe, he has learned the
ABC of giving.

Not how much we give, but how much we do not give, is the test of
our Christianity.
Oswald Chambers

Our Talents

And unto one he gave five talents, to another two, and to another one;
to every man according to his several ability; and straightway
took his journey.
Matthew 25 vs. 15

Our talents belong to God. Some are given more talents than others but everyone has a talent, none are devoid of talents. Some can sing or lead the singing. Others can teach the Bible; some have executive ability and could direct the affairs of the Church. Some have speaking ability and could preach. Whatever your talent is, are you giving it to God's work in the Church or Mission Hall? The grave significance of the parable of the talents is this: The man who had five talents used every one and doubled them by using them. He could have wasted or not used one or two and still have some left to use. But the one who had only one talent, and couldn't afford to lose it, was the one who lost it. You may have only a few, or only one talent. Don't rob God by not using the one you have. Give God the best you have, and all you have, of talents.

We will go past the Judgement Seat of Christ in single file.
John Blanchard

28 DECEMBER

Passion for Souls

Now I beseech you, brethren, for the Lord Jesus Christ's sake,
and for the love of the Spirit, that ye strive together with me
in your prayers to God for me;
Romans 15 vs. 30

He could say and say truly, "I lie not; my conscience also bearing me witness in the Holy Ghost that I have great sorrow and unceasing pain in my heart, for I could wish that myself were accursed from Christ, for my brethren." "My heart's desire and prayer to God for Israel is that they might be saved." He could say also, "I am made all things to all men, that I might by all means save some." At last he laid down his life outside Rome, saying, "I have fought a good fight. I have finished my course." As we thus consider this man whom Renan called "An ugly wee Jew," we are compelled to wonder whether we are really followers of and believers in Christ or not. What mere pigmies we are compared with Paul. How little any of us has ever done or suffered for Christ and the salvation of the lost, for whom Christ died. As we compare ourselves with this early disciple of our Lord we are put to shame. Our zeal for Christ, our works of faith and love, and our desires and efforts to win men for Christ, seem as nothing compared with Paul's.

The soul winner must first of all be a soul lover.
C H Spurgeon

A Great Privilege

Moreover as for me, God forbid that I should sin against the Lord
in ceasing to pray for you...
I Samuel 12 vs. 23

What the workers and work of God owe to sick, suffering 'shut-ins', the Judgment Seat of Jesus Christ will alone fully reveal. What a privilege this is that God has given to every saved one. To have any part in this wonderful ministry – to be God's partner in God's work – is a great honour. What condescension on God's part to have anything to do with us. When He saved us that was more than we ever deserved. If He had taken us to heaven immediately after our conversion, we could never have complained. But not only saving us, but giving us the privilege of being co-workers with Him – carrying out His purposes and plans for this world. It is beyond our comprehension, but need not be beyond our blessed experience. We are priests and kings unto God. If angels or archangels were capable of envy, they must envy us and would gladly take our place in this glorious ministry of intercession. What a privilege to have an audience with the King at any time, anywhere, about everything.

> *What a friend we have in Jesus,*
> *All our sins and griefs to bear,*
> *What a privilege to carry everything to God in prayer;*
> *O what peace we often forfeit,*
> *O what needless pain we bear,*
> *All because we do not carry, everything to God in prayer.*

Don't let us despise this great privilege by neglecting to take time, or make time, to intercede for ourselves and others.

When we miss out on prayer we cause disappointment to Christ, defeat to ourselves, and delight to the devil.
John Blanchard

Essentials

...we will give ourselves continually to prayer...
Acts 6 vs. 4

If we are to give ourselves to our priestly ministry of intercession and continue and prevail in it, there are three things that are essential. I will merely mention them and not enlarge upon them.

First – A quiet place. Jesus said, "When thou prayest, enter into thy closet, and when thou hast shut the door, pray to thy Father which is in secret." This ministry of intercession is a secret, hidden work. I believe this is the main reason why so many believers sin by ceasing from it. There is no glamour about it. There is no reward here with it, but there is a sure reward in heaven. "Thy Father which seeth in secret, shall reward thee openly." The quiet place Jesus had was either on the mountaintop or the garden of olives. If He needed such a place, how much more do we? We are creatures of habit. A place we use for prayer makes it easier to pray. Never mind what sort of a place our secret place may be, or where it is situated, just as long as it is our closet. Our Heavenly Father is no respecter of places. But we will never succeed in intercession unless we have such a place.

Second – A quiet time. We never have time to pray. We are too busy about many things. We will have to "make" time. If we haven't time to pray, we are busier than God ever intended us to be. This isn't everything, but it is the most important thing in our lives. We have to "corner" time. We will never "find" time to pray, we will have to "make" time to pray. One cannot lay down a hard and fast rule as to what time of every day is best for this ministry. You will have to do this for yourself. But do it you must if you are to succeed.

Third – A quiet heart. Keep quiet and still before God. His presence will cool our fevered heart and mind, and soothe our fretted feelings and desires. You may wait in stillness for hours before you are quiet and fit for intercession.

Three things will help you to obtain this quiet heart. First, remember your acceptance before God. You are accepted in the Beloved, and only in Him. We are unworthy in ourselves. But He is all worthy, and we are accepted in Him. Secondly, let us also remember the aid of the Holy Spirit. He will help our infirmities, for we know not "what" to pray for as we ought, and we don't know "how" to pray. The Holy Spirit is our helper. Thirdly, the precious promises. Especially repeat the promises concerning prayer. God never breaks His word. Every promise is yours in Christ Jesus. Faithful is He who has called you into this priestly ministry of intercession, who also will do it.

> It is a good rule never to look into the face of man in the morning
> 'till you have looked into the face of God.
> C H Spurgeon

Go Forward

And the Lord said unto Moses, Wherefore criest thou unto me? speak unto the children of Israel, that they go forward.
Exodus 14 vs. 15

This was the command of God to His people in that day. It is His command to us in this day. We are standing on the brink of another New Year, and the danger in all our lives is stagnation. We are so apt to settle down and be at ease. God is always on the forward move, and we are to keep in stride with Him. There will never be a time here or hereafter when we can "stay still": we should always be advancing or we will quietly but surely die. "Go forward." Never mind how many and impossible the barriers are in our way. God will see us safely through them all. It is ours to go forward. It is God's part to make it possible.

Let us go forward to a fuller possession of our inheritance in Jesus Christ. So many camp down the other side of Jordan. We are to possess our possessions. There is always more to follow. Because you are born again and baptised with the Holy Ghost and fire, you are not to remain there. Go forward into the joy and power of larger fullness's of the Spirit.

Let us go forward to a more sturdy championship of the faith once for all delivered unto the saints. We will be maligned and scorned for our stalwart stand for the truth. Never mind. Let us go forward in spite of all our foes. Ring true to Christ and His word on every occasion.

Let us go forward to more faithful personal service for Christ and the perishing souls all around us. O may we never get used to men going to hell! May the thud of their Christless feet ever sound in our ears, as long as there is a man out of Christ on the road to hell! Go forward! We are saved to save others – to show light and save souls. Go forward! Time is short – the need appalling – the loafers many – the labourers few. Go forward - winning men to Christ by all means.

I am willing to go anywhere as long as it is forward.
David Livingstone

More by the same author ...

ALL FOR JESUS

The Life of W P Nicholson
by Stanley Barnes

This is a thrilling account of the life and work of Ulster's best known evangelist, the Rev. William Patteson Nicholson. In this biography, the author seeks to introduce 'WP' as he was affectionately known, to a new generation of readers who perhaps are not aware of the achievements of this unique preacher of the Gospel.

As a result of his United Gospel Campaigns in the early 1920s, thousands were brought to Christ. Converts came from every section of the community, Protestants and Catholics, publicans and drunkards, gunmen and thieves, religious church-goers and 'down and outs'. All knelt before God in repentance, confessing their need of Christ and crying for mercy.

It was a sad day for the Devil and a glorious day for the Kingdom of God when WP Nicholson was converted and subsequently called to do the work of an evangelist.

Available from your local Christian bookshop or direct from the Publisher.

AMBASSADOR PRODUCTIONS LTD.
Providence House,
Ardenlee Street,
Belfast,
BT6 8QJ
Northern Ireland.

Phone: +44 (0) 28 9045 0010
Fax: +44 (0) 28 9073 9659

More by the same author ...

GOODBYE GOD

Twelve Stirring Messages from W P Nicholson

Includes:

✜ SAVED AND SURE

✜ REGENERATION

✜ THE NECESSITY OF REPENTANCE

✜ WHAT MUST I DO TO BE SAVED

✜ CROSS-BEARING

✜ SAVE YOURSELVES

✜ GOODBYE GOD

✜ THE UNPARDONABLE SIN

✜ HELL

✜ THE GREAT JUDGEMENT DAY

✜ HEAVEN

✜ CHRIST'S SECOND COMING

Available from your local Christian bookshop or direct from the Publisher.

AMBASSADOR PRODUCTIONS LTD.
Providence House,
Ardenlee Street,
Belfast,
BT6 8QJ
Northern Ireland.

Phone: +44 (0) 28 9045 0010
Fax: +44 (0) 28 9073 9659

More by the same author ...

THE INSPIRATIONAL TREASURY SERIES

Compiled and written by Stanley Barnes

✣ **AN INSPIRATIONAL TREASURY OF SAMUEL RUTHERFORD**

A new treasury based on the life of Samuel Rutherford, the Scottish Covenanter

AN APPRECIATION OF RUTHERFORD

SELECTED SAYINGS

LIVING INSIGHTS AND ILLUSTRATIONS

THE SERAPHIC LETTERS

THE SANDS OF TIME ARE SINKING

QUAINT SERMONS

✣ **AN INSPIRATIONAL TREASURY OF MARTIN LUTHER**

A new treasury based upon Martin Luther, the German Reformer

AN APPRECIATION OF MARTIN LUTHER

SELECTED SAYINGS

LIVING INSIGHTS AND ILLUSTRATIONS

THE PRAYERS OF LUTHER

LUTHER'S TEXT

CLASSIC SERMONS OF LUTHER

✣ **AN INSPIRATIONAL TREASURY OF D L MOODY**

A new treasury based on the life of D L Moody, the itinerant evangelist who made a lasting impact upon the religious life of Great Britain and the United States of America. The Encyclopedia Britannica refers to Moody as the 'greatest of modern evangelists'.

THE MAN AND HIS MESSAGE

LIVING INSIGHTS AND ILLUSTRATIONS

THE FINEST OF THE WHEAT

THE BEST OF MOODY'S SERMONS

WHY GOD USED D L MOODY

More by the same author ...

BEST LOVED TEXTS
OF THE BIBLE SERIES

Compiled by Stanley Barnes

✤ **SERMONS ON ISAIAH 53**

✤ **SERMONS ON THE PRAYER OF JABEZ**

✤ **SERMONS ON ACTS 16**

✤ **SERMONS ON JOHN 3:16**

Each of the above titles contains a selection of sermons by a variety of preachers including:

F B Meyer, C H Spurgeon, D L Moody, Alan Redpath, T T Shields, Thomas Manton, Alexander Raleigh, J Oswald Sanders, E E McCartney, R M McCheyne, J Sidlow Baxter, A T Pierson, Charles Finney and more!

Available from your local Christian bookshop or direct from the Publisher.

AMBASSADOR PRODUCTIONS LTD.
Providence House,
Ardenlee Street,
Belfast,
BT6 8QJ
Northern Ireland.

Phone: +44 (0) 28 9045 0010
Fax: +44 (0) 28 9073 9659